Jesus the Master Builder

Anne and Sheila
Inspiring and generous

Gordon Strachan

Jesus
the Master Builder

Druid Mysteries and

the Dawn of Christianity

Floris Books

First published in 1998 by Floris Books
Reprinted with corrections 2001

British Library CIP Data available

ISBN 0-86315-295-3

Printed in Great Britain
by Cromwell Press, Trowbridge, Wilts

Contents

III WISDOM IN THE NORTH

Acknowledgments

Whilst every effort has been made to trace the copyright holders of certain illustrations or text, this has not always proved successful. Any omissions will be corrected in future editions.

Thanks to Thames and Hudson for Figures 6, 7 and 33 from *Sacred Geometry*, by Robert Lawlor, and for Figures 43 and 56 from *Stonehenge Complete*, by Christopher Chippindale ; to Little Brown for Figures 14, 15, 16, 38 and 40 from *City of Revelation*, by John Michell (Abacus Sphere Books 1973); to Shambala Publications for Figures 3, 20, 21 and 22 from *The Power of Limits*, by György Doczi; to Vernon Jenkins for Figures 24, 25, 26 and 29 from *Figuring the Facts*, (unpublished pamphlet in author's possession); to Oxford University Press for Figures 44, 49 and 52 from *Megalithic Remains in Britain and Brittany*, by A. Thom and A.S. Thom, and for Figures 46, 47 and 48 from *Megalithic Sites in Britain*, by A. Thom; to Doctor Aubrey Burl for Figure 58 from *Stone Rows and Standing Stones, Britain, Ireland and Brittany Part ii*, by A. and A.S. Thom, collated by Aubrey Burl (BAR International Series 560 (ii) 1990), and for Figure 51 from *Megalithic Rings* by A. and A.S. Thom, with archaeological notes by A. Burl (BAR British Series 81, 1980); to Robin Heath for Figures 45 and 55 from *A Key to Stonehenge*, by Robin Heath (Bluestone Press); to The Covenant Publishing Co. Ltd. for Figures 1 and 2 from *Did Our Lord visit Britain as they say in Cornwall and Somerset?* by Rev C.C. Dobson; to Dover Publications for Figure 19 from *Vitruvius: The Ten Books of Architecture*, translation by Morris Hickey Morgan; to Rev Norman Macrae for Figure 54; to Routledge for extracts from *Imitations of Christianity among the Greeks*, by Simone Weil (Ark, 1987); to SCM Press for extracts from *Judaism and Hellenism*, by Martin Hengel.

Unless otherwise stated, all quotations from the Bible are from the Revised Standard Version.

Preface

At Midsummer 1977, my wife Elspeth and I camped beside the standing stones at Callanish. The site was almost deserted as we watched a spectacular sunset and then an equally impressive sunrise between the stones.

A few weeks later, at a wedding reception in Edinburgh, I had the good fortune to meet Professor Alexander Thom. I told him I had visited Callanish at the solstice and wondered why I hadn't been able to identify any alignments. He laughed and said 'Because it's a lunar, not a solar observatory!' Overcoming my embarrassment I tried again, 'Well, I'm obviously a beginner, but already I have come to believe your work is very important.' 'Why?' came the blunt query. 'Because it appears to turn the diffusionist theory of western culture on its head if the megalithic civilization pre-dated Greece and Egypt.' 'Quite so' — he nodded approvingly.

Since that time, I have attempted to improve my understanding of Thom's work, and the continuing debate regarding its value.

In the spring of 1986, I made my first visit to Glastonbury. During the following year, I returned several times, staying at Little St Michael's and falling in love with the Chalice Well Garden. 1 found myself unexpectedly open to the corpus of legends regarding the possible visits of Joseph of Arimathea and even Jesus.

I was contemplating making a serious study of these when circumstances conspired to carry me off to Israel for two years. I was persuaded to become the Director of the Church of Scotland's Sea of Galilee Centre in Tiberias, with Elspeth as Manager. We arrived in Israel in late August 1987, my last engagement having been at the Chalice Well Companions' Day in July.

To prepare for our duties, we had to attend Hebrew school in Jerusalem for two months. Being a hopeless linguist, I found this experience agonizing and used to slope off to the quiet shade of the Garden Tomb after classes, to recover.

On one occasion I asked the Anglican vicar on duty, where Arimathea was. He said no one knew for certain but some said it was at Ramla, south of Tel Aviv. I said I was interested because my last speaking engagement in the UK had been at Chalice Well, Glastonbury. He looked puzzled and confessed he didn't see the connection. I told him that Chalice Well and the Garden Tomb were the only two gardens in the world which were said to have belonged to Joseph of Arimathea. 'Oh,' he said, 'how very interesting.'

The following week, a young archaeologist carried on the good work of distracting me from Hebrew syntax, by taking a group of us from the St Andrew's Scots Centre, to visit the Israel Archaeological Museum. As we toured round, we passed a set of small standing stones, taken from a shrine, excavated at Hazor. 'Are those the best Israel can offer?' I quipped. 'Oh no,' our guide was quick to assure me. 'There are some great big ones at Tel Gezer.' 'Where's that?' I enquired. 'Near Ramla, south of Tel Aviv' he replied. This struck me as an odd coincidence. Within a week I had been told that Arimathea might well have been Ramla and that there were large standing stones in the vicinity. I was intrigued and decided I must investigate.

The following weekend Evelyn Simpson of the Scot's Centre staff, kindly drove Elspeth and me down to the ancient site of Tel Gezer. After negotiating many bumpy tracks we eventually found ourselves on top of the Tel and soon discovered the stones. They were very impressive; ten in all and most of them between six and twelve feet high. The scene was so reminiscent of megalithic sites in Britain that I almost felt I was back home. My only disappointment was that they were all in a straight line, not in a circle! However, as we walked round them, they seemed strangely familiar. I had seen stones in a straight line before, but where? Then I remembered. It was at Callanish ten years before! I also recalled that Professor Thom had himself been very impressed by the stone row at Callanish because it pointed due north; a very difficult feat to accomplish around 3000 BC because, at that time there was no Pole Star – and no compass. Did the stones at Tel Gezer also point north? We had brought a compass with us and, yes, we found that they did!

I was so struck by all this that I sat in the shade of the stones to mull it over. Then we had our picnic lunch during which I casually asked Evelyn 'What's that village to the north of us?' She found it on the map. 'Ayalon' she said, 'and there's an Ayalon Valley just beyond it'. 'Ayalon' I mused 'Ayalon, Ayalon'. It seemed to ring a bell. 'What does "Ayalon" remind you of?' I asked Elspeth. Immediately she said 'Avalon'. I laughed 'This is extraordinary. Do you think there could possibly have been a connection with Glastonbury?' It seemed too outrageous to contemplate, and yet I ventured to suggest that such a connection might explain why Arimathea was just down the road at Ramla. Evelyn was mystified 'How or what would that explain?' she enquired dryly.

These strange coincidences continued to intrigue me long after I needed distracting from my Hebrew classes. Over the next two years I made other discoveries which strengthened my desire to make a serious study of the evidence for the possible connections between ancient Israel and ancient Britain.

This is what I have done, off and on, since returning home in the Autumn of 1989. In the process, I have become convinced that there was indeed a very strong connection in the form of what we call the Pythagorean tradition.

Like Caesar's Gaul, I have divided this study into three parts. This seemed the best way to present material which gathered round three main topics: the Glastonbury legends, the identity of Jesus himself and the origins of the ancient wisdom tradition. In all of these, the common factor which emerged was Pythagoreanism, particularly the disciplines associated with number, later known as the Quadrivium.

In Part I, 'And did those Feet?' I maintain that the Roman and Greek consensus, that the Druids were Pythagoreans is most likely to be correct and that if Jesus came to Britain, it would have been, in the first instance, to meet with the Druids. This would provide a serious *motive* for his visit, the possibility of which, surprisingly, is not categorically denied by even the most critical historian.

In Part II, 'Jesus the Pythagorean', I present the case for an affirmative answer to the question: was Jesus himself a Pythagorean? After outlining the history of the doctrine of number from Pythagoras and Plato onwards, I show that for sixteen centuries, until the Renaissance, it was assumed by biblical scholars, that the number symbolism in the Bible was Pythagorean. Was Jesus himself aware of this dimension? Evidence from the Septuagint, the Greek translation of Old Testament, indicates that he probably was. This is strengthened by an analysis of the numerology of the Hebrew and Greek versions of his name. It is quite likely that the Essenes taught him this knowledge and that he made practical use of it as a master builder at Sepphoris, near Nazareth.

If Jesus was a master builder or craftsman, then he would also have been associated with the ancient wisdom tradition. In Part III, 'Wisdom in the North', I argue that the Pythagorean tradition was closely linked with this wisdom tradition, and that both were thought to have originated in the north. I examine evidence from Hebrew and Greek mythology which shows that the far north was believed to be the home of the gods and of Wisdom herself. This eventually leads us back to Glastonbury, Stonehenge and mega-lithic civilization, the stone circles of which may have been the earthly counterparts of the heavenly 'Pillars of Wisdom'. These heavenly pillars were probably circumpolar stars, particularly the seven stars of the Great Bear.

If Jesus embodied the Pythagorean-wisdom tradition, then he may have come to Britain not only to meet the Druids but also to return to the earthly source of that divine gnosis, of which the Druids were the heirs. It may have been in the north that Jesus first became aware of his identity as the incarnation of that Heav-enly Builder, Christ, through whom God had made the whole of creation.

A great many people have contributed to my research over the years. In Glastonbury where it began, I would like to thank Geoffrey Ashe, Patrick Benham, Marke Pawson, Leonard and Willa Sleath, Rev James and Rosemary Turnbull.

During my years in Israel, I was helped by Fr Peter du Brul, Professor Doron Chen, Dr Menashe Eyni, Emil Friedman, Richard Harper, Dr Isaac Khayutman, Rev Professor Jerome Murphy-O'Connor OP, Rev Bob Pitt and Fr Bargil Pixner OSB.

In the South of England I am particularly grateful to Philip Carr-Gomm, Robert Cowley, Elizabeth Leader, John Michell, Walter Seaman, Tessa Strickland and Patricia Villiers-Stuart.

In the Edinburgh area I have been helped in different ways by John Baker, Fiona Davidson, Maryel Gardyne, Rev Michael Jones,

Rev Norman and Dr Clare Macrae, Rev Robin Watt, Dr Nick Wyatt and my wife Elspeth.

Since 1990, the main focus for my research has been the Centre for Continuing Education at the University of Edinburgh. Those who have attended my evening classes have given me great encouragement and a valuable forum for discussion, sometimes as much outside the classes as in them: Harry Bland, Rachel Blow, Dr Anne Marie Bostyn, Alison Brown, Eileen Brownlee, Laura Chalmers, Richard Cherns, Theresa Churcher, Peggy Connarty, Madeleine Cosgrove, Annie Dale, Jim Crockett, Betty and David Cuthill, Ina Elliot, Colin Forsyth, George Fraser, Karin Gardner, Chris Garner, Ray Green, Francesca Greene, Alan Hitching, Vicky and Ali Jack, Alan Jamieson, Delia Kerr, Rev Dr John Kirk, John and Cecilia Lawrie, Michael Leslie-Melville, Marianna Lines, Alastair MacDonald, Betty MacDonald, Ranald MacKechnie, Ross McPhail, Andy Munro, Anna Munro, Dr Karen O'Keefe, Iain Oughtred, Hugh Parry, Roger Pears, Edward and Sheena Peterson, Jerry Peyton, George Rankin, Fred Robinson, Janet Romankevich, Morelle Smith, Chris Stephen, Helen Stevenson, Pete Stewart, Don Stubbings, Avis Swarbrick, Paul Turner, Hazel Wager, Bob Walker, Doris Whitley and Rev Jenny Williams.

I do not wish to imply that any of those listed above necessarily agreed with my overall thesis or the use to which I have put their particular contribution. I have valued critical discussion as much as encouragement and for both I am deeply grateful.

My secretaries Sheila Barnes and Margaret Cochran are to be congratulated on typing up a mountain of lecture notes and helping to shape them into a coherent manuscript.

Lastly my special thanks go to Anne Macaulay for practical support and for sharing her original research regarding Apollo in ancient Britain which provided the initial inspiration, and Sheila Erdal, without whose great financial generosity, I could never have finished this project.

I

AND DID THOSE FEET?

1
When did Christianity come to Britain?

Like the Somerset Levels veiled by mist, the beginnings of Christianity in Britain are shrouded in obscurity. In 1776 Edward Gibbon, using an even more oppressive meteorological metaphor, spoke of 'the dark cloud that hangs over the first age of the church' because the literary sources are 'scanty and suspicious.'[1] This opinion has been echoed since by historians even in our own time. For instance, Henry Chadwick in *The Early Church* says 'How soon Christianity reached Britain is uncertain; ... probably the Church had little serious foothold until the middle of the third century;'[2] and argues that the earliest reliable references are the presence of three British bishops at the Councils of Arles in 314 and Rimini in 359. Dom Louis Gougaud in *Christianity in Celtic Lands* agrees,[3] as does Charles Thomas in *Christianity in Roman Britain* who asserts that 'until post-Constantinian times (early fourth century) British Christianity was numerically very insignificant, had no particular geographical focus, and had up to then produced no one Christian thinker, martyr, or expatriate champion whose name could be snatched up in polished circles as that of a distant soul prominently gained for Christ.'[4]

For these and others such as W.H.C. Frend in *Christianity in Britain 300–700* and Leslie Hardinge in *The Celtic Church in Britain,*[5] the earliest sources, namely Tertullian and Origen, are taken to be merely 'travellers' tales' which 'could have little basis in fact.'[6] All of these follow the tradition of Harnack who thought 'Tertullian's notice is of no consequence.' However, there are those who disagree, taking a more positive approach.

In *Against the Jews*, written between 200 and 206 in Carthage, Tertullian said 'In whom have all the nations believed but in Christ who has already come?'[7] He then listed these nations as, among others, the Getuli, the Mauri, 'the boundaries of Spain,' 'the different peoples of Gaul,' and also 'Places of the Britons, unreached by the Romans, but subject to Christ.' This phrase

'Britannorum inaccessa Romanis loca' is not taken literally by the historians mentioned above who maintain that Tertullian was not 'concerned to ascertain either the state of the Roman frontiers in Britain in AD 200, or the exact locations of the few Christians Britain may have by then possessed.'[8] Likewise, when Origen, writing in Athens around 240 asked 'When, until the coming of Christ, did the land of Britain accept belief in one God?'[9] he also is believed to be using merely a rhetorical formula 'to hammer home the joyous fact of the triumph of the Church.'[10] However, this is not the opinion of J.R.H. Moorman in *A History of the Church in England*, who links the testimony of both these early church fathers to that of Irenaeus, Bishop of Lyons from 185 to 200, suggesting that 'when the savage persecutions broke out in Gaul in 177, a number of Christians fled northwards and ... some may have found their way to these shores.'[11] Likewise R.G. Collingwood and J.N.L. Myres in *Roman Britain* also accept that 'Christianity did reach Britain at an early date and did make very considerable progress there. By the beginning of the third century Tertullian could claim that parts of Britain inaccessible to the Romans had been conquered by Christ, which seems to imply that the new religion had not only worked its way into the more romanized parts of the country, but had already spread beyond them into the highland zone.' They are equally positive about Origen's reference saying that although it is 'vague and rhetorical,' it is 'enough to confirm us in thinking it a solid reality. It appears, then, that Christianity established itself in Britain at least as early as the second century, and that in the third it was gathering momentum.'[12]

John Foster in *They Converted Our Ancestors* goes even further than Collingwood and Myres, claiming that Tertullian actually knew about the conversion of the Getuli and Mauri in North Africa because he lived in Carthage. Likewise, he knew about Christianity in Spain which went back to Clement of Rome's assertion that St Paul had gone 'to the limit of the west,'[13] that is, Spain, and as mentioned in the Apostle's own references in Romans 15:24 and 28. Foster believes that Tertullian would also be bound to know about 'The different peoples of Gaul'[14] from Irenaeus who spent his ministry at Lyons among the Celts. So why should we assume that, when he speaks about 'Places of the Britons, unreached by the Romans, but subject to Christ,' he should suddenly have left fact for fiction? Foster answers that Tertullian would definitely have known the details about Roman Britain:

> Such a man as Tertullian would know of Hadrian's Wall, built in AD 128, He would know too of the attempt that the later Antonine Wall represents, to hold the Forth and the Clyde as civilization's frontier. A few years before Tertullian wrote, in 196, the governor of Britain had rebelled against the Emperor Septimus Severus and moved his troops into Gaul. The northern tribes rose, broke through the Antonine Wall, and ravaged as far south as York. In the years that followed, Hadrian's Wall had had to be rebuilt. In 206 the new governor of Britain called for a campaign to re-establish the Forth-Clyde line — the last campaign of Septimus Severus, who was to die at York in 211. This is the very period, 200–206, of Tertullian's writing. Whichever the actual year, Britain was in the news. Tertullian, living in Carthage, was almost as near the centre of the Empire as in Italy itself. And in the midst of these events Tertullian is claiming that the Church reaches farther than the might of Rome. His enthusiasm may have carried him away; he often does exaggerate. But one cannot easily say that he had no facts to go on.[15]

From this brief survey it is already obvious that scholarly opinion is deeply divided about the reliability of these sources. This division continues when we move on to consider the next two authorities, Eusebius and Gildas. Eusebius, writing his *The Proof of the Gospel* in Caesarea in 330, said 'The Apostles passed beyond the ocean to the Isles called the British Isles,'[16] and Gildas, the British historian, in 560 wrote in *The Ruin of Britain*, 'Meanwhile these islands, stiff with cold and frost, and in a distant region of the world, remote from the visible sun, received the beams of light, that is the holy precepts of Christ, the true Sun ... in the latter part, as we know, of the reign of Tiberias Caesar.'[17]

Both these famous British historians make what appear to be extravagant claims for a very early apostolic mission to Britain. This is particularly the case with Gildas, because Tiberias Caesar died in AD 37. Margaret Deansley in *The Pre-Conquest Church in*

England, dismisses them both together as worthless. Gildas' date, she says:

> ... is a mere guess, an inference indeed from the widely
> held theory that the Twelve Apostles had divided up the
> world by lot and proceeded to preach in the parts allotted
> to them. Eusebius was aware of this theory, and certain
> passages in his Ecclesiastical History are apparently based
> on it: and Gildas had read the Ecclesiastical History in
> Rufinus' Latin translation.[18]

However, John McNeill in *The Celtic Churches* has a different opinion and is not at all dismissive. He concedes that Gildas is not verifiable:

> ... but when we realize the busy traffic on Roman roads and
> western seas, we can hardly think it certainly false.
> Christians of Tiberias' time were too early to be converts of
> St Paul, but according to the Book of Acts, there were many
> of them and 'they that were scattered abroad went
> everywhere preaching the word.'[19]

Geoffrey Ashe in *King Arthur's Avalon* is even more positive, maintaining that Gildas was not guessing. Like John Foster's interpretation of Tertullian, Ashe believes that Gildas knew something definite and represented a tradition:

> One does not get the impression that he is merely
> speculating. It sounds more as if he were referring to a
> familiar idea. The inference is easier to draw than to reject.
> Sixth century Britons in the unconquered west, with a
> continuity of tradition back to the first Christian landing,
> held this to have taken place extremely early.'[20]

Ashe then goes on to list other references which help to give credence to Gildas. First, as already mentioned, Clement of Rome spoke of St Paul arriving 'at the extremity of the West' which was probably Spain, but later, Theodoret in 435, said 'St Paul brought salvation to the islands that lie in the ocean' meaning Britain.[21] Second, in Romans 16:10 St Paul says 'My greetings ... to the household of Aristobulus' and Aristobulus is called 'Bishop of Britain' according to a fourth century text ascribed to Dorotheus of Tyre.[22] Third, King Lucius (*c.* 170 AD) is said by British historians Bede and Nennius, to have sent to Pope Eleutherius for missionaries Faganus and Deruvianus who were successful in widespread conversions and church organization. Ashe thinks Lucius was fictitious but not the mission. Fourth, St Philip: around 638, Isidore of Seville claimed that Philip the Apostle came to Gaul.[23] This was repeated two hundred years later by the historian Freculfus. Fifth, according to various Dark Age stories, St Simon Zelotes and St Peter were both said to have come to Britain.

These scraps of evidence are enough to convince Ashe that Gildas was not 'merely speculating' about a very early mission to Britain. He thinks that the Roman context is crucial for a fair judgement in this matter:

> Claudius's conquest, during the 40s of the Christian era, brought Britain forcibly into the Roman orbit and into the news. Imperial enterprise opened up the island to a rapid economic invasion. The Romans' quarrel with Druidism gave their new province a special religious interest, and Boadicea's rising excited the capital itself. Neither St Paul nor St Peter nor any other alert resident in Rome could have helped hearing constantly about British affairs. That a mission was contemplated is very likely. That it actually happened within the Apostles' lifetimes we have no reason to affirm, but only a negative reason to deny. There are only rumours, no record worth calling a record. But, after all, plenty of real happenings fail to get recorded.[24]

Ashe has gone as far as the meagre evidence will allow, to say that an early mission was most probable. John McNeill takes up Ashe's point about the likelihood of unrecorded missions having taken place. He refers specifically to the case of Epaphras: 'We are justified in assuming that in Britain as elsewhere there was much early Christian activity that remains undocumented. St Paul has high praise for Epaphras as the teacher of Christianity to the Colossians (1:7), but gives us no narrative of this pioneer mission. There must have been many an Epaphras whose name and work went wholly unrecorded.'[25]

We can thus fairly conclude from this general examination, that while the majority of historians are sceptical about Christianity having arrived early in Britain and would not trust sources before the early third or fourth centuries, there is a significant minority who think otherwise. These are prepared to accept that it is possible, even probable that there were Christians in Britain in the second or even the first century. Some of these would also concede that while it is not possible to prove, the question of an actual apostolic mission cannot be entirely ruled out.

This cautious openness is given an unexpectedly positive twist by John McNeill and Margaret Deansley, neither of whom can resist the temptation to shift the discussion of beginnings to Glastonbury. Having done so, they both find evidence for a very early foundation, even if they don't accept the historicity of the visit of Joseph of Arimathea. McNeill writes,

> Although the Joseph legend must be held to be fiction, Glastonbury, from very ancient times an active seaport on the Severn estuary, was well situated to be the entrance point for a new religion into western Britain. it was most likely 'Trade-borne,' as Margaret Deansley suggests, and may have come as early as the second or even the first century. Miss Deansley notes 'the curious appositeness of the site selected by tradition as that of the oldest church in Britain.'[26]

So we find that the door which was only sightly ajar when literary sources alone were being considered, is now beginning to open up, once the evidence at Glastonbury is taken into account. Deansley develops this at length and we will return to it in the next chapter. It is sufficient for the moment to give her summary of the cultural argument:

> The claim made for the church of Glastonbury to an antiquity beyond memory was, in fact, a claim that the old Celtic, La Tène culture had contact with Christianity independently of the Romans, who brought it to Britain via London and Kent. There is no historical evidence to support the claim except the words of Tertullian, but one or two points can be made in its favour.[27]

It would appear that the study of the ancient site of Glastonbury offers more evidence for the possibility of first century Christianity in Britain, than the literary sources. If this is the case, why must the Joseph legend be held to be fiction? Why don't we hear of Joseph of Arimathea in the early sources?

2
Did Joseph of Arimathea come to Britain?

If the mist and dark clouds which obscure the origins of Christianity in Britain, seemed to be lifting for a moment to reveal the clear features of a first or second century landscape, they return with added opacity when we turn to the alleged visit of Joseph of Arimathea. Most of the historians we have consulted so far, if they mention him at all, do so in a disparaging manner, as if even to consider the matter were more than their professional reputation was worth. For instance Moorman says 'But where history is silent, legend and tradition have produced strange and wonderful stories of journeys to this island made by St Paul or St Philip or St Joseph of Arimathea and of the founding of a Christian Church at Glastonbury.'[1] Collingwood and Myres call these stories 'pious inventions,'[2] while Charles Thomas says 'they attempt to fill a vacuum, to explain the unascertainable by the incredible' and by the later concoction of 'retrospective apostles.' Even John McNeill who, as we have seen, is otherwise open to an early mission, states that 'the Joseph legend must be held to be fiction.'[3]

Why is this? Why are most historians so dismissive of the Joseph stories? The answer is not hard to find. It is because there are no early sources that even so much as hint at Joseph or his connection with Britain, let alone Glastonbury. His first mention comes as late as 1240, about twelve hundred years after the events in which he was said to have played such an important role. That is why he and his legends are not taken seriously by most professionals in the field.

Even when Joseph did make his debut in 1240, it was in a manuscript which had been tampered with, thus giving sceptics further cause for serious doubt as to the story's authenticity. The manuscript concerned was *De Antiquitate Glastoniensis Ecclesiae* (*The Antiquities of Glastonbury Church*) by William of Malmesbury. The original version of this, published in 1135, had made no mention of Joseph.

In 1125 William of Malmesbury had published *De Gestis Regum Anglorum* in which he had said that Glastonbury Abbey was founded by Ine, King of Wessex (688–726). The Abbey monks told him he was wrong and invited him to do further research in their great library, which he did. He found so much material there that he had to rewrite the early chapters. The Abbey was far older than he had thought. It was after this discovery that he wrote *De Antiquitate Glastoniensis Ecclesiae* in which he accepted that 'Glastonbury was the first church in the Kingdom of Britain, and the source and fountain of all religion.' The monks loved this. They copied it and copied it and, according to the sceptics, they began to alter it to suit their growing pretensions.

The only surviving copies of the *De Antiquitate* are the altered versions of a century later. It is only in this final, much altered, later edition that Joseph makes his first appearance. Hence the dubiety about the reference. This is the story:

> St Philip, as Freculfus attests in the fourth chapter of his se-
> cond book, came to the land of the Franks where he con-
> verted many to the faith by his preaching and baptized
> them. Desiring to spread the word of Christ further, he sent
> twelve of his disciples into Britain to teach the word of life.
> It is said that he appointed as their leader his very dear
> friend, Joseph of Arimathea, who had buried the Lord.
> They came to Britain in 63 AD, the fifteenth year after the
> assumption of the blessed Mary ... In the thirty-first year
> after the passion of the Lord ... they completed a chapel as
> they had been instructed, making the lower part of all its
> walls of twisted wattle, an unsightly construction no doubt
> but one adorned by God with many miracles. Since it was
> the first one in that territory the Son of God dignified it
> with a greater honour by dedicating it in honour of his
> mother.[4]

The story goes on to tell how the local king was not amenable to conversion but nevertheless granted the disciples land on the island of Ynys-vitrin. Two of his successors also added grants to make up the traditional Twelve Hides. They lived devout, monastic lives there until they died. Evidently no converts were made because after their death the land reverted to being a 'covert for wild beasts.' The narrative then tells how King Lucius sent to Pope Eleutherius for the missionaries Phaganus and Deruvianus, as mentioned in the last chapter. The usual dates for this are between 174 and 189. It was only after that that the earlier Christian site was discovered and re-inhabited.

As noted, there are no surviving manuscripts of the original, unrevised *De Antiquitate*, but William of Malmesbury did refer to Glastonbury in the final revision of his earlier work *De Gestis Regum Anglorum* (*The Acts of the Kings of England*) which he completed in 1140:

> Moreover there are documents of no small credit, which
> have been discovered in certain places to the following
> effect: 'No other hands than those of the disciples of Christ
> erected the church of Glastonbury.' Nor is it dissonant from
> probability: for if Philip the Apostle, preached to the Gauls,
> as Freculfus relates in the fourth chapter of his second
> book, it may be believed that he also planted the word on
> this side of the channel also. But that I may not seem to
> balk the expectation of my readers by vain imaginations,
> leaving all doubtful matter I shall proceed to the relation of
> substantial truths.[5]

The tentative nature of this reference, together with the alter-ations in the later version of the *De Antiquitate*, have given rise to a scholarly consensus, itself of some antiquity, that in these documents we are dealing in the first case with fraud and in the second with William's own scepticism. The late Professor R.F. Treharne is one of the most recent protagonists of this consensus and pulls no punches in *Glastonbury Legends*, as he comments on the last quotation:

> It will be seen that William carefully recounts what his
> Glastonbury hosts had told him, and what the documents
> which he saw purported to say; but his interpretation of the
> evidence is critical and detached. He lived in what has been
> called 'the great age of forgery,' when great churches, not
> to speak of princes, statesmen and lawyers, thought it at
> least their right, if not their duty, to manufacture
> documentary evidence so as to fill the gaps in existing

documents when proof was needed to make good their
claims to material possessions, rights or even prestige.
Living among men who employed itinerant professional
forgers of documents, highly skilled in their art, William
can hardly have been unaware of the practice of forgery or
unskilled in the science of recognizing forged documents.
He did not believe all that he saw or was told.[6]

Treharne then goes on to show in detail just how suspicious
William obviously felt about the material the credulous Glastonbury monks had shown him, and how he was much more
convinced by the later story about the mission sent by Pope
Eleutherius between 174 and 189.

Almost the whole of Treharne's book is an extended exposé of
the fraudulent nature of the Glastonbury legends. It is obvious
from his style that he greatly enjoys mocking every aspect of the
genre. For instance, as he draws towards his conclusions, he has
his tongue firmly in his cheek as he feigns grief that the whole of
Joseph's spurious life in Britain must be thrown out:

Much more grievous is the disappearance of St Joseph of
Arimathea himself. Transplanted to Glastonbury early in
the thirteenth century along with the rest of the newly-
localized Arthurian legend, Joseph, like his famous staff,
has flourished mightily under our varying skies, far from
the land of his birth. Not merely the first evangelist of
Britain, the founder of Glastonbury, the planter of the
Glastonbury Thorn, the builder (by proxy) of the *Vetusta
Ecclesia* (the Old Church), and the bringer of the 'cruets'
and the Grail, he has become, in modern times, a wealthy
Jewish merchant importing tin into Palestine from the
Cornish tin-mines before ever the Romans conquered
Britain ... In the fullness of time St Joseph was buried at
Glastonbury and so joined the countless throng of the
Abbey's saints — probably in the later thirteenth century ...[7]

On and on he goes, relishing the ease with which it is possible to discredit, with a historian's rigour, the legends' pretensions to historicity. For over 100 pages his tone is confident, his
mastery flawless and his conclusions obvious. It is therefore very

surprising, not to say disconcerting, to find him having a change of heart. He suddenly becomes unexpectedly cautious. Within sight of total victory his trumpet gives an uncertain sound 'We must be careful of the words we use: we may not flatly assert that Joseph never came to Glastonbury, for this is one of those negatives which cannot be proved.'[8] This comes as a shock but he reassures us at once by saying for the hundredth time that there is no evidence whatsoever for the claim. But then almost immediately he is once again stricken with another attack of doubt: 'it is well to reflect that, thanks to the *Pax Romana* and, especially after AD 43, to the Roman conquest of Britain, a wealthy Jew, especially if he happened to be a merchant, could have travelled more easily from Palestine to Glastonbury in the thirty years following the Crucifixion than at any later time until well into the nineteenth century. Strictly speaking, it is not impossible that Joseph of Arimathea came to Glastonbury.'[9]

This extraordinary *volte-face* would carry no more conviction than a death-bed conversion were it not for the fact that, despite his continued protestations that 'there is not a scrap of evidence,' he is now manifestly arguing with himself. The open-minded reader has already been convinced by his scepticism. His marshalling of the evidence for the lack of evidence, has been impressive. He alone can weaken his own case which he continues to do off and on for the last ten pages of his book. His concluding paragraph is worth quoting in full because it brings us back to Margaret Deansley and John McNeill both quoted in the last chapter. For all his scholarly rigour, Treharne leaves us in no doubt about his final position:

> We should remember the economic importance, both before
> and for some forty years after the beginning of the
> Christian era, of the thriving community of craftsmen and
> traders living in the lake villages of Glastonbury and
> Meare, and we should keep in mind the well developed
> trade-routes which they established ... Scholars in recent
> years have familiarized us with the idea that Christianity
> may first have reached these islands, not by the easy and
> obvious short sea-route to Dover and London, but, like so
> many earlier cultures and some religions of the pre-historic
> age, in the little boats of traders and adventurers braving

the stormy western approaches between the Armorican and the Cornish Coasts. We cannot prove it and probably we never shall: but if we accept this idea as a possibility, is there anything incredible in the thought that, coming from the south-west, and along the south coast of the Bristol Channel, it was under Glastonbury Tor that Christianity found its first secure shelter and abiding place in our remote land?[10]

This is a most remarkable conclusion from one who, more than any, was set to disprove everything Josephan. Significantly it is his own rigorous standards which, in the end, have prevailed and forced him to be fairer than expected. He found ultimately that he could not deny that the political circumstances of the time favoured Joseph's coming. Neither could he deny the evidence of western trade routes with Armorica and Cornwall and the positive cultural implications of the archaeological findings at the Lake villages of Glastonbury and Meare. In so doing he is following Margaret Deansley, who, five years earlier, in 1961 had written:

When Julius Caesar raided Britain in 55 and 54 BC, London was non-existent, and Britain's trade with Gaul and the Mediterranean was conducted by the way of the Severn mouth and Glastonbury. Economic historians stress the importance of Glastonbury as the focal point of track ways from the Midlands, Wilts and Somerset, as well as the near neighbour of the lead workings carried on in the region of Meare, and the tin-workings of Wales ... Glastonbury was the Bristol of the day ... The speed with which Christianity spread from eastern Europe to Edessa and Persia along a great trade route, and that in the first and second century, renders it not impossible that a similar expansion along a trade route should have occurred in the west, through the Mediterranean, Massilia and the Rhone valley to north Gaul and Britain, or round the western promontories to the Severn mouth.[11]

Such are the similarities between this and Treharne, it would appear that Deansley has had a strong influence on the latter's acceptance of the ease with which 'a wealthy Jew, especially if he happened to be a merchant,' could have travelled from Palestine to Glastonbury. So much for his confident assertion 'Joseph ... must go.' It is evidently not so easy to get rid of this wealthy Arimathean merchant. If he must go anywhere, it now looks ironically as though he must go back to Glastonbury! Deansley then makes another telling point with regard to the possible authenticity of the earliest Glastonbury tradition:

> Again, it is strange that early medieval tradition in Britain should have asserted that the church of Glastonbury was the oldest in the land, when the men who made the tradition were without any predilection for a western origin, without the evidence of Glastonbury's economic and cultural importance available to modern archaeologists, and without the pointer that Glastonbury and the Severn mouth were indeed the places where a trade-borne Christianity was likely to have arrived in the second or even the first century. There were no obvious Roman remains in Glastonbury to prompt the rise of a tradition. No early claim was made on behalf of any other church in Roman Britain to have been the earliest founded: when one was made much later, in the twelfth century, by the abbey of Westminister, it was easily demolished by William of Malmesbury.[12]

This is a strong argument from the tradition of the early Middle Ages, made on behalf of the primacy of the Glastonbury church. Deansley does not mention Joseph specifically and appears to be at pains not to do so. However, all that she says about Glastonbury in the *early* medieval period is applicable to Joseph in the *later* Middle Ages as it is recorded at Pisa in 1409, Constance in 1417, Sienna in 1424 and Basle in 1434. At these Church Councils it was consistently maintained that 'the Churches of France and Spain must yield in points of antiquity and precedence to that of Britain as the latter church was founded by Joseph of Arimathea immediately after the passion of Christ.'[13] This phrase *statim post passione Christi* is very reminiscent of Gildas' claim that the gospel reached Britain before the death of Augustus Caesar in AD 37, but unlike Gildas, it specifically mentions Joseph as its bringer. It would appear that, sceptical though most modern scholars are about the authenticity of the late Joseph material, as detailed above, this claim was nevertheless considered to be sufficiently strong by the early fifteenth century to prevail over competition from St Denis of Paris or St Philip of France. This is a remarkable development, suggesting that, as noted earlier, Gildas represented a tradition and was not merely guessing. Evidently this acknowledgement of British Josephan primacy was no passing fashion because it is mentioned in the sixteenth century by Cardinal Pole who accepted that 'this Island before all islands received the light of Christ's religion' and Polydore Virgil who believed that 'Britain, partly through Joseph of Arimathea ... was of all kingdoms the first that received the Gospel.'[14]

At last, it would seem, the dark clouds and impenetrable mists that surround the question of Joseph of Arimathea's visit to Britain, have begun to disperse. The sun is about to break through to reveal the majestic silhouette of Glastonbury Tor, Wearyall Hill, the Holy Thorn and the Abbey ruins. The sceptics have done their best to prove there was nothing behind the thick veil of legend but they have been unsuccessful. In the event, the corpus of Glastonbury and Josephan material is not so easily disproved. It somehow just manages to survive the severest critical onslaught and has done so for many hundreds of years. In fact, its very existence over the centuries has itself become a part of history.

There is one more question to be asked about Joseph. It is this: why was it specifically Joseph and not somebody else, who was said to have been the bringer of Christianity, the cruets of Christ's blood and sweat, the Holy Thorn, the Chalice and the Holy Grail? Why was it Joseph and not one of the Apostles such as Paul, Peter, Simon Zelotes, Philip or even Aristobulus, 'the Bishop of Britain,' all of whom had a much higher standing, and all of whom at some date were said to have come to Britain? Why was it the shadowy Joseph who featured so large in the Arthurian romances of the late twelfth and thirteenth centuries and not some important, well-known apostolic leader? Geoffrey Ashe in *King Arthur's Avalon* asks this question and gives a surprising answer. He says it is the very oddness of the choice of Joseph, a virtual 'nobody,' unconnected with any known mission, which he finds strangely convincing. He says 'it is hard to avoid the feeling of an obstinate fact underlying the fable ... St Joseph's presence on British soil is too odd, under the circumstances, to have quite the air of pure invention.'[15] He argues that the flowering of the Joseph material in the early Middle Ages couldn't have arisen from nothing. There is far too much of it and it is too varied for it all to have been a late invention. It must have originated in earlier times: 'There must have been a prior belief lurking somewhere, a belief too stubborn to dismiss, a belief which there was good reason to use.'[16]

Ashe, I believe, has made a very astute point which finally brings the sun to the Glastonbury scene. He strengthens his argument by making a most intriguing comparison between Joseph and King Arthur whose tradition was dormant for hundreds of years:

> Throughout the Dark Ages the English had many scribes
> and scholars, but not one so much as hints at the existence
> of Arthur, or even the existence of an Arthurian legend. Yet
> there was such a legend: the Welsh hoarded it for six
> hundred years before the English discovered it ... So with
> Joseph of Arimathea ... I find it easier to believe that such a
> fancy existed from early times than to accept the sudden
> contrivance of the whole business in the Middle Ages.[17]

Ashe's argument here is most convincing. His comparison between the lost Joseph tradition and the lost Welsh Arthur tradition is a strong one. However, by using the concept of a 'lost tradition' doesn't he open up the possibility *in principle* of there also having been a lost Jesus-in-Britain tradition? After all, at least one of the sources yet to be cited claimed that the *Vetusta Ecclesia*, the Old Church at Glastonbury, was 'constructed by no human art, but by the hands of Christ himself, for the salvation of his people,'[18] while the Jesus legends as a whole claim that he came with Joseph. Since the Jesus-in-Britain tradition is thus part of the Joseph-in-Britain tradition, isn't it reasonable to extend Ashe's argument to cover both? Isn't it reasonable to suggest that it is easier to believe that at least some of the Jesus legends existed from early times than to accept that they were all contrivances of a later age? Couldn't Ashe's conclusion regarding Joseph's presence on British soil being too strange 'to have quite the air of pure invention' apply equally to the persistence of the belief that Jesus came with Joseph?

3

Did Jesus and Joseph come together?

It is, I believe, eminently reasonable to propose that if the Arthurian legends could have been lost for six hundred years, then the Joseph legends could have been lost for eleven hundred. It is, I believe, also legitimate to extend this comparison to the Joseph-with-Jesus legends. And yet to do so is to stray beyond the bounds of academic acceptability. Treharne for instance, warns that those who believe Joseph 'sent his "nephew," Jesus, to Cornwall, while still a young lad, to look after the Cornish end of his "uncle's" business,' are merely 'enthusiasts for the more extreme forms of the Glastonbury legend.'[1] Even Geoffrey Ashe, whose trenchant question: Why Joseph? has led directly to this comparison, will not speculate further. In his *Mythology of the British Isles*, he gives his summary of the Jesus-in-Britain legends:

> Some say that Jesus himself visited Britain during the hidden years before his public ministry. He was in Somerset, perhaps for an appreciable time. The Druids were prepared for him because they had a god Esus or Yesu. On the future site of Glastonbury Abbey, he put up a small building which was his home for a while. He walked over the Mendip Hills to the north where Priddy now is. He may also have been in Cornwall, where the Jesus Well near the mouth of the Camel is said to commemorate him, and there are scraps of folklore about his visit in other places, such as St Just-in-Roseland. If he did come to Britain it was probably as a youth, in the company of Joseph of Arimathea, the rich man who, after the crucifixion, obtained his body from Pilate and laid it in the tomb. Glastonbury Abbey had nothing to say of any visit by Jesus, but its account of its beginnings makes much of Joseph.[2]

This is Ashe's short, objective summary. Later in the Chapter, following the model of Robert Graves in *The Greek Myths*, he gives a commentary. This is mainly concerned with his views on the Joseph-in-Glastonbury material, as already outlined. He has very little to say about Jesus, and what he does say is thoroughly sceptical:

> The legend concerning Jesus is linked with the tin theory.
> Its advocates assert that Joseph was related to the Holy
> Family and took Mary's son with him on one or more of
> his voyages. The problem is to decide how old the legend
> actually is, and how it started.[3]

His problem about deciding how old the legend is, proves not to be a serious one, because in almost the next sentence he says that it probably 'arose from a too literal reading of the story about the Old Church being of divine foundation.' He says that the difficulty of such literalism is that if Jesus built it, then Joseph didn't. Enthusiasts have therefore had to claim that 'the reference is to a small house which Jesus did build and which became a chapel.' He also thinks that the story associated with St David, who had a vision in which Christ told him that he had dedicated the Old Church to his mother, has been taken too literally. He then goes on to reject any literal content in William Blake's 'And did those feet?' which is to be taken symbolically. He follows this with a rejection of all the other items in his earlier summary:

> The Priddy variant is dismissed by sceptics as Victorian.
> The village schoolmistress wrote a play for the children in
> which she imagined Jesus coming to Priddy, and this
> harmless fancy, like other fancies, became an 'ancient
> Somerset tradition.' The Druids did have a god called Esus,
> though in Gaul rather than Britain, but so far as he was
> identified with anyone else, it was with Mars or Mercury.
> Since the main fact known about him is that he was
> worshipped with human sacrifice, he seems an
> unpromising character to bring in.[4]

It could be argued that this paragraph is too brief to do justice to the extensive reflections, on this and related topics, which have come from Ashe's pen over many years . Nevertheless, I have it on his own authority that, of all he has written, he is happiest with this account. It is therefore disappointing to find him quite so negative. It might be understandable for him to disregard the Priddy legend but to rid himself in two sentences of any possible Druid connection, could be said to be unacceptably dismissive. From his annotated references it is clear that, at this point, he is rejecting C.C. Dobson who, in *Did Our Lord Visit Britain as they say in Cornwall and Somerset?* puts forward an intriguing case for a possible Druid link with Jesus. Why doesn't he at least give this an airing and tell us a little more about it? Is it because Dobson's thesis depends largely on the acceptance of an oral tradition? His omission is uncharacteristic because in other books he combines his erudition with a positive acknowledgement of non-literary realities such as the oral tradition, the spirit of place and the Glastonbury mystique. Could it be an inability to face the possible consequences of his earlier question: why Joseph? He says that if there had been a genuine Jesus-in-Britain or Jesus-in-Glastonbury tradition, the monks would have mentioned it, and they never do. Therefore the tradition must be false:

> It [the Jesus tradition] cannot have been known at Glas-
> tonbury during the Abbey's lifetime, because the monks
> would have exploited such a splendid distinction, and they
> never so much as hint at it.[5]

This is a more moderate, but just as definite an opinion that he had put forward some years before in *Avalonian Quest*:

> Glastonbury's great Christian establishment was always
> Catholic and never separated from Rome, and it was killed
> by the very king who began the Reformation in England.
> The need to exorcize the spectre underlies the fantasies
> about Joseph or Jesus getting there first and founding a
> distinct British Church.[6]

This is in essence, an extreme form of the same doubtful position we are considering here. There is a flaw in the assumption that the Jesus tradition could not have been known at Glaston-bury 'because the monks would have exploited such a splendid distinction, and they never so much as hint at it.' If the monks had known about it, would they necessarily have spoken about it? Ashe must be aware of what happened to many Celtic monks when Roman Church practices prevailed in the seventh and eighth centuries. Basically they had to toe the line or else they were out of a job — or worse. He must remember what happened at Glastonbury when the Normans took over from the Saxons: how the appointed Norman abbot Thurstan had a bloody confrontation with the Saxon monks in which some lost their lives and others were seriously injured.[7] It seems strange that he has overlooked the ethnic conflicts which are written into the church history of Glastonbury. The Celtic or ancient British monks had to keep quiet about their distinctive Celtic or British beliefs when the Anglo-Saxons took over. Likewise the Anglo-Saxon monks we know, had to obey their new Norman ecclesiastical superiors or suffer dire consequences. This is so central to Glastonbury's history and to church history in general, that to foreclose the debate without even mentioning it, is a serious weakness.

It is much more likely that by the time written records appeared during the Anglo-Saxon period, the distinctive elements of the Celtic oral tradition had long been suppressed. Ashe is inconsistent for he says that on the one hand, regarding the dormant Arthur tradition, no English scribe 'so much as hints' at its existence 'yet there was such a legend,' while on the other hand, referring to the Jesus tradition, the fact that the monks 'never so much as hint at it' explains why there was *no* legend. He uses the same argument to reach completely opposite conclusions. However, like the Arthur legends, the Jesus legends *are there*. They *do* exist. Yet the implication of his logic is to deny they are there at all. His earlier position in *Avalonian Quest* as quoted above, does at least have the virtue of acknowledging that the legends do exist, even if they are no more than Protestant 'fantasies.'

There is little justification for treating the history of the Abbey as a continuous whole. This is the implication of Ashe's position. It is just not so. There was in all probability considerable disconti-nuity during the Celtic, Saxon and Norman periods. Throughout each of these huge changes, revolutions and invasions, some of the indigenous tradition and lore would have been lost.[8] Contentious beliefs would have been suppressed and what could have been more contentious than the claim that Joseph, let alone Jesus, founded the Abbey. Contrary to what he says, it is the very silence of the monks which speaks the loudest. It tells of men who were afraid because they knew what happened to anyone who stepped out of line and favoured an alleged early British foundation which might appear to threaten the primacy of the Roman Church. The monks said nothing because they were obliged to 'know nothing,' and they were obliged to 'know nothing' because they and their predecessors over many centuries had been ordered not to say anything if they wanted a quiet life. Consequently, the argument based on their silence points in the opposite direction to Ashe. It is much more likely that the monks never so much as hint at the Jesus tradition because it was there, in a residual form, and had been, since the first centuries, before the distinctive beliefs and practices of the Celtic Church were pronounced heretical by Rome and stamped out. It could only begin to re-emerge after the Reformation.

I believe Ashe is nearly right, but not entirely. He has not followed up his powerful comparison between the lost Arthur tradition and the lost Joseph tradition. He has retreated to safer ground. Did he see, with characteristic perception, where that particular comparison could lead? Perhaps if he were to have developed that comparison, he would have had to face up to the question: why do religious traditions get lost? Why do they disappear? Since this has now become a central issue in our enquiry, it is, I believe, pertinent to look briefly at two other religious traditions that were lost for longer than either Arthur or Joseph, and which have been rediscovered in our own day. Perhaps we can learn something from them.

The Lost Traditions

The two lost religious traditions which have been rediscovered in modern times are the Gnostic texts of Nag Hammadi which were found in the sands of the Upper Nile in 1945 and the Dead Sea Scrolls, initially found in the caves of Qumran in 1947. Both of these unexpected discoveries have been more precious to scholars in the field than gold because they have provided evidence, hitherto unavailable, for alternative interpretations of who Jesus was believed to be and the times in which the early Church developed. The thirteen Coptic papyrus books at Nag Hammadi have shown clearly the many ways in which the Gnostic interpretation of Jesus differed from the orthodox view, and how this centred on a highly spiritualized perception of his risen presence. On the other hand, the 800 Hebrew and Aramaic manuscripts found at Qumran have given evidence of a more down-to-earth Jewish, Essene and possibly even Zealot dimension to the Gospels.

Why were these documents hidden? Why were they stuffed into earthenware jars and buried in the sand and desert caves? The answer is the same for both. Because they belonged to persecuted groups. They were the sacred writings of people who in my first example, had been pronounced heretical by the church and in the second, declared subversive by the state. They had therefore been condemned to destruction. They were all that could be saved from religious communities who were doomed to be expunged from the pages of history. They were the holy relics of losers in a history written by winners. In the case of the Nag Hammadi manuscripts, the losers were the Gnostic heretics and the winners were the fourth century persecuting orthodox Christians in league with the Roman Imperial authorities. In the case of the Dead Sea Scrolls, the losers were the Qumrani sectarian Jews who were put to the sword by the all-conquering Roman legions around AD 68. In both cases the documents were hidden because the beliefs of their authors threatened the winners. The Gnostic Gospels threatened the ascendancy of the newly defined Church orthodoxy and the Qumran texts threatened the political ascendancy of the Roman Empire. Since they were perceived as threatening to church and state, they would have all been burnt had they been discovered. In order to survive, they had to be well hidden and they were.

It is strange that, during the long years of delay between the initial rediscovery of these hoards and their eventual publication, the same motives for their having been hidden in the first place were reactivated, at least to a certain extent, in the opinions of some commentators. The Nag Hammadi texts took thirty-five years (from 1945 to 1980), and the Dead Sea Scrolls forty-five and thirty-six years (from 1947 and the second find in 1956, to 1992), to be published completely. Elaine Pagels in *The Gnostic Gospels*, quotes Professor Hans Jonas, the eminent authority on gnosticism, as complaining that, with regard to the gnostic texts, the massive delays were due to the 'persistent curse of political roadblocks, litigations and, most of all, scholarly jealousies."[9] As regards the Dead Sea Scrolls, there are many who came to believe that pressure from the Vatican inhibited the International Team, centred on the Ecole Biblique in Jerusalem, from publishing the majority of the Scrolls for fear of Inquisatorial reprisals. There are those who believe that but for the determination of certain scholars and journalists over many years, much of the Scrolls' material would once again have been 'lost' because it posed a threat to Catholic doctrine. Michael Baigent and Richard Leigh's notorious account of all this in *The Dead Sea Scrolls Deception*, denounced by interested parties as mere sensationalist journalism, documented too much evidence from other sources to be wholly dismissed.[10] It is sobering to reflect that after lying buried in the desert for sixteen and nineteen hundred years respectively, these texts should reemerge into a world in which their power to alarm is still considerable. Have there ever been time bombs with longer fuses?

Is it possible to draw a comparison between these sagas of the Nag Hammadi and Qumran manuscripts on the one hand, and the Joseph-with-Jesus-in-Britain material on the other? Obviously the answer is 'yes' as far as ecclesiastical motives for its suppression are concerned. If we take such scraps of evidence as there are, whether written or oral, as all that remains of a suppressed tradition, then we can see that the early foundation of the Old Church at Glastonbury, whether by Jesus or Joseph, would clearly have been a major threat to Roman claims to primacy. The Roman Church would probably have denied that there had ever been any apostolic visit from Peter, Paul, Simon Zelotes, Philip or even Aristobulus, the reputed 'Bishop of Britain.' Such early Christianity as there might have been, would have been attributed to an offshoot of Philip's mission to Gaul and been subsumed under that. If Joseph was known to have come, the claim that he had established a church could have been dismissed because he was not an Apostle and in the technical sense, only Apostles could found churches or ordain successors. Also, there would have been no report of any converts or martyrs which would have been thought highly suspicious. How could there have been a mission without converts or martyrs? Both were essential components of all other authentic churches. Then there would have been the enormous cultural and ethnic gap between the Mediterranean and north-west Europe. How could the denizens of the Greco-Roman world,

Christian or no, have been expected to believe that a non-Apostle had settled happily with his fellow Christians among northern barbarians, not only without bloodshed, but also on land gifted to him by heathen princes? And all this *before* Peter or Paul had settled in Rome. It would have been unthinkable. This would have applied even more to any hint that Jesus himself had visited Britain. It would have been, as indeed it still is, greeted with laughable derision, despite the fact that, then as now, nobody knows what Jesus did or where he went between the ages of twelve and thirty.

So, yes, as far as motives for its suppression are concerned, there is every reason for maintaining that there is a valid comparison to be drawn with the Nag Hammadi and Qumran sagas. Can this be carried further? Surely not, because in order to do so, some new evidence regarding Joseph and Jesus-in-Britain would have to have been produced and it has not. The Nag Hammadi finds added new knowledge to smaller earlier finds and the extensive polemical writings of Irenaeus and other Gnostic-haters. The Qumran finds added to earlier knowledge going back to Philo, Pliny and Josephus. Certainly there is no new literary evidence to call on. No lost manuscript has been dug up in Glastonbury, St Just or Looe. Neither has anyone added to the scraps of oral tradition gathered by eccentric Anglican vicars earlier this century. And yet I believe, for all that, there is indirect, circumstantial evidence to be looked at which is based on inferences from recent archaeological discoveries and theories. It may not be sufficient in itself to prove anything, but I think it can be legitimately included in the material which must be looked at before the discussion can be adequately concluded. I do not claim that Dobson's thesis, following on from Geoffrey Ashe, contains the necessary element to complete a true analogy between a possible lost Jesus-with-Joseph tradition and the lost Gnostic or Qumran traditions, but I do believe that if it is aired fairly, it could open up a way of looking at certain recent archaeological research which could be held to impinge on this question. It could prepare the way for a different attitude to the topic, a different approach and a potentially new paradigm. This must be taken in stages and the first stage is to summarize Dobson who himself comes from a line of speculation which goes back to the eighteenth century. He, like his mentors, has been marginalized because it is now thought that his sources lack historicity to such an extent that he is guilty of unacceptable credulity. He has therefore been discredited, for having fabricated the modern equivalent of 'monkish fables.' However, in the light of the recent archaeological theories which I shall come to later, it may be that the speculations of Dobson and his ilk, were not as unfounded as has been thought. It is at least my intention to use him as an introduction to a neglected option.

This examination of the reasons why religious traditions get lost, with particular reference to Nag Hammadi and Qumran, has made me more curious to find out the reasons why not only Dobson but also H.A. Lewis and R.W. Morgan, whom Ashe also draws on, have been so completely rejected. A summary of their contribution will tell us and lead on to unexpected avenues of inquiry.

4

Why would Jesus have come to Britain?

In his small but influential booklet *Did Our Lord Visit Britain as they say in Cornwall and Somerset?* published in 1936, the Rev C.C. Dobson gratefully acknowledges his sources. The first is the Rev Sabine Baring-Gould's *A Book of Cornwall.* The second is *St Joseph of Arimathea at Glastonbury* by the Rev Lionel Smithett Lewis, published in 1922 and revized in later editions. The third is *Christ in Cornwall?* by the Rev H.A. Lewis, published in 1939, whom he quotes only in later editions. The fourth is *St Paul in Britain* by the Rev R.W. Morgan, first published in 1860. All these were Anglican clergymen tinged with Celtic sympathies, who quoted each other as authorities, and it could be claimed that they all betray bias. I would accept that they all had a vested interest in attempting to prove the primacy of the ancient British church and that some of their arguments are extremely tenuous. I am inclined to agree with Ashe when he says 'Much of the recent Glastonbury literature has unfortunately a crankish flavour,' and when he chides the Rev Lionel Smithett Lewis:

> Ardent, painstaking, and more nearly right in spirit than many a wiser author, he spoiled both books by an utter inability or unwillingness to criticize evidence ... When guesswork has been discounted, Lewis's books have a certain value in suggesting lines of research. But anyone who follows these up will be distressed to find that Lewis's authorities are largely outmoded, and that he is capable of quoting a document with name, date and an air of scholarship, but with no hint whatever that all scholars regard the document as a forgery.[1]

Since the Rev H.A. Lewis and the Rev C.C. Dobson both cite the Rev Lionel Smithett Lewis uncritically, it would seem to be legitimate for anyone, following Ashe, to dismiss all these vicars as unworthy of further serious consideration. While I would go a long way with this, I would have to stop short of total scepticism because I cannot see in principle why Jesus should not have come to Britain with Joseph. No one knows where he went during his silent years and he could just as well have come to Britain as stayed at home or gone to Egypt or India as others have proposed. If he came with Joseph it could easily have been in a boat to St Just-in-Roseland, Falmouth, or St George's Island off Looe, as the Rev H.A. Lewis claims, or to Glastonbury up the River Brue from Burnham or Uphill on the Somerset coast, as the Rev C.C. Dobson suggests. This last possibility would agree entirely with Professor Treharne and Margaret Deansley as quoted earlier, while the first option would agree with the traditional interpretation of the tin route as described by Diodorus Siculus in the first century BC, when he stated that 'On the island of Ictis the merchants purchase the tin of the natives and carry it from there across the Straits of Galatia or Gaul.'[2] While the exact location of the Isle of Ictis has been disputed, it is usually thought to be somewhere on the south Cornish coast, most probably St Michael's Mount, as R.D. Penhallurick asserts in *Tin in Antiquity*. Interestingly, while Penhallurick rejects the deeply rooted belief that the ancient Phoenicians were involved in the Cornish tin trade, he is surprisingly open to the possibility of a Jewish connection, although, unlike the Rev H.A. Lewis *et al*, he dismisses the link between Marazion and Zion and of Trejewas or Market Jew, Penzance, being of Jewish origin.[3]

It seems to me that the weakness of all these stories, whether from various sites in Cornwall or Somerset, does not lie ultimately in the absence of ancient literary sources to back them up. For if we are to accept the oral tradition as an important part of the Celtic heritage, then all the legends collected by these Anglican vicars must be considered to derive more likely from historical fact than not. In her article 'St Joseph in Britain: Reconsidering the Legends. Part 2,' Deborah Crawford makes the pertinent point that the oral transmission of sacred stories was actively preferred to the written word by the Celts. She quotes Caesar's *Conquest of Gaul*: 'The Druids believe that their religion forbids them to commit their teachings to writing, although for most other purposes, such as public and private accounts, the Gauls use the Greek alphabet.'[5] Amazing feats of memory continued to be a distinctive feature of

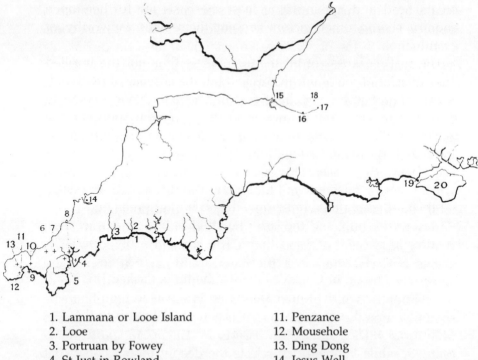

1. Lammana or Looe Island	11. Penzance
2. Looe	12. Mousehole
3. Portruan by Fowey	13. Ding Dong
4. St Just-in-Rowland	14. Jesus Well
5. Falmouth	15. Burnham
6. Redruth	16. Glastonbury
7. St Day	17. Pilton Hills
8. Carnon Downs	18. Priddy
9. St Michael's Mount	19. Hurst Castle
10. Nancledra	20. The Isle of Wight

Figure 1. Places in the West of England associated with Jesus' visits

the bardic storytellers until well into the Christian era. Thus 'allegedly early stories without an early manuscript history become the norm, rather than being automatically suspect.' She cites examples from the historian Jan Vansina of 'the surprising ability of oral information to survive indefinitely in recognizable forms' and of one from Southern Libya which 'appears to have survived by oral transmission for two and a half millennia.'[6]

If we add this preference for the oral transmission of sacred teachings to the model of a 'lost tradition' as outlined earlier, then all we would expect to have come down to us, would be the few, varied scraps which we do in fact have. There is therefore a case for turning the sceptical assessment, as represented by Ashe, on its head and making it at least the basis for further, open enquiry should other factors present themselves as worthy of examination.

The real weakness of all these stories is thus not the implied inadequacies of the oral transmission but the absence of motive. It is the lack of any compelling reason for Jesus having come to Britain, that stands out as the serious flaw. The only popular one given is that he accompanied his 'uncle' Joseph in the tin trade, as recounted by Sabine Baring-Gould:

> Another Cornish story is to the effect that Joseph of Arima-
> thea came in a boat to Cornwell, and brought the child
> Jesus with him, and the latter taught him how to extract the
> tin and purge it of its wolfram. This story possibly grew
> out of the fact that the Jews under the Angevin kings
> farmed the tin of Cornwall. When the tin is flashed [in
> smelting], then the tinner shouts 'Joseph was in the tin
> trade,' which is possibly a corruption of 'St Joseph to the
> tinner's aid.'[7]

This is plainly an insufficient reason, implying that Jesus was at a loose end, hanging about, waiting for his Messianic call to come through, so, to fill in the time, he became gainfully employed in the family business overseas. While this is acceptable at a certain level, it is nevertheless trivial in its understanding of Jesus' possible reason for coming.

The only serious motive given is that he came to Glastonbury to build a church. This is the story we have already heard about and which Geoffrey Ashe has dismissed as arising from a:

> ... too literal reading of the story about the Old Church
> being of divine foundation, though there is an evident diffi-
> culty here, because if Jesus built it, Joseph did not. Enthu-
> siasts have had to argue that the reference is to a small
> house which Jesus did build and which became a chapel.

The source of this is a letter written by St Augustine to Pope Gregory some time after he settled at Canterbury. For all Ashe's scepticism it is worthy of close scrutiny:

In the Western confines of Britain, there is a certain royal
island, called in the ancient speech Glastonia ... dedicated to
the most sacred of deities. In it the earliest (English)
neophytes of the Catholic rule, God guiding them, found a
church, not built by art of man they say, but prepared by
God himself for the salvation of mankind, which church,
the heavenly Builder himself declared — by many miracles
and many mysteries of healing — he had consecrated to
himself and to the holy Mary, Mother of God.

Another version of this concludes '... found a church constructed
by no human art, but by the hands of Christ himself, for the
salvation of his people.'[8]

Whether taken literally or purely spiritually, this text appears to
indicate that Augustine, perhaps with some surprise, had heard of
the tradition that the first church in Britain was at Glastonbury and
that it was reputed to have been built by Jesus himself. The
reference to 'the heavenly Builder himself declaring' referred
particularly to St David of Wales who had come to dedicate the
Old Church in Glastonbury, but who had been warned sternly by
Jesus in a vision the night before not to do so because he had
already dedicated it to his mother. All this is narrated in the later
edition of William of Malmesbury's *De Antiquitate*, as referred to
in Chapter 2.

The Rev C.C. Dobson makes much of this text. Indeed, it is he
particularly who is criticized for literalism, as in the following:

The translation 'hands of Christ himself' has been
questioned ... In the ancient MS used by William of
Malmesbury the Latin expression is 'a Deo Paratam,'
'actually by God Himself.' In one of the two ancient Mss,
used by Bishop Stubbs, that of the anonymous Saxon priest
'B,' the expression is 'Coelitus paratam,' 'divinely constructed.' Whichever version is preferred, 'the divine hand'
is obviously Christ Himself, because a material building is
being referred to, and because in contrast, 'The Almighty' is
mentioned as subsequently watching over it ...[9]

However, to my mind, this comment appears reasonable
enough. Literalism would seem to be as valid an interpretation

here as any other. Dobson goes on to note that William of Malmesbury records in his earlier book *The Acts of the Kings of England*, that Paulinus, St Augustine's companion, covered the Old Church with protective boards in order to preserve it: 'This certainly shows a very marked reverence on the part of St Augustine and his mission for the old church. What cause had he for showing such high reverence, when he might quite well have regarded it as a rival to his mission? Does not his letter to Gregory supply the reason, and the fact confirm the latter?'[10]

Dobson thinks that this authenticates the literal truth of Gildas' assertion that 'Christ, the True Sun, afforded His Light' to Britain before the last year of Tiberius, AD 37. In other words, he was not referring to an early preaching of Christ's teachings by an apostolic mission but to the actual presence of Jesus in the flesh and his own personal teaching. He says that it is only this literalism which can explain the saying attributed to the bard Taliesin, circa AD 550 : 'Christ, the word from the beginning, was from the beginning our Teacher, and we never lost his teaching.' He argues that if Jesus had indeed stayed at Glastonbury, then 'we never lost his teaching' would refer to an unbroken witness to his actual teaching through Joseph and his disciples.[11] These are staggeringly literal interpretations of both Gildas and Taliesin, yet I cannot see why they should not in principle be taken as seriously as the usual symbolic explanation.

One of the reasons why Ashe rejects the possibility of either Jesus or Joseph having built the Old Church is that 'buildings for Christian worship were unknown till much later,'[12] but couldn't it have been the exception which proved the rule? After all, as he and other historians admit, the Old Church did exist and had stood on the site 'from time immemorial, so long that there was no authentic record of its foundation.'[13] And couldn't the use of the appellation 'the heavenly Builder,' *coelorum Fabricator* in St Augustine's letter in this instance have been meant to signify something a little more particular than a general attribute of God? Can't the possibility be acknowledged that in this instance the link being made between an earthly building and 'the heavenly Builder' was no more accidental than it was appropriately pious? Do we have to face the possibility that in assessing the age, authenticity and importance of the Old Church, we may have to take into account categories of interpretation which so far have not been used, notably those of sacred architecture and the esoteric wisdom tradition? I believe we have because there is clearly a secret hidden somewhere in the antique veneration which surrounded this unique building. Even Ashe is tempted to speculate: 'Its dedication, unparalleled in Britain till long after, was to the Virgin Mary, a fact that may hint at pre-Christian Glastonbury having been a goddess sanctuary.'[14]

I believe that this speculation can be taken further, from its dedication to Mary to its possible construction by Jesus himself as the tradition represented by C.C. Dobson and company maintains. My reason for this does not spring from any covert Celtic sympathies or any desire to establish the primacy of the British church. It arises in general from the study of the ancient principles of sacred architecture, and in particular from the knowledge that while Jesus is popularly believed to have been a carpenter, in the esoteric tradition he is understood to have been a builder and to have led an earthly life analogous to that of 'the heavenly Builder.' It is not necessary to develop this further at this point because it will be explained fully in the second part of this study. Nevertheless it is appropriate to note here that there is another instance in which the esoteric tradition makes an appearance with reference to the architecture at Glastonbury. This occurs in the *Domesday Book* where it is said that within the monastery there was 'the Home of God' which was called 'the Secret of the Lord.' The full quotation runs: 'The Domus Dei, in the great Monastery of Glastonbury, called the Secret of the Lord. This Glastonbury Church possesses in its own Villa XII hides of land which have never paid tax.'[15] By any criterion, this is a very strange text which, if taken by itself, only serves to heighten the sense of mystification surrounding the foundation. But if it is taken together with the other texts we have looked at, it is possible to see it as yet another piece of evidence for the presence of a secret tradition, which had been 'lost' because it had been suppressed. It was also clearly esoteric insofar as it testified not only to the fact that Jesus came to Glastonbury but that as a builder who was also 'The Builder,' he had constructed a house himself.

Such an interpretation is strengthened by the cryptic reference to 'some holy secret' which William of Malmesbury makes when he is describing the Old Church in his earlier book *The Acts of the Kings of England*. Round the altar he says 'we may note in the pavement on either side, stones carefully placed, either in triangles or squares, and sealed with lead; beneath which, if I believe some holy secret to be held, I am doing no harm to religion.'[16] We shall return to this in Part III. In the meantime, it need only be noted that, if read literally, there is another sentence in William of Malmesbury which could be taken to refer to the ancient belief that the physical Jesus came and ministered at Glastonbury. This is in part of the famous charter given by King Ine circa AD 700, which William gives in full:

> To the ancient Church, situate in the place called Glaston-
> bury (which Church the Great High Priest and Chiefest
> Minister formerly through His own ministry, and that of
> angels, sanctified by many an unheard-of miracle to
> Himself and the ever-virgin Mary, as was formerly revealed
> to St David) do grant ... etc.[17]

It is on the basis of a literal interpretation of all these extraordinary texts that C.C. Dobson constructs his definitive restatement of what Professor Treharne calls 'the extreme form of the Glastonbury legend.' It goes like this: Joseph of Arimathea, the 'honourable counsellor' of Mark 15:43 in the Authorised Version, is the 'Nobilis decurio' of St Jerome's Vulgate Latin translation. This can be taken to mean that he was a member of a provincial Roman Senate as well as or instead of, a member of the Jewish Sanhedrin and Decurions were known to be in charge of mining districts.[18] He is therefore presumed to have come on business to trade with the rich tin, lead and copper mines of Cornwall and Somerset. It is significant that there are no legends in Devon. This is because the trade route in these metals did not go through that county. He took Jesus with him because he became his guardian after his father's early death. This and the claim that he may have been Jesus' uncle or a close kinsman is inferred from the fact that later Pilate readily granted him Jesus' body after the crucifixion. They followed the trade route as described by Diodorus Siculus. They landed at St Michael's Mount or some other trading port on the south Cornish coast. Business then takes them on a tour to mining areas in Cornwall and Somerset, the journey to the latter being accomplished by boat as indicated on his map.

They arrived eventually at Glastonbury, 'the Bristol of its day'

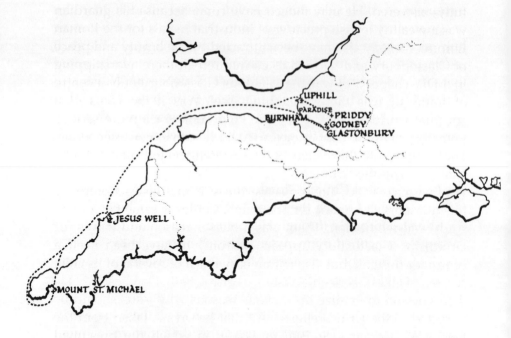

Figure 2. Traditional route taken by Jesus and Joseph of Arimathea

according to Margaret Deansley. Here, says Dobson, Jesus was
attracted by the peace and beauty of the island. Evidently it was
not such a busy trading crossroads that quiet corners could not be
found. He later decided to return as a young man:

> Seeking a quiet retreat in which to spend some years alone
> before His Ministry, He returned here as a young man,
> erected His own small hermitage of mud and wattles, of
> which houses were erected in the neighbourhood, and then
> in prayer and meditation, prepared for His work and
> Passion. This house afterwards may have been used by
> Joseph and his eleven companions as a private chapel.[20]

I confess that I consider all this to be well within the bounds of
possibility. I know it cannot be proved but nevertheless, bearing
in mind the number of anomalous references and otherwise
unaccountable components of the history and legends as outlined,
I find it, on balance, easier to believe than to doubt. Yet I am still
dogged by the feeling that the question of motive has not been

fully answered. He may indeed have come because his guardian was a wealthy Jewish procurer of industrial metals for the Roman Empire. He may also have been attracted by the beauty and peace of Glastonbury and decided to go into retreat there, worshipping in a DIY chapel. But was that all? Was Glastonbury only a centre of trade, or was there something else? Was it the focus of a spiritual world as well? Could he have come for a more serious exchange than tin, copper or lead? Did he come, not to be alone, but to share with the leaders of the Old Religion in Britain? Did he come to meet the Druids?

What makes C.C. Dobson so pertinent is that he asks precisely this question. For him it is not enough that Jesus came for retreat, study and meditation. There was a deeper reason and it was for Druidism. 'Glastonbury appears not only to have been itself a centre for this cult, but also within easy reach of several of its chief centres, such as Caerleon, Salisbury, Bristol, Bath, Dorchester.'[21] He then goes on to itemize the various reasons why Jesus should be attracted to the Druid religion. All that he says is taken from the Rev R.W. Morgan's *St Paul in Britain* in which the presumed doctrines of Druid theology are presented in detail. To summarize, he makes eleven main points: First; Druidism is an ancient, reputable religion, as exemplified in the triad 'Three duties of every man. Worship God: be just to all men: die for your country.' Second; it was widespread and powerful as witnessed by its major role in the resistance to the Roman invasion of Britain. Third; it believed in a Trinity and was not polytheistic. The Godhead was Duwa and the Trinity were Beli the Creator, Taran the preserver and Yesu the coming Saviour. Fourth; the oak was the sacred tree of the Godhead. Fifth, the mistletoe with its three white berries, represented the Trinity but especially Yesu. Sixth; Druidism thus anticipated Christianity. Seventh; it is similar to the law of Moses. Eighth; it was a strictly oral, secret faith like the Masons today. Ninth; Caesar said 'The Druids teach that by no other way than the ransoming of Man's life by the life of man is reconciliation with the Divine Justice of the Immortal Gods possible.' This means they had a Doctrine of Atonement as well as a Saviour Yesu. Tenth; there were forty Druidic Universities with 60,000 students each spending twenty years studying. Eleventh; the subjects studied were natural philosophy, astronomy, arithmetic, geometry, jurisprudence, medicine, poetry and oratory.[22]

With such an impressive list of attractions, it is easy to see why Jesus would have wanted to come. In fact it is difficult to imagine how he could have stayed away! This of course is precisely the conclusion Dobson has reached:

> Here was a faith propagated by profound oral teaching, enshrining the truth, proclaiming the coming Christ under the very name Jesu and the principle of Atonement. Do we wonder that Jesus came to reside in a land thus ripe to receive His Truth? When Joseph of Arimathea subsequently came to proclaim the Saviour under the very name familiar to every Druid, and as having fulfilled in the Atonement their basic principle, we do not wonder that he received a welcome at the hands of the Druids. It is a remarkable fact that Druidism never opposed Christianity, and eventually became voluntarily merged with it.[23]

Dobson then quotes John 7:15 where it says that 'the Jews marvelled, saying, How knoweth this man letters having never learned?' He suggests that the answer to their question is that he had studied the Mosaic law in conjunction with the Druidic oral secrets at Glastonbury and that this combination was what made his message so wonderful. He then concludes:

> In Britain He would be free from the tyranny of Roman oppression, the superstition of Rabbinical misrepresentation, and the grossness of pagan idolatry, and its bestial, immoral, customs. In Druid Britain He would live among people dominated by the highest and purest ideals, the very ideals He had come to proclaim.[24]

Here, at last, we are presented with a sufficiently serious motive for Jesus to have come to Britain. It is to Dobson's credit that he has seen that such a profound motive is needed in order to justify the presence of the traces of the lost Jesus-in-Britain tradition as outlined. It is also to his credit that he puts forward such a strong case for the Druid connection. He presents his case so succinctly and so clearly that it is difficult not to find it compelling. Yet there are many, as indicated, who would doubt the reliability of his sources, particularly of the Rev R.W. Morgan, on whose *St Paul in*

Britain he draws so heavily. There are many who would agree with Ashe's criticism of the Rev L.S. Lewis, that 'his authorities are largely outmoded'[25] and would apply it equally to Dobson with regard to Morgan. Indeed it has been claimed that most of what Dobson got from Morgan can be traced back to Edward Williams (1747–1826) better known as Iolo Morganwg of whom Stuart Piggott said 'his Druidic fabrications were to poison the well of genuine scholarship in early Celtic literature for generations to come.'[26] Piggott is not alone in believing that Iolo Morganwg and other late eighteenth, early nineteenth century Celticists were 'economical with the truth.' There is still a general feeling among scholars that the well of genuine Druidic studies remains so polluted by these men and Morganwg in particular, that to drink from it at all is to risk damaging your intellectual health.

We must therefore ask the question: to what extent can Dobson and Morgan be trusted? Have they painted a romantic picture of what they wanted to believe? Have they re-invented rather than rediscovered Druidism, recreating it in the image of their own predilections? Have they made it fit their own needs? Have they conveniently Christianized it? In order to answer these questions we must look deeper into the history of the earlier Celtic literature before turning to the classical texts to answer the question: who were the Druids?

5
How Reliable Are the Sources?

It could well be that the details of the Rev R.W. Morgan's Druid theology which the Rev C.C. Dobson summarizes, came from the highly suspect, if not fraudulent world of Iolo Morganwg. Stuart Piggott outlines the main features of this world succinctly. After the publication of James Macpherson's *Ossian* translations in 1762–63, themselves deeply suspect, Thomas Percy published his *Reliques of Ancient English Poetry* in 1765. He was in touch with the Rev Evan Evans who was collecting old Welsh poetry and had published his own *Specimens of the Poetry of the Ancient Welsh Bards* the previous year. This was a time of growing enthusiasm for early Celtic poetry and others were also making important contributions to serious studies such as Edward Jones in his *Musical and Poetical Relics of the Welsh Bards* of 1784 and *The Bardic Museum of Primitive British Literature* of 1802.[1]

Evan Evans admitted that some of these early poems, particularly those attributed to the sixth century poet Taliesin, were extremely difficult to translate. Nevertheless he cautiously but unwisely claimed that they represented the 'Druid's Cabbala.' But, as Piggott shows, Iolo showed no such restraint and went much further:

> Iolo went much further, with the advantage that he had no compunction in inventing sources where none existed, and in his *Poems, Lyric and Pastoral* (1794) announced that the poems of Taliesin 'exhibit a complete system of DRUIDISM,' and that 'by these (undoubtedly authentic) writings it will appear that the *Ancient British* CHRISTIANITY was strongly tinctured with DRUIDISM.' There is indeed a group of very obscure poems, attributed to Taliesin but more probably of later date, and free 'translations' of these could yield, to Iolo and many others, an unlimited degree of mystic nonsense, but he set the matter on a firm basis of forgery

with his thirty 'aphorisms' defining the mysterious
doctrines and philosophy of the Druids, allegedly set out in
a sixteenth-century manuscript and as unconvincing as the
twenty Druid Ordonnances of Noel Taillepied. 'Dedication,
learning, self-delusion, mischief and error characterize this
phase of Welsh studies,' Dr Owen has sadly written.[2]

From this we can infer that R.W. Morgan most probably got his
dubious Druid theology at least in part from Iolo's understanding
of ancient British Christianity and thirty Druid aphorisms. This
certainly is the implication since he quotes from the Iolo MSS
Principles of Prediction of Gildas the Prophet.[3] And yet he need not
have done so entirely because there were others from whom he
could have obtained it just as easily. Iolo was not alone. The belief
that the Druids' religion was similar if not identical to the
Patriarchal religion of the Old Testament was widely held. Piggott
goes on to itemize other notable proponents of this hypothesis, for
instance Rowland Jones who published *The Origin of Language and
Nations* in 1764, *Hieroglyfic* in 1768 and *The Circles of Gomer* in 1771.
For Jones, as for many others, the Welsh were the Children of
Gomer and Japhet, son of Noah, was himself a Druid. Piggott
continues:

> ... in *The Way to Things by Words* (1766) he presents Celtic as
> the parent of all European languages, with primeval
> wisdom preserved and transmitted by the Druids, who so
> successfully permeated early Christianity with their
> doctrines that the Mass took its name not from the words
> *missa est*, but from the Druids' 'mistletoe.' The Druids had
> now acquired their own literature, concealed and obscure,
> but apparent to the eye of faith and recoverable by
> sympathetic translation, in early Welsh literature.[4]

The Patriarchal religion of the Welsh Druids was developed in
a series of books such as William Cooke's *An Enquiry into the
Druidical and Patriarchal Religion* (1754), D. James' *Patriarchal
Religion of Britain* (1836), Edward Davies' *Celtic Researches* (1804)
and *The Mythology and Rites of the British Druids* (1809).
Morgan could have found the substance of his Druid theology
in any of these or in the progeny they spawned, not just in Iolo.

This is implied by another reference where he quotes Godfrey Higgins' *Celtic Researches* (1827).[5] However irrational it may now seem to Piggott and other modern scholars, this avenue of studies was broad and fertile and there were many who were only too happy to walk down it. In view of the more extravagant theories of these enthusiastic Celticists, it is therefore surprising that they stop short of claiming that Jesus came to Britain to enjoy fellowship with their congenial Druidical Patriarchs. This might have been because even their daring speculations wavered at that outrageous possibility. Morgan's book is called *St Paul in Britain* not *Jesus in Britain* and he nowhere suggests that he came. It is left to the Rev C.C. Dobson to take that final adventurous step. Yet there was one famous Celticist of this period who had asked the question: did Jesus come to Britain? and who had done so with such vivid imagery and poetic grandeur that thereafter not even the deepest sceptic could wholly dismiss the idea. However, as Piggott shows, even Blake's *Jerusalem* was inspired by yet more eccentric proponents of this genre.

Rowland Jones had a great influence on William Owen Pughe, through whom it has been said, in terms reminiscent of Iolo, 'he [Roland Jones] helped to pollute the stream of Welsh scholarship throughout the nineteenth century.' Piggott laments that it is at this point that the Druids 'begin to move away from scholarship, however eccentric, and offer themselves as symbols within a non-rational universe in which every form of unreason may meet.'[6] He blames Pughe and his friend William Sharp for perverting the mind of William Blake with Rowland Jones' Celticist extravagances and Joanna Southcott's 'religious mania.' He agrees with Robert Southey: 'Poor Owen found everything he wished to find in the Bardic system, and there he found Blake's notions, and thus Blake and his wife were persuaded that his dreams were old patriarchal truths, long forgotten and now revealed.' Blake's *Prophetic Books*, *Jerusalem* and Druidical engravings were the poetic expression of this:

> Blake had been strongly influenced by the speculative mythologists, especially Bryant in his *New System: or An Analysis of Ancient Mythology* (1774–6): 'the antiquities of every Nation under Heaven' Blake was to write, 'is no less sacred than that of the Jews. They are the same thing, as

Jacob Bryant and all antiquaries have proved.' Though the
Druids change their character as Blake's own vision
changed during the writing of the *Prophetic Books* between
1797 and 1804, they have their apotheosis in the context of
his revolutionary discovery that Britain was the original
Holy Land, and Jerusalem not so far from Primrose Hill
where Iolo had initiated his first Gorsedd. At first Druids
are the priests, law-givers, philosophers and
mathematicians of Urizen, but by *Jerusalem*, 'All things
Begin and End in Albion's Ancient Druid Rocky Shore' ...
'Was Britain the Primitive Seat of the Patriarchal Religion?'
Blake asked, and straightway gave his answer: Patriarchal
Druids originated in Britain and spread their doctrines far
and wide, even to the oak-groves on the Plain of Mamre.
'Your ancestors' he told his readers (actually the Jews)
'derived their origin from Abraham, Heber, Shem and
Noah, who were Druids, as the Druid Temples (which are
Patriarchal Pillars and Oak Groves) over the whole Earth
witness to this day.'[7]

For all the other Celticists, the Druids were derived from the
biblical Patriarchs. They, like the Welsh, were descended from
Noah via Gomer and Japhet. Blake took the outrageous step of
turning this theory on its head and claiming that the Patriarchs
were Druids; that Abraham, Heber, Shem and Noah were descended from the ancient wise men of Britain. It was Britain, he
claimed, not Canaan that was the 'Primitive Seat of the Patriarchal
Religion.' If Britain, not Palestine, was the original Holy Land then
what was more logical than to pose the question: 'And did those
feet ...?' The answer was obvious. The question was rhetorical.
Jesus had come to Britain in order to return to the source of his
distant forebears' religion.

For Piggott, as for most modern Celtic scholars, all this is no
more than the *reductio ad absurdum* of a logic of supreme unreason
of which all those mentioned above were guilty. Blake may
perhaps be exonerated for having been no more than an inspired
eccentric, but the rest cannot. R.W. Morgan and C.C. Dobson, as
recognizable followers of this disreputable tradition, would
therefore have to be condemned along with all the rest. The
answer to our question: can they be trusted? would thus have to

be a resounding 'No' if this was the only possible assessment of
what became known in the nineteenth century as the helio-arkite
theology. But is it? Does Stuart Piggott speak for all reputable
scholars? By the number of editions of his book and the number
of times it is quoted, one could be forgiven for thinking so. But
does he? More pertinently, does his totally negative judgement
stand up to detailed scrutiny? I believe the answer to this is 'No'
and my reasons for so believing will emerge if we submit his
thesis to close inspection.

Piggott follows T.D. Kendrick in *The Druids* of 1927, who
appears to be just as damning of the helio-arkite tradition as
Piggott. Nevertheless, he in fact does leave the door open to the
possibility of there having been a genuine continuity between the
ancient Druids, the medieval Welsh bards and the Celtic revivalists
saying 'this is not by any means an extravagant or ridiculous
belief.'[8] Piggott accepts this, admitting that the medieval Welsh
and Irish bards had 'genuine roots in the ancient past of the Celts
and Druids.' He also admits that 'the links of this tradition in the
eighteenth century with that of the Middle Ages were genuine
enough.'[9] Now if this is indeed the case, that there were genuine
links among the Celticists of the eighteenth century, the bardic
tradition of the Middle Ages and the ancient bards and Druids,
why don't we hear more about them? Why doesn't he make this
the basis of a more positive assessment? His answer is that this
genuine tradition is so tenuous and the fabrications of the likes of
Iolo, Rowland Jones and Owen Pughe, so vast, that it has become
impossible to refine the gold from the dross. Consequently Piggott
dwells too much on the negative side of things, and leaves us with
the conviction that we are only dealing with fraud or fantasy in
the whole of early Celtic studies.

Surely, if there was any trace of truth in the assertion that there
was a genuine element of continuity, then that should be presented
to us as an option. But it is not. All we get is an endless catalogue
of criticism which implies that there were in fact not only no
genuine links with the medieval or ancient past, but that there
were no reliable scholars in this field at any period. Such a totally
sceptical assessment arouses the suspicion that he is not as
objective in his judgement as he makes himself out to be or would
like us to believe. This suspicion increases when we realize that his
attitude to the ancient Roman and Greek references to the Druids,

is as critical as it is to the helio-arkites of the eighteenth and nineteenth centuries. It is one thing to condemn the interpreters of the classical texts for having distorted and misinterpreted their sources, but it is quite another to blame the Roman and Greek authors themselves for having known very little about their subject and of having perpetrated the initial distortions and misrepresentations about the Druids, which their later interpreters have merely perpetuated. Yet this is his avowed position, which he states in his introduction and consistently maintains :

> ... the understanding of, and comments on, the barbarians round about them by the classical *literati* were inevitably coloured by contemporary modes of thought and current philosophical schemes, and here ... we must endeavour to detect where concepts and motifs have been unconsciously imposed on the Druids by those who first wrote about them, and who on occasion did them the honour of finding in them convenient vehicles for the exemplification of a philosophic concept.[10]

The concepts and motifs which Piggott believes the classical authors unconsciously imposed on the Druids were those of the Noble Savage and the Primitive. It was these which changed the Druids-in-themselves into the Druids-as-wished-for, and began the distortions which have been perpetuated and added to ever since. The concept of the Primitive, he maintains, manifests itself as Hard Primitivism if the author wished to stress the barbarity of human sacrifice, magic or extreme nationalism. This, he claims, tends to be the particular weakness of the Latin commentators. If the author wished to idealize the Druids, not mentioning human sacrifice etc. but presenting them as the repositories of ancient wisdom, then he says they were guilty of Soft Primitivism. This was the habitual shortcoming of the Alexandrian Greek writers. It is important to realize that *all* the classical authors, according to Piggott, were, without exception, guilty of one or the other. He develops this into a general theory of historical ideas regarding Golden Ages and Noble Savages:

> This complex of ideas has profoundly affected Western thinking and feeling since Homer and Hesiod, and by a

very slight enlargement, also came to comprehend the idea
of Utopian societies. It has all the vitality of a great
commonplace, and today provides a theme for much
science fiction for, as modern geographical knowledge now
precludes the existence of undiscovered terrestrial Utopias,
intelligences superior to frail and incompetent man have to
be sought for in inter-galactic space. We shall see, too, how
these same ideas were powerfully effective among those
who rediscovered and reconstructed the Druids from the
late seventeenth century onwards.[11]

This theme of the 'idealization of primitive peoples by those of
more complex societies' is obviously a very powerful one. No one
would wish to minimize this in the history of ideas or in any
consideration of important ideas about history, and Piggott has
massed an impressive amount of detailed evidence with which to
back up his theory. But my reservation about his position is not
that I doubt the importance of what he says, but that he claims
that it explains *everything*. I believe it explains much but not all,
and that in claiming to have explained all, he effectively explains
the Druids away altogether. Not only that, he gets so carried away
by the apparent success of his Noble Savage and Primitive models,
that he feels justified in being abusive about all those who believe
anything positive about the Druids whatsoever. These he sneers,
chase 'Moonbeams from the Larger Lunacy' seeking 'the Comforts
of Unreason.' They are credulous about 'almost unbelievably
fatuous speculations and fantasies.'[12] Their ranks are filled with
'many a psychological misfit and lonely crank.'[13]

Piggott should not be so dismissive since his own position is not
as unassailable as he believed it to be. This becomes clear when he
deals with the texts which speak of the Druids as having been
associated with, and having had many attributes of, the Greek
Pythagoreans. This is no marginal matter as it would appear from
his treatment of them for, apart from their Hard Primitive
condemnation of human sacrifice, magic and extreme nationalism,
the Romans are fairly consistent in likening the Druids to Pythagoreans. Likewise, the Greek Alexandrians who, Soft Primitivists to
a man, also consistently portray them as such. This is upsetting for
Piggott because, if the Druids were Pythagoreans, then they
couldn't have been Noble Savages and since they obviously were

Noble Savages, they couldn't possibly have been Pythagoreans. So in order to preserve this theory, he has to accuse those Romans and Greeks who make this claim, of the unforgivable sin of Soft Primitivism. They just have to be wrong. They just have to be idealizing these Primitive Savages. Their evidence has to be discredited. His theory must prevail over all these primary references. This is what he has to demonstrate. He is very ingenious in doing so but I believe he is nevertheless unfair, biased and guilty of as grave a distortion as many of those whom he criticizes so severely. In doing so I believe he is, like Rowland Jones or Owen Pughe, effectively saying, 'these are the theories on which I base my facts.' He only mentions the Pythagoreans rarely in any detail so let us look at two of his references in order to expose his unacceptable procedures.

The first I have chosen is with regard to the many times in which the Roman and Greek writers say that the Druids were like the Pythagoreans in their belief in the immortality of the soul. Piggott says that these are all guilty more or less of idealization because the Celtic doctrine of immortality 'is not in fact Pythagorean in content at all.' Why is this? Because 'it does not imply a belief in the transmigration of souls through all living things ... but only a naive, literal and vivid reliving of an exact counterpart of earthly life beyond the grave.'[14] Now, I do not doubt that he may have a point here, but notice the use he makes of it. The Celtic-Druid belief is made out to be naive and simple, meaning Primitive, whereas the Pythagorean is sophisticated and complex. He drives a wedge between the two, stressing the contrast rather than the similarity: 'What is surely significant is the very real contrast between the Celtic and classical vision of eternity.' The similarity which so many of the classical authors claim, has been based on their recognition that the Celtic belief in the afterlife is actually so strange and alien 'as to be necessary of explanation in some familiar philosophical terms.' In other words, they could only explain the strange by means of the familiar. They were guilty of crediting the Noble Savages with complex civilized ideas. They were guilty of Soft Primitivism. In this way Piggott has proved that although they said their beliefs were similar, they either knew they weren't or they were wrong. Thus the many references which link the Druids to the Pythagoreans on this doctrine are successfully discredited.

The other example I have chosen concerns the classical descriptions of the Druids as natural philosophers, theologians and wise men, similar to the Pythagoreans. None of these appellations fits Piggott's model of Savage barbarians at a primitive stage of evolution, so they must also be shown to be no more than the ill-founded speculations of a literary class who approached the subject 'with a number of pre-suppositions already in the minds of the most unprejudiced.'[15] Needless to say the presuppositions of the most unprejudiced concerned the irresistible appeal of 'the idea of sages as rulers among remote primitive peoples.' In their eagerness to describe them, the classical literati could not escape using terms associated with their own highly developed, technical, profound and subtle thought which, despite its 'overtones of intellectual complexity and sophistication,' nevertheless still 'had to be used in recording the simplest beliefs, superstitions, traditional lore and institutions of the barbarian peoples beyond the Alps.'[16] Piggott makes us feel really sorry that they had to come down from such lofty heights to describe such lowly affairs. The air is heavy with *noblesse oblige*. By implication we are also sorry for Piggott because it is obvious that he has to do the same. What a wearisome business it is to have to expend so much brilliant, subtle, sophisticated scholarship on such a trifling matter:

> They could not escape from writing of *philosophoi* and *theologoi*, philosophers and theologians; who studied *physiologia* and *ethike philosophia*, natural and moral philosophy; investigated *quaestiones occultarum rerum alterumque*, problems of things secret and sublime; and were *magistri sapientiae*, professors of wisdom. It would surely be a mistake to think that such phrases, when applied to the Druids, should necessarily be interpreted in the same sense as in a Socratic dialogue or a passage of Seneca or Cicero.[17]

Now I do not deny that there might have been an element of truth in this and that some romanticizing of the Druids may well have been evident, but to say that that was *all* there was to it and that the titles 'philosopher,' 'theologian' and 'professor of wisdom' were only used inadvertently because there were no others available, is surely going too far. Once again, his method is to accuse and excuse his sources of Soft Primitivism. As on the subject of the immortality of the soul, Piggott blames the classical authors for idealizing the Druids but explains why this was inevitable. It would surely be a great mistake to think classical authors were using these subtle, profound, sophisticated appellations in the same way as they used them of Socrates, Seneca or Cicero. But why? There is only one reason. If they were savages, however noble, they would have been far too uncivilized, uncouth, crude, naive, simple and barbaric to be capable of such intellectual achievements. This has already been proved. They were Primitive and anyone who doubts it, is himself guilty of Primitivism. This is Piggott's theory and his facts have demonstrated it. The same argument is also employed to discredit the many references to the Druids' considerable knowledge of astronomy and cosmology. Such expertise we are told 'is in fact common to many relatively barbarian societies' and could still be found until the last century among such primitive illiterates as the Tamils of South India.[18]

Thus Piggott has cleverly demolished every single classical text, and there are around twenty of them, which either state definitely, or infer, that the Druids were Pythagoreans. We have seen that he needs to do this, in order to preserve his theory. It is in many ways an attractive theory and he is to be congratulated for the thoroughness and astuteness with which he expounds it. But is it fair? Does it do justice to all the evidence? I think not. I think it sounds more like something between sophistry and speciousness. For there seems to me to be no other reason for such wholesale scepticism than his determination to hold on to an untenable position at all costs. I cannot for one moment believe that *all* the Classical authors were so guilty of Primitivism whether Hard or Soft, that *none* of them may be regarded as in any way balanced or trustworthy. All of them some of the time or some of them all the time perhaps, but not all of them all of the time. This is plainly ridiculous for it puts Piggott in the unique position of being the sole arbiter of their veracity. This makes him arbitrary. He assumes he can do what he likes with all the source material because it is all suspect, but this is not convincing scholarship. We have seen that he has an unacceptable motive for discrediting the Pythagorean option. This is all the more reprehensible because at no point in his book does he rise to the challenge of Nora Chadwick who, in *The Druids*, published a few years before, put forward a strong case for the Druids having been Pythagoreans as the classical authors describe. Although Piggott mentions Chadwick three times on minor points, he does not address, reply to or criticize her scholarly Pythagorean presentation. It would seem as though he were not writing an objective study at all but a polemic helpful no doubt to those with anti-Druid prejudices, like those responsible in recent years for banning modern Druids from Stonehenge at midsummer, but decidedly unhelpful to those who are looking for a fair assessment.

While not wishing to dismiss Piggott's contribution, it is important not to accept the substance of his thesis which is so clearly biased, particularly with regard to the Pythagorean option. Likewise, while not wishing to accept much of the helio-arkite theology, it would be as wrong to reject it all as to reject the authenticity of all the classical sources on which it is ultimately based. What has come out of this examination is that the Pythagorean interpretation of the classical texts on the Druids has not yet been assessed. Until this has been done, it would not be fair to assume that Dobson's, or even Blake's proposition that Jesus might have come to Britain to meet the Druids, was wholly misguided. For if the Druids were in fact Pythagoreans, this would present us with an unexpectedly strong link between ancient Britain and Greece and indeed the whole of the Middle Eastern world from which Jesus came.

6

The Pythagorean Option

Turning from Stuart Piggott to Nora Chadwick's *The Druids* is a shock. Right from the *Preface* her approach is completely different. After Piggott's sustained polemic, her affirmation is refreshing:

> The Druids are the most advanced of all intellectual classes among the peoples of ancient Europe beyond the Greek and Roman World. They were the most distinguished members of the Celtic communities of Gaul. We cannot fail to be impressed by their pre-occupation with spiritual and intellectual matters.[1]

One suspects that had she been writing after Piggott, not before, she would have wanted to have been a little more critical of the classical sources, but this is not necessarily the case because his negativity comes largely from T.D. Kendrick's *The Druids* of 1927, which was available to her and to which she refers in passing but does not follow in substance. Behind Kendrick, she also had J.A. MacCulloch's *The Religion of the Ancient Celts* in a similar vein, which she chose to ignore. In fact, she too is critical, admitting that such sources as we have, are rightly suspected of being either badly informed or second-hand. None of them, except Caesar and Cicero, had even met a Druid, and they had only met one — the same one, Divitiacus. Yet, for her, the perceived limitations of the classical texts are not due so much to their propensity for romanticizing the Druids as to their desire to misrepresent them for political purposes. She is also well aware that opinions vary as to the reliability of Posidonius (c. 135–50 BC) the presumed earlier source for Strabo, Diodorus Siculus, Caesar, Pomponius Mela, Pliny and Lucan. Did they quote him accurately? To what extent were he and his tradition concerned primarily with the bizarre, curious aspects of Druidism and not with serious appraisal? She comes close to Piggott's Soft Primitivism when she suggests they might all have been guilty of writing, to some extent, like tourists.[2] However, she turns away from accepting this in favour of acknowledging that we owe them a debt for their curiosity and that, most importantly, they are to be considered trustworthy because in many ways they paint a consistent picture. They are to be believed when they tell us that there were three orders of Druids:

1. Bards, who were panegyric or lyric poets (Diodorus, Strabo, Ammianus).
2. Ovates, who were sacrificers, diviners and seers (Strabo).
3. Druids, who were natural philosophers (Diogenes Laertius, Cicero, Clement); moral philosophers (Strabo); theologians (Diodorus, Tacitus, Lucan); interpreters of nature (Ammianus); diviners (Dio Chrysostom, Pliny, Diodorus, Hippolytus); magicians (Pliny, Hippolytus); doctors (Pliny); 'most just men' (Strabo); judges (Caesar, Strabo); arbiters in war (Diodorus, Strabo); settlers of manslaughter suits (Caesar, Strabo); educators (Caesar, Pomponius Mela): professors of wisdom (Pomponius Mela).

Likewise the Alexandrian Greek, Dio Chrysostom, Hippolytus, Clement, Cyril and Diogenes Laertius, following their main source, Alexander Cornelius Polyhistor (c.105 BC), are to be believed when they liken the Druids to the magi of the Persians, the priests of Egypt, the Brahmins of India and the Pythagoreans. She treats them with respect, unlike Piggott who says their accounts are 'all second-hand library work, with no new empirical observations from first-hand informants or from field-work among the Celtic people.'[3] Even if we accept that this may well be so, his own bias is evident in his failure to address, let alone refute, the grounds on which Chadwick bases her position, namely, that the Alexandrians probably went back to sources behind Polyhistor, to the third and fourth centuries BC, and that they were therefore much the earliest.[4] He also ignores her when she comments perceptively that it was not in the interests of the Alexandrians, who after all were Christians, to say positive things about the Druids: 'The later Alexandrian writers were Christians, and are not likely to have seriously falsified the tradition of the heathen Druids to their advantage.'[5]

As will become clear in later chapters, many of the categories used to describe the Druids, whether by Romans or Greeks, fit the Pythagorean model. Natural and moral philosophers, interpreters of nature, theologians, doctors, magicians, educators and professors of wisdom, were all descriptions which could as easily be recognized for being Pythagorean or Druidic. Quite apart from these implicit similarities, Chadwick is impressed by the many explicit connections which are recorded, such as that given by Hippolytus (c. 200 AD):

> The Druids among the Celts having profoundly examined the Pythagorean philosophy, Zalmoxis, a Thracian by race, the slave of Pythagoras, having become for them the founder of this discipline, he after the death of Pythagoras, having made his way there, became the founder of this philosophy for them. The Celts honour them as prophets and prognosticators because they foretell matters by the cyphers and numbers according to the Pythagorean skill.[6]

Chadwick is not convinced by Kendrick's assertion that there is 'no assured record of any intercourse between Pythagoras and the Kelts' and that the legend of Zalmoxis is pure fable.[7] It may not be history as such but it is legendary evidence for an acknowledged ancient connection. Her over-all assessment of the classical sources comes to precisely the opposite conclusion. The Druids she maintains can best be understood as Greek Pythagoreans:

> The *outstanding* features of druidical training may be summed up as natural philosophy and natural science — the nature of the physical universe and its relationship to mankind. This branch of human knowledge was characteristic of the early Greek philosophers of Ionia, and it is probable that the Druids and seers of Gaul, representing the backward but not wholly uncultured peoples on the periphery of Greek civilization, have preserved and transmitted late echoes of early philosophy and knowledge derived from the common property of the ancient Greek world which probably penetrated Gaul in the first place through the Greek colony of Marseilles. The form of this knowledge and this philosophy ... was associated by

the Alexandrian Greeks in particular with 'Pythagoreanism'
... How otherwise can we account for Druidism by any
explanation consistent with the facts? ... A relationship
between Druidism and the Greek world such as I have
suggested, would be consistent with the use of the Greek
alphabet by the Druids to which Caesar refers and with the
Greek personal names in the family of Phoebicius of
druidical ancestry, as reported by Ausonius.[8]

In fairness to Piggott, it must be admitted that he also makes a
passing acknowledgment of the possibility that 'some elements of
Greek mathematics found their way into the Celtic world through
the Massaliot contacts from *c.* 600 BC' but he immediately goes on
to sneer that if any Pythagorean doctrines really were transmitted,
it was probably only to do 'with such mundane affairs as the value
of the square on the hypotenuse of a right-angled triangle.'[9] This
sarcasm has provoked Peter Beresford Ellis in *The Druids* to make
the important observation that such a dismissive judgement can
only be made if the evidence of the megaliths and stone circles is
ignored. He says he knows that these constructions were not built
by the Celts because they pre-date Celtic civilization by at least one
thousand years. Nevertheless he quotes Christopher and Jacquetta
Hawkes who argued that they were built by the forebears of the
Celts. He is aware of various theories as to who built the megaliths
but he follows Neven Henaff, (1908–1983) who studied Stonehenge
in relation to the ancient Druidic Coligny Calendar and who,
following R.J.C. Atkinson's *Stonehenge* (1956) argued in *Carn* that
the mathematics of the numbers of stones at Stonehenge corresponded to the numbers on the Coligny Calendar. He quotes
Henaff: 'So that, after all, popular tradition and "primitive"
archaeologists, in persistently relating Stonehenge to the Druids,
may well have been correct from the start.'[10]

This is a very brave response to Piggott, and indeed to the
majority of contemporary archaeologists and prehistorians, among
whom Piggott's opinions still prevail. Beresford Ellis is sailing into
the eye of a storm which has been raging for many years on this
topic and risks being sunk or shipwrecked by the academic
establishment. Even though he is a respected Celtic scholar
himself, he has ventured into dangerous waters. For he is recognizable as one who should know better than to cite controversial

authorities to support arguments which appear to be harking back to romantic Soft Primitivism and Noble Savagery which, as we have seen, is considered to have polluted earlier Celtic studies. Yet it is obvious he is taking a calculated risk because he goes on to cite Gerald Hawkins' *Stonehenge Decoded* (1966) and others whose highly debatable theories gave rise to the new science of archaeo-astronomy, the study of the possible astronomical alignments of megalithic monuments. This, he says, led on to a positive re-assessment of Celtic building capabilities:

> In 1967 the archaeologist Patrick Crampton, in *Stonehenge of the Kings*, became the first to overturn the popular idea that the British Celts had little idea of sophisticated building techniques before the coming of the Romans, by showing the excavations of Clickhimin as an example, and then pointing to a tradition of sophistication in building from the time of Stonehenge to the Roman Conquest, showing a continuum. But whether these great astronomical constructions were built by pre-Celts or proto-Celts, the evidence is that they became part of Celtic tradition and certainly the building knowledge was inherited by later Celtic culture.[11]

Although elsewhere Beresford Ellis expresses doubts about a link between the Druids and the Pythagoreans, all that he and his authorities claim, supports a literal interpretation of the classical references, such as Caesar, who refers to the importance of cosmology to the Druids: 'Besides this, they have many discussions as touching the stars and their movements, the size of the universe and of the earth, the order of nature, the strength and the powers of the immortal gods, and hand down their lore to the young men.'[12] He is sceptical about a Pythagorean connection because he certainly would disagree with Piggott's and even Chadwick's contention that the Druids were the residue of 'backward but not wholly uncultured peoples on the periphery of Greek civilization.'[13] He would argue for an indigenous Celtic culture predating any possible Greek influence.

Radical though this position is compared with most contemporary archaeological opinion, it is nevertheless strangely similar to certain Alexandrian texts which claim not that the Druids were derived from the Pythagoreans as described, but that the Pythagoreans were derived from the Druids. Piggott predictably regards such ideas as the expression of the worst extremes of the Soft Primitive 'dream-world' and Chadwick, although respecting these texts, is unable, sadly, to make anything of them. It is left to Beresford Ellis to identify the monuments of the pre-Celts or pre-Druids of the megalithic age, as evidence of an indigenous ancient British culture from which the Pythagoreans could have been descended.

This seems to be the only interpretation which makes sense of Clement of Alexandria's claim that Pythagoras himself learnt his philosophy from the barbarians, among whom were the Druids: 'Alexander (Polyhistor), in his book "On the Pythagorean symbols," relates that Pythagoras was a pupil of Nazaratus the Assyrian ... And will have it that, in addition to these, Pythagoras was a hearer of the Galatae (Gauls) and the Brahmins.'[14] It would also make sense of Clement's other similar statement:

> Thus philosophy, a science of the highest utility flourished
> in antiquity among the barbarians, shedding its light over
> the nations. And afterwards it came to Greece. First in its
> ranks were the prophets of the Egyptians; and the
> Chaldeans among the Assyrians; and the Druids among the
> Gauls; and the Shamans among the Bactrians; and the
> philosophers of the Celts; and the magi of the Persians.[15]

Clement was evidently not alone in implying that Pythagoras could have been called a Druid *manqué* in so far as he was said to have learned from the Druids of Gaul, because Diogenes Laertius, Cyril and Stephanus of Byzantium also agree with his assertion to some extent.[16] Echoing Chadwick we may ask: how otherwise can we account for these far-fetched claims by any explanation consistent with the facts?

Extraordinary, nay outrageous, though it may seem, it would appear that these Alexandrian texts testify to a universal wisdom which pre-dated Pythagoras and from which he learnt. The representatives of this wisdom were called by various names in different countries but among the Celts they were known as philosophers and among the Gauls, as Druids. Furthermore, from the recent authorities to whom Beresford Ellis has referred, such as Atkinson, Henaff, Hawkins and Crampton, it would appear that these classical texts, as far as the Celtic philosophers and Gaulish Druids were concerned, might well have been referring to the proto-Celtic, proto-Druidic wisdom which had originated with the megalithic culture in the Neolithic Age. Just how Pythagorean this was and how contentious this issue is, will emerge in Part III when we look at the theories of Professor Alexander Thom and the controversy surrounding them, for although Beresford Ellis doesn't mention him, all he has proposed points in that direction.

It is important to mention that Beresford Ellis is not alone in holding that there was continuity of culture between the Celtic Druids and their distant Neolithic and Bronze Age predecessors. There are others who have also come to believe that the reaction against 'popular tradition and "primitive" archaeologists' went too far, and that recent research is now showing that after all they may not have been so wrong. For instance Euan Mackie in *Science and Society in Prehistoric Britain* has no difficulty in accepting cultural continuity from Stone Age to Druidic times. In contrast to Kendrick, Piggott and Chadwick, he maintains that if the Druids had acquired their knowledge of *physiologia* from the Greeks, then the centre of Druidism could be expected to have been Gaul, because the Greek influence came, as we have noted, via Marseilles (Massilia). But this, he reminds us, is not what Caesar says. He tells us that the Druidic *disciplina* 'developed first in Britain, and thence was introduced to Gaul; and to this day those who wish to pursue their studies of it more deeply, usually go to Britain for the purpose.' Mackie argues that this suggests a much older, British origin of the *disciplina* which, in turn, implicitly suggests the possibility of a link going right back to megalithic culture.[17]

John Edwin Wood in *Sun, Moon and Standing Stones* is another who would accept in principle the likelihood of such a link. Speaking about the transition from late Neolithic to Early Bronze Age Britain around 2500 BC, when the Beaker Folk arrived with their new knowledge of bronze metal working and distinctive pottery, he says that there seems to be evidence of a peaceful assimilation of the old with the new 'with apparently no break in continuity.'[18] Earlier archaeologists thought that the Beaker Folk conquered the indigenous tribes and forcibly established their own culture, but now this has been contested. 'The Beaker Folk and their successors took over the techniques for handling large blocks of stone, and although they no longer built communal graves, they set up stones in circles, and rows and as solitary megaliths from Shetland to Brittany.'[19]

From Wood's observations two points about continuity of culture can be made. First, there is no reason why, in principle, when a new wave of immigration and technology sweeps a country, it should necessarily imply the rejection of significant elements of an earlier culture. Second, even if there is conquest by immigrants, this does not in itself imply complete discontinuity of cultural systems, as evidenced by many of the wars between different European nations, or the Crusades when the western Christian conquerors found themselves 'conquered' or assimilated to a considerable extent by the culture and science of Islam. The implication of Wood's point is that there was most probably continuity of culture throughout the whole period of megalith building, that is from around 3000 BC to 1200 BC. This still leaves a gap between 1200 BC and 750 BC, the earliest date usually given for the arrival of the Celts and hence the Druids, but there is other evidence for continuity during this period to which we shall return later. It has been sufficient here to establish that Beresford Ellis is by no means alone in proposing that, if not the Druids, then at least their predecessors, were responsible for building Stonehenge and all the other stone circles; that they were the heirs of a tradition going back to at least 3000 BC and that not only was this tradition Pythagorean but, because of its vastly greater age, the Pythagoreans themselves may be thought of as a later expression of it. With all this in mind, we can now turn to Thom.

Alexander Thom

Alexander Thom had a long and distinguished academic career. He was, among other distinctions, Professor of Engineering at Oxford from 1945 to 1961, but he is best known for his surveys of megalithic sites in England, Scotland, Wales and Brittany. These began in the 1930s, on a sailing trip up the west coast of Scotland, when he noticed that the famous avenue of stones at the Callanish circle was aligned due north: 'a very difficult thing for people to achieve in those times because the Pole Star wasn't where it is now.' Thus began thirty years' field work at over three hundred sites during which he produced various articles on his results. In

1967, his first book *Megalithic Sites in Britain* was published in which, as well as startling conclusions regarding solar and lunar astronomical alignments, he put forward the theory that some of the stone circles were not round but egg-shaped or elliptical. These, he claimed, had been constructed by means of notional Pythagorean triangles, that is to say, right-angled triangles in which all the sides were whole numbers. He maintained that he had identified these as triangles where the sides were units of 3, 4 and 5; 5, 12 and 13; 8, 15, 17; 12, 35 and 37. He believed that he had also discovered the units of measurement which the builders had used and which had thus enabled him to find so many Pythagorean triangles. These were units of 2.72 feet which he called the Megalithic Yard (MY) and 6.8 feet, that is two and a half Megalithic Yards, which he called the Megalithic Rod (MR). He was impressed with his findings: 'It is remarkable that 1000 years before the earliest mathematicians of classical Greece, people in these islands not only had a practical knowledge of geometry and were capable of setting out elaborate geometrical designs but could also set out ellipses based on the Pythagorean triangles.'[20]

Thom's theories were greeted with incredulity and derision by most archaeologists and prehistorians. Professor Richard Atkinson summed up the general reaction at the time: '... it is almost inconceivable that mere barbarians on the remote north-west fringes of the continent should display a knowledge of mathematics and its applications hardly inferior, if at all, to that of Egypt at about the same date, or that of Mesopotamia considerably later.'[21] Later Atkinson was to change his mind. He realized that the problem Thom posed was not so much the nature of his data, although his complex mathematical and astronomical calculations were incomprehensible to most, but that its very sophistication upset 'the conceptual model of the prehistory of Europe.' He admitted: 'It is hardly surprising, therefore, that many prehistorians either ignore the implications of Thom's work, because they do not understand them, or resist them because it is more comfortable to do so. I have myself gone through the latter process; but I have come to the conclusion that to reject Thom's thesis because it does not conform to the model of prehistory on which I was brought up involves also the acceptance of improbabilities of an even higher order.'[22]

Although Atkinson's conversion is now over twenty years

old and has itself become part of the history of the archaeo-
astronomical debate, his statement and analysis is still definitive.
For instance, the eminent archaeologist Aubrey Burl, in *Prehistoric
Stone Circles* wrote quite recently 'many archaeologists remain
sceptical of theories of an intellectual elite setting out right-angled
triangles and computing the irrational Pi two thousand years
before Pythagoras,'[23] and 'Geometrical and astronomical theories
obtained from rings like these are likely to be misleading.'[24] Since
he goes on in this Shire Publication to call Stonehenge 'an
architectural disaster'[25] and 'an impressive but ramshackle
edifice,'[26] we may suspect that he suffers from more than a mild
form of Piggottry, nevertheless, his opinions are highly regarded
and widely accepted. Although he worked closely with Thom as
exemplified in their joint BAR publication *Megalithic Rings*, he has
remained consistently sceptical about the possibility of geometric
layout or a standard unit of megalithic measure. This is all the
more remarkable because his own surveys in many cases differ
only fractionally from those of Thom's whose actual surveying
skills he greatly respects. In *Prehistoric Avebury* he gives vent to his
anti-Thom-and-company sentiments and in doing so, speaks for
many of his colleagues:

> Modern over-emphasis on the mathematical and astrono-
> mical intentions of stone-circle builders, and the omission of
> archaeological evidence in several books about megalithic
> monuments, has transformed the animistic and living world
> of these prehistoric people into a kind of laboratory whose
> clinical walls were covered in Euclidean computations. The
> single support for this comes from statistics. There is no
> anthropological parallel for such a society. There is not one
> aspect of Neolithic and Bronze Age life amongst the
> thousands of artefacts, monuments, settlements, the
> economies, burial practices, rituals even the personal
> ornaments of the dispersed communities in Britain to
> suggest there was an island-wide culture bonding all these
> societies together, with a national yardstick and an all-
> powerful priesthood dedicated to a study of the heavens.[27]

It is certainly very strange that there is no archaeological evidence to back up Thom's conclusions — except of course the

evidence from the three hundred surveys on which his conclusions are based. And Thom is not alone. Quite apart from Professor Atkinson and others already mentioned, his research was developed from earlier surveys such as those of Admiral Boyd Somerville and Sir Norman Lockyer. Their work in turn goes back to pioneers like Stukeley and Aubrey and other Soft Primitivists of the seventeenth and eighteenth centuries. Bearing this in mind, can we say that Burl himself is without bias? May he not still be resisting Thom because he does not want his 'conceptual model of the prehistory of Europe' to be upset? This would appear to be the case because nowhere in his book on Avebury for instance, does he consider a Pythagorean interpretation either of astronomy or geometry. This is the case among all those who reject Thom's findings. At no point do they seriously consider his propositions from within the disciplines of mathematics or astronomy. Atkinson's indictment that they actually ignore the details of Thom's work 'because they do not understand them, or resist them because it is more comfortable to do so' would still seem to be correct. Christopher Chippindale in *Stonehenge Complete* admits this with refreshing candour:

> Neither the particular schemes of Stonehenge astronomy nor the larger vision of megalithic science have found favour with archaeologists. I am not sure they were ever given a really fair consideration, or that they could have been. Although some astronomers tried to grasp the archaeology, and some archaeologists the astronomy, practically no one had or has sufficient grasp of *both* subjects fairly to explore them together. And the statistical issues, far beyond the mathematics of most archaeologists, taxed the methods of first-rate statisticians.[28]

It is highly significant that when serious attempts have been made by those who are qualified to assess Thom's work from an astronomical and mathematical point of view, the results have by no means been as negative as those of the archaeologists. For instance Professor Douglas Heggie in *Megalithic Science*, although ambivalent and ambiguous in many of his conclusions, admits that he 'found satisfactory evidence for something like' Thom's megalithic units of length 'in the sense that the distribution of diameters is significantly non-random in a manner consistent with Thom's quantum hypothesis.'[29] Likewise he gives qualified acceptance to the geometry: 'There can be little doubt that some megalithic sites, especially rings of standing stones, were set out to careful geometrical designs.'[30] As regards the astronomical alignments he is equally if cautiously positive:

> Having sifted through a great deal of evidence on megalithic science and rejected what seems not to be significant, we find that there remains a small but interesting core of results. These are the results which are difficult to reconcile satisfactorily with the view that megalithic sites were *not* laid out using certain designs and that their orientation was *not* determined astronomically.[31]

Heggie attempts to sit firmly on the fence but is surprised at himself for having such relatively positive results after submitting Thom's work to such rigorous analysis. He is even tempted to interpret his conclusions by asking daringly why the megaliths were built. As he threads his way cautiously between possible answers, he admits that perhaps it may be time to change the old model of primitive prehistoric man, or if not change it, modify it. Such modification he believes has been put forward by Euan Mackie who 'has shown how a great deal of orthodox archaeological evidence can be re-interpreted in a way that offers no apparent conflict with the claims of megalithic science. Not only is this re-interpretation possible; some aspects of it, according to Mackie, seem "inescapable".'[32]

It is clear that Heggie is attracted by Mackie's ideas for he goes on to examine them with cautious but clear approval:

> Mackie supposes that the practice and knowledge of megalithic science were restricted to an élite class in society, of whom Lockyer's term 'astronomer-priests' is a quite accurate description. They lived in dwellings set apart from the ordinary people and enjoyed a higher standard of living, and it is they who organized the great projects such as the building of Stonehenge. According to Mackie, there may even be evidence for them in legend.[33]

This is a most remarkable affirmation of Mackie by Heggie, giving the lie to prehistorian Ronald Hutton's outburst of polemical Piggottry in *The Pagan Religions of the Ancient British Isles* where he contends falsely that Heggie has only negative things to say about Thom and Mackie.[34] For the legends to which Mackie, with Heggie's approval, points us, are those concerning the Druids. Indeed Mackie is not afraid to bring the Druids into his, or rather Lockyer's, picture of astronomer-priests. Commenting on Caesar's other observation that the youths who are sent by their parents to the Druidic colleges 'are said to learn by heart huge quantities of verse. Some spend twenty years in this *disciplina*,' he says he has no doubt that this verse 'contained all the Druids' accumulated wisdom, including data on astronomy and cosmology.' From similar oral transmissions in Polynesia and elsewhere, he finds it 'easy to see how the presence of an intellectual class in Late Neolithic Britain having such abilities ... could have led to most of the achievements that Thom has inferred.'[35]

Mackie goes on to cite evidence from the measurements of the Iron Age brochs in Scotland to clinch his case for a 2,000 year continuity of astronomer-priests and wise men:

> Not only has an independent mathematical analysis of the internal dimensions of the brochs revealed that a unit of length almost identical to the megalithic yard was used to set out their circular plans on the ground, but it is also clear that a few brochs were built around more complex geometrical figures also seen in the stone circles. Unless broch metrology was an Iron Age invention which by chance is identical to that of the Late Neolithic period — surely a far-fetched notion — this would seem to be a decisive demonstration that the learning of the stone circle builders was handed down intact across two millennia to the time of the Druids. There is not much reason to doubt now that the non-literate learned order of Iron Age Britain and Gaul had at least part of its origins in the wise men who inhabited the giant henges and who built the stone circles and Stonehenge.[36]

We may conclude that however contentious all this is among archaeologists and prehistorians, the fact remains that it is still an open debate. Sides may still be taken and points may still be argued. However much the majority may not like it, there is still a strong minority who view the work of Alexander Thom very favourably and who have used it to put forward a revised or modified model of the prehistory of Britain. This revised model suggests that what we call Pythagoreanism, or something very like it, can be traced back through the Druids to the astronomer-priests or wise men who built the megalithic stone circles. This opens up a staggering vista of some 3,000 years in time and 3,000 miles in distance between the eastern Mediterranean and Britain. It also opens up an equally staggering possibility with regard to Jesus, for if he can be shown to be connected in any way to the Pythago-reans of the Middle East, then, by implication, it could also be inferred that he might have been connected to the Druids. Furthermore, in a certain sense, what has been proposed by Euan Mackie could be seen as an archaeological ratification of something like Blake's position when he claimed that the Jewish Patriarchs were descended from the Druids. When this was considered under the scathing eye of Piggott, it seemed laughable, but now that it has been shown that the proto-Druid tradition pre-dated the Pythagoreans by two millennia, all it needs is to demonstrate that the Jewish Patriarchs might have had Pythagorean or proto-Pythagorean connections for Blake's crazy notions to seem at least feasible. Strange as it may seem, this is not hard to substantiate because, from the first century to the Renaissance, there was a tradition of biblical interpretation which held that, at least as far as number symbolism and cosmology were concerned, the Bible was permeated with Pythagorean and Platonic ideas. It is to this that we must now turn.

PART II

JESUS THE PYTHAGOREAN

7
The Pythagorean Tradition

Pythagoras was born between 580 and 570 BC to Mnesarchus of Samos and died at Metapontum, southern Italy, around 500 BC. Although much was written about him in later centuries, many of the details of his life are of disputed authenticity.[1] However, it is generally agreed that he left Samos in middle life because of the tyranny of its ruler Polycrates, and sailed to Croton in Southern Italy where he founded a religious and scientific community which was greatly influenced by the Orphic mysteries. This community soon acquired great political power but was eventually destroyed by a popular uprising against its authoritarianism. Those of its members who escaped were scattered, some going over to mainland Greece. After many years however, the community revived and continued its activities in Italy, notably at Tarentum, where, during the first half of the fourth century BC, Archytas, Philolaus and Eurytas flourished as eminent teachers.

The most important, distinctive teaching of Pythagoras and his school was that all things are numbers. As Aristotle says: 'the Pythagoreans, as they are called, devoted themselves to mathematics, they were the first to advance this study, and having been brought up in it they thought its principles were the principles of all things.'[2]

The Origins of the Pythagorean Doctrine

It is not known where this doctrine came from. Some say it was developed by inference from Pythagoras' experiments with the monochord, the one-stringed musical instrument on which he is said to have discovered the numerical ratios which underlie the musical scale.[3] Some, like his later biographer Iamblichus, claimed that the 'Pythagorean number theology was clearly foreshadowed, to some extent, in the Orphic writings' in which Orpheus had taught that 'the eternal essence of Number is the most providential principle of the universe of heaven and earth, and of the intermediate nature.'[4] Others say there was some influence from Anaximander who taught that everything was derived from the Unlimited (*Apeiron*) and to which Pythagoras added the notion of the Limited (*Peras*), the principle of form-giving through number as expressed in the ratios of musical harmony. The connection between number and music recurs in many sources. As Aristotle, the most reliable source of all says, they, the Pythagoreans: 'saw that the attributes and the ratios of the musical scales were expressible in numbers; since then all other things seemed in their whole nature to be modelled after numbers, and numbers seemed to be the first things in the whole of nature, and the whole heaven to be a musical scale and a number.'[5]

There is another possible origin for this doctrine and it is that Pythagoras learnt it from the extensive travels he is reputed to have made round the ancient world. Iamblichus (*c.* AD 250–325) says that he conversed with the Hebrew prophets on Mount Carmel, was initiated into the mysteries of Byblos and Tyre, spent twenty-two years in Egypt learning astronomy and geometry, was taken captive by Cambyses to Babylon, where he learned arithmetic, music and other sciences from the Magi, and then returned home after another twelve years.[6] Porphyry (*c.* AD 233–305) gives much the same itinerary, saying:

> As to his knowledge, it is said that he learned the
> mathematical sciences from the Egyptians, Chaldeans and
> Phoenicians; for of old the Egyptians excelled in geometry,
> the Phoenicians in numbers and proportions, and the
> Chaldeans in astronomical theorems, divine rites, and
> worship of the Gods; other secrets concerning the course of
> life he received and learned from the Magi.[7]

Diogenes Laertius (third century AD) repeats this in outline adding that he went also to Crete and descended into the Idaean cave.[8] Many scholars have been sceptical about the authenticity of these supposed voyages of instruction. The three biographers quoted above, writing 800 years later during the Neo-Pythagorean revival, are often criticized for having embellished legends and presented them as historical facts. As J.A. Philip caustically remarks: 'it is only as they become more distant in time from Pythagoras that the accounts grow more precise and more detailed; after a millennium they tell us the composition of the cakes that were his principal sustenance.'[9] He says that although tradition has value, Pythagoras' voyages are 'intrinsically improbable.' He holds that they were based on the fact that later, from Plato onwards, philosophers did journey abroad to study but that in the earlier case of Pythagoras 'there is no reason for believing that there is a historical basis for any such journeys.'[10]

Yet such radical scepticism may not be entirely justified. In the case of J.A. Philip, it is based on his belief that all the sources are unreliable except Aristotle. Others would say that this was too strict because many of the writings of Plato, as we shall find later in this chapter, have been generally accepted as being heavily Pythagorean, not least by Aristotle himself! And once the concept of the Pythagorean Plato is accepted, then at least some of the later sources have to be taken more seriously. It may also be unfair to single out Aristotle as the only reliable source, because he was an unsympathetic critic and is known to have been writing, at least in part, from a polemical point of view. There are those who would say that it has to be conceded that it is ultimately not possible to separate the concept of 'source' from that of 'tradition.' Among these, Jamie James represents a fairer position when he says:

> However, primarily because none of his works survive, Pythagoras's achievement languishes in obscurity. Everything we know about the man and his philosophy comes down to us secondhand, through the writings of his followers and the commentaries of later philosophers. Modern scholarship is deeply divided on the question of the extent to which the Pythagoras venerated by Western humanists may be identified with a historical individual, born on the island of Samos in the sixth century BC. Furthermore, the Pythagorean tradition itself holds that the Master, as he was known to his disciples, travelled widely in Egypt, Mesopotamia, and Persia when he was a young man, and there is reason to think that he picked up many of the important concepts attributed to him on these wanderings.[11]

This opinion is acceptable to mathematicians such as John McLeish who has no difficulty in saying that Pythagoras as a young man 'settled in Babylon where for 20 years he studied and taught astronomy, mathematics and astrology.'[12] He does not at this point, state his source, and in the light of J.A. Philip's strictures, we may wonder whether he is mistakenly referring to Iamblichus' claim that Pythagoras spent twenty-two years in Egypt. However this may be to quibble over detail for as an historian of mathematics, he is well aware, as his chapters on Sumeria, Babylon and Egypt show, that Greek mathematics developed from these earlier civilizations. He may be referring indirectly to the seminal work of Otto Neugebauer, who has established that in the third millennium BC, the Babylonians were so advanced in mathematics that they knew all about:

> ... reciprocals, multiplications, squares and square roots,
> cubes and cube roots, the sums of squares and cubes, ...
> exponential functions, coefficients giving numbers for
> practical computation ... and numerous metrological
> calculations giving the area of rectangles, circles etc.

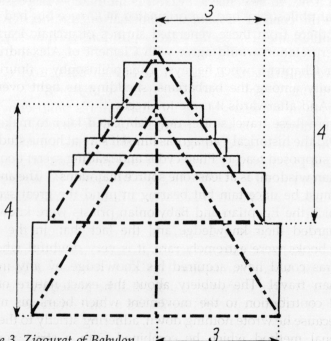

Figure 3. Ziggurat of Babylon

Neugebauer specifically mentions that the famous theorem of Pythagoras was known in Babylon 'more than a thousand years before Pythagoras.'[13] This has been corroborated by the work of Livio Stecchini who has reconstructed the basic geometry of the Ziggurat of Babylon from the information given on the cuneiform text of the Smith Tablet and has shown it to consist of a series of 3:4:5 'Pythagorean' triangles.[14]

We may therefore confidently assume from these revelations that the so called Pythagorean mathematics, was discovered in Babylon at least a thousand years before Pythagoras and that it was also known in Egypt, as demonstrated in the proportions of the pyramids to which reference will be made later. This being so, we can deduce that the purpose of the later stories about the travels of Pythagoras, was to show that he was not the originator, but the transmitter of an ancient wisdom based on number, different aspects of which had been expressed in the earlier civilizations of Phoenicia, Egypt, Babylon and Chaldea. Whether he actually travelled to these places or not, the main point would have been to demonstrate that the Master had been a student of the sciences and an initiate of the mysteries of all these sacred cultures. That he had made voyages to study, emphasized the point that philosophy had not originated in Greece but had been brought there from these venerated shrines of archaic learning. This interpretation would agree with Clement of Alexandria, as quoted in Chapter 6, when he says: 'Thus philosophy ... flourished in antiquity among the barbarians, shedding its light over the nations. And afterwards it came to Greece.'[15]

But were these travel stories only fabricated later to make this point? Did the historical Pythagoras himself stay at home studying with his supposed teacher Pherecydes and reading secret books of Phoenician wisdom, as at least one source maintains?[16] The answer to this must be uncertain but bearing in mind the great secrecy with which the Egyptian and Babylonian priests were known to have guarded their knowledge and the fact that, in the sixth century, books were extremely rare, it is very doubtful whether Pythagoras could have acquired his knowledge by any means other than travel. The dubiety about the exact nature of his personal contribution to the movement which bears his name, arose, because he wrote nothing down, adhering strictly to the oral educational method which he combined with a strict vow of secrecy, as evidenced by the story of the hapless Hippasus, who it is alleged, was drowned for giving away secrets. We may lament this, yet his success as a teacher may have been based on the integrity he displayed in committing himself to keeping his promises to those who had taught and initiated him in all these foreign lands. For he may well have had to promise under oath that he would not write anything down and only divulge the mysteries to initiated disciples. Thus his strict adherence to the secret, oral tradition, may be the best evidence we have that he was merely transmitting the wisdom of those from whom he had received it, in the way in which he had received it.

If there is any merit in this conclusion, then it can presumably be extended to lands not listed by Iamblichus, Porphyry or Diogenes Laertius but mentioned by Clement of Alexandria. It will be recalled that although Clement's immediate source, Alexander Polyhistor, only takes us back to the second century BC, he was himself, according to Nora Chadwick, based on earlier sources from the third and fourth centuries BC, thus making him reputable even by the strict standards of J.A. Philip. As cited in Chapter 6, Clement believed that Pythagoras, being the one who had first brought philosophy to Greece, had learnt it not only from all the countries listed above, but also from, among others 'the Druids among the Gauls.' Thus we have arrived at a remarkable confirmation of the possible historical connection between Pythagoras and the Druids as then put forward. Add to this the fact that Caesar said the Druids' religion 'forbids them to commit their teachings to writing'[17] and that other Roman commentators stressed their strict secrecy, and the comparison between the Druids' and Pythagoras' teaching methods begins to look quite striking.

The Pythagorean doctrine that all things are numbers, was widely influential in subsequent centuries particularly through Plato, whose later writings are permeated with Pythagorean numbers, cosmology and mathematical allegories as Ernest McClain has demonstrated.[18] It is now generally accepted among scholars that:

> Plato was strongly influenced by the mathematical
> speculations of the Pythagoreans — even if it is difficult to
> determine the precise extent of his debt to them in this
> respect. And to say of the Pythagoreans that they were one

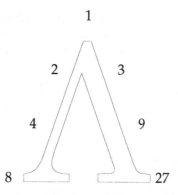

Figure 4. Lambda

of the determining influences in the formation of the
thought of Plato, is to pay them no mean tribute.[19]

This influence was nowhere more profound than in the *Timaeus*
in which, following Pythagoras, Plato states that true morality
springs from a harmony in the soul and that this reflects the Soul
of the World. For Plato, as for Pythagoras, the cosmos itself is a
God. It is a living being with soul in its body and reason in its
soul. It is shaped from chaotic materials by the divine Demiurge.
Plato also deals with the Body of the World, which is divided up
and put together proportionally with the World Soul in proportions which are linked to the numbers 1, 2, 3, 4, 9, 8, 27, which
together make up his famous Lambda. He speaks of the music of
the soul, elaborating on the Pythagorean connection between the
music of the spheres and the orbits of the soul. He also describes
the creation of the regular solids and allocates them to the
elements: the cube to earth, the pyramid or tetrahedron to fire, the
icosahedron to water and the octahedron to air. The fifth figure,
the dodecahedron, he assigns to the sphere of the heavens.

The influence of the *Timaeus* on the philosophy and theology of
the ancient world, was immense. Its emphasis on mathematics
introduced a most important concept to first Hebrew, then
Christian theology; namely that God created by geometrical rules
which were harmonic and universal. As Christopher Butler says:
'The ideas of Pythagoras and Plato proved to be so influential
largely because these mathematical ideas were brought into so
many spheres of knowledge. As Spitzer reminds us, in the *Timaeus*:

"the world soul (a religious concept), the regulation of the cosmos (a concept of physics), world harmony (a musical concept) and the soul of man (a psychological concept) are fused".[20]

From this introduction we can now turn to the Bible as it was later interpreted by those who subscribed to these Pythagorean and Platonic teachings.

Pythagorean Number Symbolism in the Bible

As implied from what has been described above, numbers for the Pythagorean-Platonic tradition were not merely quantitative, they were also qualitative. Each was associated with certain attributes and universal principles. Aëtius said that the Pythagoreans proclaimed that the numbers were *archai*, meaning that they were first principles which had been there from the beginning of time (*arche*), and as such were divine. Today, we would call them archetypes and it is significant that C.G. Jung, through his extensive analysis of dreams, came to regard numbers as intelligences. Arnold Ehrhardt tells us it is appropriate in this connection, to speak theologically:

> When, therefore, Pythagoras and his disciples concentrated upon number as the principle of the 'cosmos' (a word which Pythagoras was reputed to have employed as the first for the description of the universe) it was a theological decision which they took. At the same time his followers were motivated in doing so by the discovery of the fact that numbers follow their own, intrinsic, logical law, not imposed upon them by human fancy, but pre-established independently, a discovery which even Aristotle ascribed to them.[21]

Through this theological dimension came the belief that the Gods were numbers, and through this intrinsic, logical discovery came the realization that therefore all things were essentially numbers. The attributes or qualities of the numbers arose from the marriage of the theological and the intrinsic. Thus the number one was symbolic of the One, the Monad, God, the potentiality of all number, a point, or a circle within which the attributes of all the other numbers could be geometrically inscribed. Two was the Dyad, associated with division and strife but also with the potentiality of harmony. Three was harmony, the ubiquitous and wondrously good 'third term' about which more will be said later. Four, the first square number, was associated with justice because justice involved reciprocal personal relationships and that reciprocity was symbolized by square numbers. Five symbolized marriage because it was the sum of two, the first feminine number and three, the first masculine number.

There were also certain numbers which were revered for their factorizing properties. Among these, special importance was given to what are called 'perfect' numbers. A 'perfect' number is defined as one which is the sum of its divisors, exclusive of itself. They are very rare and the lowest of them is six $(1 + 2 + 3 = 6)$ which was regarded as the most important.

It is easy to see how such numerical symbolism could be used to interpret the Bible for, on every page, from *Genesis* to *Revelation*, numbers are obviously being used for symbolic purposes. Indeed, so much is this the case that it seemed reasonable to presume that the underlying symbolic system being used was Pythagorean in origin. This assumption was demonstrated to have been the case in the extensive writings of Philo, the first century Alexandrian Jewish philosopher (*c*.30 BC — AD 50) who succeeded in reconciling Jewish with Hellenistic thought, largely through his realization that the Old Testament could indeed be interpreted in this way. This is nowhere more evident than when he is explaining why in *Genesis*, God created the world in six days:

> ... because for things coming into existence there was need of order. Order involves number, and among numbers by the laws of nature, the most suitable to productivity is 6, for if we start with 1, it is the first perfect number, being equal to the product of its factors (i.e. $1 \times 2 \times 3$) as well as made up of the sums of them (i.e. $1 + 2 + 3$) ... For it was requisite that the world, being most perfect of all things that have come into existence, should be constituted in accordance with a perfect number, namely six.[22]

Philo was widely influential, more among Christian than Jewish theologians. This was particularly the case with St Augustine

(354–430) who echoes Philo almost word for word in his interpretation of the six days of creation:

> Six is a number perfect in itself, and not because God
> created all things in six days; rather the converse is true;
> God created all things in six days because the number is
> perfect and it would have been perfect even if the work of
> six days did not exist.[23]

Through St Augustine, much Pythagorean and Platonic teaching was transmitted to the Christian Church throughout Europe. He was by far the most important Western theologian for the next thousand years and gave an enduring ecclesiastical imprimatur to the Pythagorean interpretation of number symbolism in the Bible when he said:

> We must not despise the science of numbers, which, in
> many passages of Holy Scripture, is found to be of eminent
> service to the careful interpreter. Neither has it been
> without reason numbered among God's praises 'thou hast
> ordered all things in number and measure and weight.'[24]

The Neo-Platonic and Neo-Pythagorean revival in the third and fourth centuries associated with Plotinus, Proclus, Macrobius, Porphyry, Iamblichus and Diogenes Laertius, the last three of whom as we have seen, all wrote lives of Pythagoras, had already had a great impact on Christianity by the time of Augustine. Although it was to a considerable extent the expression of a revival of pagan beliefs as in the case of Plotinus, Iamblichus and Porphyry, it also resulted in the reinterpretation of Platonic and Pythagorean thought in ways which were considered to be compatible with Christianity. This was so much the case with regard to the debate about the doctrine of the Trinity, which raged among theologians during the fourth century, that it has been argued that the influence of Pythagorean number symbolism was decisive in ensuring that the Christian God would be eventually defined as Three in One. For instance V.F. Hopper claims:

> The paramount doctrinal weakness ... was the duality of the
> Godhead. The acceptance of Philo's 'logos,' and its

identification with the Son, was the first step towards a
solution, but the addition of the third person, the Holy
Ghost, provided indisputable evidence of unity. The
presence of divine triads in all the Gnostic creeds was
certainly a determining factor in the creation of the Trinity,
but the underlying Pythagorean basis of contemporary
philosophy necessitated the doctrine. That the Father and
Son were One was questionable upon numerical grounds.
But Father, Son and Holy Spirit were unquestionably One
by virtue of being Three.'[25]

The logic behind this would be unintelligible without the realization that the number two, the Dyad, was associated with division, strife and the breaking away from Unity, while the number
three, the Triad, was associated with all things good. As Proclus
said, 'Every divine order has a unity of threefold origin from its
highest, its mean and its last term.'[26] The doctrine of the Trinity
was finally ratified at the Council of Constantinople in 381.

Christopher Butler cites many leading theologians throughout
the Dark and Middle Ages such as Boethius, Cassiodorus and
Hugh of St Victor (d. 1141), who carried on this Pythagorean-
Platonic tradition. Far from dying out, it gathered strength through
the centuries, so that by the time of the early Renaissance,
philosophers, theologians and men of culture could call on such a
huge repertoire in this field, that the Renaissance itself can be seen
as this tradition's most brilliant flowering in fifteen hundred years.

With the invention of printing and the massive increase in
translations from the classics, the Renaissance humanists had a
much greater range of sources on which to draw than any of their
medieval predecessors. Neither were they restrained by narrow
religious orthodoxy. This resulted in a syncretism of many expressions of ancient wisdom which included the Orphic, Egyptian,
Chaldean, Hebrew, Pythagorean, Platonic, Hermetic, Cabbalistic,
Christian Patristic, Gnostic and Neo-Platonist, especially Proclus
and Plotinus.

This eclectic syncretism led to what Butler calls a 'totally
ahistorical conflation of doctrines,'[27] which makes it very hard to
discover exactly what men like Ficino or Giordano Bruno believed.
They seemed to have the ability to hold so many apparently
disparate strands together. For the specifically Christian thinkers

a 'root conflation' was made between the Hebrew and the Greek traditions, so that it was said: 'What is Plato but an Athenian Moses? ... either Plato was "Philonizing," or Philo was "Platonizing," so familiar is his mode of thinking and speaking to the platonic one.'[28]

In similar vein, it was also said:

> What is Plato but Moses Atticus? And for Pythagoras it is a thing incredible that he and his followers should make such a deal and doe with the mystery of Numbers, had he not been favoured with a sight of Moses his Creator of the world in six days and had the philosophick *Cabbala* thereof (not been) communicated to him, which consists mainly in numbers.[29]

Butler concludes that 'The indebtedness of Plato to Moses was the prime ahistorical assumption made by Renaissance thinkers who believed that it was possible to trace a single tradition of *prisca theologia* in all preceding thought.'[30]

Thus Platonism was held to be at the centre of both Pythagorean and Hebrew systems, as Ficino stated 'our Plato, together with the Pythagorean and Socratic doctrines, followed the law of Moses and prophesied the Christian law.'[31]

Butler has only a grudging sympathy for this syncretism, the complexity of which he explains with consummate skill. He basically disapproves of its 'pick and mix' superficiality, in much the same way as people today, who are committed to a specific religious path, disapprove of so-called 'New Agers' who are reputed to have an *hors d'oeuvre* attitude to spirituality. He certainly has the right to hold this position, based as it is on such erudition, but whether it is the only one which arises legitimately out of the sources, is another question. Perhaps being educated presumably in a system which was mainly analytical, he would naturally want to tease out the distinctive features of the various theological and philosophical strands, stressing their differences, whereas if he had been open to a more synthetic approach he might have considered it just as important to stress what they had in common. A fair compromise between these two approaches might perhaps be found by holding that synthesis is just as important as analysis in the assessment of any great cultural epoch. For it cannot be doubted that the Renaissance was an enormously creative time for Europe and the rest of the world. Its great figures, as mentioned above, need not necessarily be considered to have been 'guilty' of syncretism. They could just as easily be seen as having revelled in their discovery of unity behind all diversity; of finding how the One was connected to the Many in true Platonic fashion and of how they could discern common features and themes, even in the great variety of ancient traditions to which they had access for the very first time in history.

It is, I believe, very important that just such a balance between analysis and synthesis be kept, for it is crucial in any fair assessment not only of the motives and achievements of the Renaissance humanists but of any comparison we may wish to make between the Greek and the Hebrew traditions as a whole, and their possible common inheritance from other more ancient civilizations as discussed above. We shall be returning to this theme again in subsequent chapters, but for the meantime it is sufficient to assert that while Christopher Butler is not justified in being quite so categorical, he must be respected when he states that a 'root conflation' was made by the Renaissance Christians between the Hebrew and the Greek traditions, and that this was 'totally ahistorical.' As examined earlier, the third century biographers of Pythagoras have also been accused of what amounts to a 'totally ahistorical' 'root conflation' among the cultures of Egypt, Babylon and Chaldea, and yet, as argued, this accusation may not be entirely justified. We are dealing here with very large issues about which there is still much uncertainty

It is important not to foreclose the discussion about cultural origins and cross-cultural influences before the various options have been examined. It is all too easy to laugh in a superior way at the supposedly naive belief that Pythagoras and Plato got their wisdom from Moses. It would be easy to claim that this was not only ahistorical but unhistorical because modern biblical scholarship has assured us that Moses did not write the Pentateuch, which was probably not completed in its final form until after Pythagoras and Plato. Yet we would still have to face the difficult question: where did the Hebrews learn their number symbolism? Did they get it from the Egyptians? This is certainly implied in Acts 7:22, which was used so often in the Renaissance as 'proof' that 'Moses was educated in all the wisdom of Egypt.' As we have seen, it is also stated in the later biographies of Pythagoras, that he, Pythagoras, got his wisdom, at least in part, from Egypt, thus echoing the earlier opinions of Heroditus, Plato and Aristotle regarding the origins of Greek mathematics,

Without carrying this discussion further at present or coming to any final conclusions, the importance of Butler's work is that while he doesn't answer the 'how' question, he definitely makes it impossible to deny that for seventeen centuries of biblical scholar-ship it was believed that the Bible, especially the Old Testament, following Philo, was Pythagorean in its number symbolism. The fact that this has been forgotten or ignored by most modern scholars, does not detract from the overwhelming evidence which Butler has adduced to substantiate this assertion. There can be no doubt that whether or not the Bible *was* Pythagorean in the historical derivation of its number symbolism, it may be *taken* to have been so because the similarities between the two systems are so extensive as to be considered either identical or as having originated from a common source. So we may effectively speak about a 'Pythagorean Bible' even if at this stage we cannot point to any definite historical links.

The last chapter ended with the question: did the Jewish Patriarchs have any Pythagorean or proto-Pythagorean connec-tions? The assumption was that if the answer was in the affirma-tive, then William Blake's notion that Abraham, Heber, Shem and Noah were Druids, would seem at least feasible. The reason for this was that it has been demonstrated from Professor Thom's surveys of stone circles, that a form of proto-Pythagorean geometry and astronomy could be identified in Britain as early as 3000 BC, and that the Druids were most probably the heirs of this tradition. The assumption made by the Roman and Alexandrian sources, that the Druids were Pythagoreans, seemed therefore to have been turned on its head. For if there was any historical or prehistorical transmission, it would have been more likely to have been from the older to the younger culture, that is, from the Megalithic Age in north-west Europe to the Greeks. This question has now been answered unequivocally in the affirmative and it is highly intriguing that from Philo to Ficino the first *locus classicus* of biblical Pythagoreanism is the creation story of Genesis and the second is Moses, meaning the Pentateuch, the first five books of the Old Testament. In other words, while the whole of the Bible was considered to be Pythagorean in this respect, it was the early portions in particular which exemplified it best. But it was these early books, especially Genesis, which told the stories, not only of the creation in six days, but also of the Patriarchs Abraham, Heber, Shem and Noah!

We may therefore conclude from this examination, that not only is Blake's notion feasible, but that it might be the clue we need to press the further question, also raised at the end of the last chapter with regard to Jesus, namely: did Jesus himself, coming out of and being steeped in the biblical tradition, have any knowledge of or connections with the Pythagoreans? If so, did he have any knowledge of, or links with, the Druids as those from whom, among others, Pythagoras was reputed to have learnt his wisdom? Leaving the second part of this question until later, let us begin to address the first part by examining certain features of his teaching which, according to Simone Weil, have a distinctly Pythagorean flavour. In doing so it is important to note that while the Pythagorean tradition of biblical interpretation has been in eclipse since the seventeenth century, that eclipse has never been total. There have always been those who have subscribed to it and, in the twentieth century, none of them have shone with such brightness as Simone Weil whose insights bring the light as of a new Renaissance, to certain important passages of the New Testament.

8
Simone Weil and
the Pythagorean Doctrine

Simone Weil (1909–43) was a brilliant French, Jewish, Catholic philosopher who died at a tragically young age and is still remembered with great admiration by many of an older generation, not only for her thought but also for her life. Her reflections on Greek philosophy were published posthumously as *La Source Greque* and *Les Intuitions Pré-Chrétiennes*. They were republished in English as *Intimations of Christianity among the Ancient Greeks* in 1957 and have been in print since then. Her chapter on 'The Pythagorean Doctrine' is so germane regarding the theme of Pythagoreanism in the Bible especially in the New Testament, that it must be examined in some detail. She begins with a eulogy on the diversity of Pythagorean pre-eminence throughout the Greek world:

> Pythagorean thought is for us the great mystery of Greek civilization. It recurs everywhere, again and again. It impregnates almost all the poetry, almost all the philosophy — and especially Plato, whom Aristotle regarded as a pure Pythagorean. The music, the architecture, the sculpture, all the sciences of ancient Greece proceeded from it; so did arithmetic, geometry, astronomy, mechanics and biology ... Plato's political thought (in its most authentic form, which means as it is formulated in the dialogue, the *Statesman*) also derives from the Pythagorean doctrine. It embraced almost all secular life.[1]

Echoing our findings in the last chapter, she says that the origins of this Pythagoreanism go back to very ancient times. Plato has no doubts about the fact that philosophy did not originate with the Greeks but was derived from 'the ancients.' He speaks about this in his *Philebus* (16b):

... the ancients who were better than we are, and lived
nearer the gods, have transmitted this tradition to us. Here
it is: that the realities called eternal derive from the one and
the many, and carry, implanted within them, the
determinate and the indeterminate. We should therefore,
since this is the eternal order of things, seek to implant a
unity in every kind of domain. We shall find it, for it is
there. Once we have grasped this unity, we should examine
duality, if that is present, or else trinity, or some other
number. Then the same subdivisions must be made upon
each one of the subordinate unities. Finally, what at the
beginning appeared not only as one, and many, and
unlimited at once, appears also as a definite number.[2]

What Plato appears to be describing, on the basis of the
presumed Pythagorean or proto-Pythagorean origins of the 'eternal
order of things,' is a unitary understanding of knowledge. All
things derive from the one and the many. The many are related to
the one. All things are connected. Today we would call it a holistic
or systems theory of knowledge. All things are related to each
other by number. This is not only number as quantity but as
quality or symbol as we have seen. It is also number in space
which is geometry, number in time which is music and number in
space-time which is astronomy-astrology. Plato explains this all
elsewhere in the *Republic*.

It is gratifying to note that, as Weil goes on to review the
possible origins of this unitary theory of knowledge, she puts the
Druids high on her list and is obviously referring to the same
sources as those cited in earlier chapters when she refers to
Diodorus Siculus and Diogenes Laertius:

Another ancient historian, Diodorus Siculus, I believe,
points to the analogies between Pythagorean thought and
Druidic thought, which, according to Diogenes Laertius,
was considered by certain people as one of the sources of
Greek philosophy.[3]

However, she turns away from this option in favour of Heroditus who held that it was derived from the Egyptians. Adducing
other evidence of her own she asserts that 'a current of perfectly

pure spirituality would have flowed across Antiquity from prehistoric Egypt to Christianity. This current flowed through Pythagoreanism.'[4] Thus she places herself fairly and squarely in the tradition outlined in the last chapter in which Plato was seen as the Greek Moses, and in which both Greek and Hebrew wisdom were believed to have derived from Egypt.

Weil is as certain as J.A. Philip that only certain texts are authentic, but unlike him relegates Aristotle to a minor place on a team dominated by Plato, for besides his *Philebus* quoted above, she includes passages from his other works — *Gorgias, Epinomis, Timaeus* and *Symposium*. She also lists some fragments from Philolaus, some formulae and equations given by Aristotle and Diogenes Laertius and a formula from Anaximander. She tells us that in this regard we should also not forget 'the totality of Greek civilization.' Her definition of authentic texts while selective, is thus also enormously far-reaching.

What is very unexpected and of great importance from the point of view of this enquiry is that her list of authoritative passages also includes certain sayings of Jesus, some of which she likens unequivocally to Pythagoran *akousmata* or axioms:

> 'That he who leaves his country does not return' (cf. Luke 9:62: 'No man, having put his hand to the plough, and looking back, is fit for the kingdom of God.') And again: 'Let the man who enters a temple adore, and not speak, nor be occupied with anything temporal.' 'He who follows the divinity is before all things master of his tongue.' (cf. Epistle of St James: 'look not at thyself in a mirror beside a lamp,' and 'If any one thinks he is religious, and does not bridle his tongue, this man's religion is vain.' James 1:26 and 3:1–12)[5]

What is even more surprising is that she likens other New Testament texts from St John's Gospel to the Pythagorean doctrine in an altogether more profound way. These texts all refer to Jesus' sayings about his relationship to God and to his disciples:

> St John 17:11, 21-23: 'Holy Father, keep through thine own name those whom thou hast given me, that they may be one, as we are ... That they may all be one; as thou,

Father, art in me, and I in thee, that they also may be one in us ... And the glory which thou gavest me I have given them; that they may be one, even as we are one: I in them and thou in me, that they may be made perfect in one.'

St John 17:18: 'As thou hast sent me into the world, even so have I also sent them into the world.'

St John 10:14f: 'I am the good shepherd, and know my sheep and am known of mine. As the Father knoweth me, even so know I the Father.'

St John 15:9f: 'As the father hath loved me, so have I loved you: continue ye in my love. If ye keep my commandments, ye shall abide in my love; even as I have kept my Father's commandments, and abide in his love.'[6]

The Pythagorean doctrine of which these passages from St John are examples, according to Weil, is that of the theology of proportion. It was this theology of proportion which lay at the heart of Pythagorean and Platonic thinking and which linked together the knowledge of all things. Weil believes that the writer of St John's gospel has used analogies from geometry to state profound theological truths, thus expressing what is best described as geometrical or mathematical theology:

When the son of God is in a reasonable creature, as the Father is in the Son, that creature is perfectly just. Plato says in the *Theaetetus* that justice is assimilation in God. Similarity, in the geometrical sense, means proportion. The mysterious equation of the Pythagoreans (that 'justice is a number to the second power'), and that of Plato (that 'friendship is an equality made of harmony') which seems clear, have the same meaning. Whoever is just becomes to the Son of God as the Son is to his Father. Doubtless this identity of relations is not literally possible. However, the perfection proposed to man should be something like that, for in many of St John's precepts the same words are repeated to designate the relationship of the disciples to Christ and of the Christ to his Father. The allusion to a mathematical equation of proportion is evident.[7]

In justification of this mathematical interpretation, Weil cites Plato in the *Timaeus* where he speaks of the most beautiful of bonds being established between the terms of the geometrical proportion. This might be thought to be applicable only to mathematics, were it not for the fact that in the *Symposium* he uses the same bonding image 'to define the mediatory function of Love between the divinity and man.' Since this passage from the *Timaeus* is important not only for its description of geometrical proportion but also for its being the probable origin of the Christian doctrine of the Trinity, or Three in the Oneness of God, referred to in the last chapter, it is worth quoting in full:

> It is impossible that the disposition or arrangement of two
> of anything, so long as there are only two, should be
> beautiful without a third. There must come between them,
> in the middle, a bond which brings them into union. The
> most beautiful of bonds is that which brings perfect unity
> to itself and the parts linked. It is geometrical proportion,
> which, by essence, is the most beautiful for such
> achievement. For when of three numbers, or of three
> masses, or of any other quantity, the intermediary is to the
> last as the first is to the last and reciprocally, the last to the
> intermediary, as the intermediary to the first, then the
> intermediary becomes first and last. Further, the last and
> the first become both intermediaries; thus it is necessary
> that all achieve identity; and, being identified mutually,
> they shall be one.[8]

Put in simple terms, the geometrical proportion is defined as being composed of three terms in which *A* is to *B* as *B* is to *C*. Applying this to St John's texts we get: 'And the glory which thou (*A*) gavest me (*B*), I (*B*) have given them (*C*).' Likewise 'As thou (*A*) hast sent me (*B*) into the world, even so have I (*B*) also sent them (*C*) into the world.' And 'As the Father (*A*) hath loved me (*B*), so have I (*B*) loved you (*C*).'

Weil points out an important distinction between proportions which have three terms and those which have four. Those which have four, that is *A* is to *B* as *C* is to *D*, like those derived from Thales' similar triangles, have proportion but not mediation. Only those proportions, principally the geometric but also the arithmetic and harmonic, which have three terms, relate to the concept of mediation. It is only the third term, not third and fourth, to which the notion of mediation applies. This notion is also called the mean proportional. This is the heart of the Pythagorean doctrine which Weil reiterates throughout her essay. All this explains not only the doctrine of the Trinity but also the concept of Christ being the Mediator. The following paragraph makes this abundantly clear:

> When Plato, in the *Gorgias*, speaks of geometric equality, this expression is doubtless exactly equivalent to that of harmonious equality employed by Pythagoras. Both terms constitute without doubt technical expressions whose meaning was rigorously defined by the equality between two ratios having a common term, of the type A is to B as B is to C. For the adjective geometric, in such terms as 'geometric mean' and 'geometric progression,' indicates proportion. The phrases from St John cited above have so clearly and insistently the aspect of an algebraic equation that this is manifestly what is meant and what allusion is made to. Plato could certainly and legitimately say: 'Geometric equality has a great power both over the gods and over men.' Following the definition of friendship, the other expression from the same passage, 'Friendship unites heaven and earth, the gods and men,' has exactly the same meaning. By inscribing over the door of his school 'Let no one enter who is not a geometer,' Plato was doubtless affirming in the form of an enigma, and therefore as a pun, the truth which the Christ expressed in the saying, 'No one cometh unto the Father except by me.' The other Platonic equation, 'God is a perpetual geometer,' obviously has a double sense and refers at the same time to the order of the world and to the mediatory function of the Word. To sum up, the appearance of geometry in Greece is the most dazzling of all the prophecies which foretold Christ.[9]

To which we might add that the appearance of such writing as this is probably the most dazzling expression of the Pythagorean interpretation of the New Testament in this or indeed any century.

It must thus be concluded that Simone Weil is correct in her assumption that the Johannine texts which she cites have been constructed on the basis of Pythagorean and Platonic principles of proportion. We would therefore agree with her when she concludes:

> If the passage from the *Timaeus* on proportion has, besides its obvious sense, a theological sense, this meaning can be none other than that of Christ's words cited by St John, which are so very similar.[10]

But what are we to make of her next conclusion:

> The allusion is evident. Just as the Christ recognized Himself as Isaiah's man of sorrows, and the Messiah of all the prophets of Israel, He recognized Himself also as being that mean proportional of which the Greeks had for centuries been thinking so intensely.[11]

We are used to assuming that, because the New Testament references to the Old Testament prophets are so numerous, Jesus might have recognized himself as Isaiah's 'man of sorrows.' But because there are no similar references in the New Testament, at least of an overt nature, to any Greek sources, we are not at all accustomed to the idea that he might also have thought of himself as the embodiment of the Greek concept of the mean proportional. Having now had this possibility pointed out to us by Simone Weil in such a convincing way, we would be inclined to accept that there is indeed a Pythagorean-Platonic substructure to these and probably other New Testament texts. But is it legitmate to infer from this that Jesus himself knew about these things? Is it reasonable to deduce that Greek theories of proportion and mathematical theology were in his consciousness? We can certainly accept that such theories might well have been in the minds of the Gospel writers, especially the writer or writers of St John's Gospel. However, we have been taught by biblical scholars to be so careful before attributing any of the sayings of Jesus, in the form we have them, to Jesus himself, rather than to those who wrote them down later, that we would need more evidence before we could arrive at this particular conclusion of Weil's.

What we can settle for at this stage as a result of her insights, is that there is apparently a much greater amount of Pythagoreanism in the New Testament than we might have suspected and that it is of such a profound nature, bound into the very fabric of linguistic form and theological proposition, that it would appear to be there by design and not by accident. This in itself is extraordinary enough but it also opens up the possibility that there might be more Pythagorean treasure hidden away, waiting to reveal its arcane secrets to those who are prepared to follow in her pioneering footsteps.

Is there a Secret Knowledge?

Do the verses from which Simone Weil has so convincingly deduced a substructure of Pythagoreanism, imply that there is a secret Gospel within the Gospel, hidden in the New Testament texts? Although she doesn't herself address this question, being more of a theologian and philosopher than a literary critic, may we not infer from her discoveries that the New Testament contains an esoteric as well as an exoteric teaching? Certain other passages which she does not quote make this seem most likely. For instance where Jesus says:

> Woe to you lawyers! For you have taken away the key of knowledge; you did not enter yourselves and you hindered those who were entering. (Luke 11:52)

In the original Greek, the word for knowledge here is *gnoseos*. It is preceded by the definite article and should read 'you have taken away the key of *the* knowledge.' This alters the meaning of knowledge from a general to a specific kind. Jesus blames the lawyers for having taken away the key to this knowledge thus raising four questions namely: what was the key? Why had the lawyers taken it away? What was the knowledge which they were supposed to have entered into, and why hadn't they done so? These questions open up vistas of speculative possibilities, supposing that this is indeed an authentic saying of Jesus and not the sentiments of a later writer with a grudge against lawyers. Whatever the wider ramifications of this verse, we can at least assume that there was indeed a gnosis, *the* gnosis, which Jesus believed the lawyers should have known and to which they had the key. It was clearly a gnosis about which he knew and which he felt was very important. The traditional interpretation of this verse has been akin to the evangelical Christian who castigates the rank and file of his denomination for not being born again, of being nominal Christians who have not entered into an experience of the living Christ. So Jesus castigates the lawyers for not entering into the living heart of spiritual experience and thus by implication, not being able to recognize who he is. Curiously enough, Simone Weil, in an uncharacteristically traditional moment, accepts this position, about this text, later in her essay:

> The Christ is that key which locks together the Creator and creation. Since knowledge is the reflection of being, the Christ is also, by that same token, the key of knowledge. 'Woe unto you, lawyers!' said he, 'for ye have taken away the key of knowledge.' He was that key, He whom earlier centuries had loved in advance, and whom the Pharisees had denied and were going to put to death.[12]

This interpretation is acceptable in a general, homiletic and theological sense, but it is not actually what the verse says. There is no reason to imply that Jesus was referring to himself as the key or as the knowledge. The definite article before knowledge precludes that possibility. Is that why the translators from Jerome onwards left it out, so that we would not be left wondering whether there was a secret gnosis to which Jesus was referring and if there was, what the key to it was?

It is apparent that there has been some sort of suppression of evidence or streamlining by later translators because the original Greek has also been altered to achieve a similar denial of esoteric knowledge in other texts. For instance, in St Paul's famous hymn to love where he says 'And if I have prophetic powers and understand all mysteries and all knowledge ...' (1Cor.13:2), the Greek reads 'all *the* mysteries and all *the* knowledge.' Thus once again what was specific has been generalized and robbed of its contextual meaning. Paul was referring to *the* mysteries not mysteries in general. Thomas Simcox Lea writing with Frederick Bligh Bond earlier this century, saw this clearly:

But it can hardly be denied that the words *'ta musteria panta'* convey a very specific meaning and would have done so to the Greeks of the day, who would have connected the words with the religious rites of a secret nature to which they had been accustomed. Similarly *'pasa he gnosis'* would mean to them a certain body of knowledge associated with those mysteries.[13]

There are however other passages in the New Testament which indicate the presence of an esoteric or 'insider' tradition even more clearly and without any suppression. For instance in Mark 4:10–12:

And when he was alone, those who were about him with the twelve asked him concerning the parables. And he said to them 'To you has been given the secret of the kingdom of God, but for those outside everything is in parables; so that they may indeed see but not perceive, and may indeed hear but not understand; lest they should turn again and be forgiven.'

Commentating on this in *The Beginnings of Christianity* Andrew Welburn says that the latter part of Jesus' saying refers to Isaiah's condemnation of Israel as no longer being worthy of God's favour. He goes on to say that this is 'among the most uncompromising statements of esotericism in the New Testament.' Those who would merely look in from the outside will be excluded:

The words express the demand for a leap from 'outside' to the 'inside' view, which alone reveals the true interpretation. There can be no in-between. To the outsiders all things happen in parables; 'but privately to his own disciples he expounded everything.'[14]

Like Simcox Lea above, Welburn cites other texts where Paul implies that there is a secret wisdom for the insiders. For instance, in his letter to the Corinthians, having vehemently denied that there is any wisdom in his own proclamation of the gospel, he then admits 'Yet among the mature we do impart wisdom' (1Cor.2:6) This wisdom he makes clear, is not the wisdom of this transitory age, but 'a secret and hidden wisdom of God' (RSV) which Welburn translates:

> For we speak a wisdom among the initiated, a wisdom not of this aeon, nor of the world-rulers of this aeon who are passing away. We speak a wisdom of God in a mystery, an occult wisdom which God ordained before the aeons for our glory.

He comments dryly: 'The claim to esoteric knowledge is put, one might suppose, clearly enough!' Later Welburn shows how the apocryphal Gospels of Thomas and Philip, the Dead Sea Scrolls and the Nag Hammadi Gnostic texts all indicate that there was an editing out of references to this esoteric dimension as certain manuscripts came to be considered canonical and others heretical. The most spectacular example of this is the letter, discovered at Mar Saba monastery in 1958 by Morton Smith and written by Clement of Alexandria between AD 180 and 200, in which reference is made to a secret Gospel of Mark. Writing to an unknown friend called Theodore, he said:

> Mark, then, during Peter's stay in Rome, wrote an account of the deeds of the Lord, not however declaring all of them, nor yet hinting at the secret ones, but selecting those he thought most useful for increasing the faith of those who were being instructed. But when Peter died as a martyr, Mark came over to Alexandria, bringing both his own notes and those of Peter, from which he transferred to his former book the things suitable to whatever makes for progress towards knowledge (*gnosis*). Thus he composed a more spiritual gospel for the use of those who were being perfected. Nevertheless, he yet did not divulge the things not to be uttered, nor did he write down the hierophantic teaching of the Lord, but to the stories already written he added others and, moreover, brought in certain sayings of which he knew the interpretation would, as a mystagogue, lead the hearers into the innermost sanctuary of that truth hidden by seven veils. Thus ... when he died, he left his composition to the church in Alexandria, where it is even yet most carefully guarded,

being read only to those who are being initiated into the great mysteries.[15]

Clement's letter also contained extracts from this secret Gospel. As Welburn observes:

> ... certain passages of the original Gospel of Mark had been regarded as esoteric. The publicly circulated version of Mark did not contain the 'secret' deeds of the Lord, since the full 'Gnostic' version of the Gospel was 'carefully guarded' and read only to those being initiated into the 'great Mysteries.'[16]

Another arresting example, from *The Secret Book of John* and the *Acts of John*, is the mention of the physical nature of Jesus, that he was not always present in a tangible form. This also comes from Clement:

> For in the (esoteric) traditions it is reported that John touched the outward body (of Jesus) and put his hand deep inside and that the solidity of the flesh in no wise offered resistance but yielded to the disciple's hand.

Like many other unacceptable references, all indications that Jesus' body was changeable in this way, were removed by the firm hand of a later orthodoxy. Commenting on this process of editing out, Welburn writes:

> The imposition of a standard, 'orthodox' belief came only later, with the concentration of authority in the hands of the Roman Church. And we can in fact observe how the Church introduced its own literature, opposing the diversity of apostolic traditions with a colourless amalgam in the name of 'the Twelve Apostles.' This had two consequences: on the one hand it unified and strengthened the collective belief of the organized Church, and so helped the spread of Catholic Christianity; and on the other, it actually drove those who held to the older apostolic traditions outside the Church ultimately turning them into 'heretics.'[17]

Enough evidence has now been presented to demonstrate that there is a secret, inside or esoteric teaching within the canon of the New Testament. It would also appear from the apocryphal Gospels that some if not much of similar esoteric teaching was deliberately left out of the canon. It also seems to be apparent that the translators over later centuries have in certain instances, done their best to hide references to the presence of this secret knowledge.

What was this secret knowledge, *the* knowledge, and why was it to some extent suppressed or marginalized? The simple answer is of course that during the second and third centuries, the early Christian church engaged in a huge and bitter controversy over the whole concept of gnosis in which those who believed in the possibility of experiencing an esoteric higher knowledge of God were called Gnostics. They were eventually condemned as heretics by an increasingly inflexible and intolerant orthodoxy, their teachings were misrepresented and their experiences caricatured. Such was the legacy of acrimony over the centuries, and so complete was the destruction of their writings that it has only been in recent years, since the discoveries of Gnostic texts at Nag Hammadi, that any fair reappraisal of their understanding of gnosis has been possible.

However, what we are looking at is what *has* been left in the New Testament canon, not what has been left out. We are not concerned with later Gnostic literature as such but with the canonical writings which were not condemned as Gnostic, although the omissions of the definite article in the later translations of *the* knowledge and *the* mysteries might well be attributable to the fear that there were still some unacceptable traces of Gnosticism in the New Testament which had to be suppressed.

If it is therefore anachronistic to call these New Testament references trace elements of a later Gnosticism, to '*the* knowledge,' '*the* mysteries,' 'the secret of the kingdom,' 'the hidden wisdom', what can we call them? To what esoteric yet acceptable tradition, contemporaneous with the first century, can we attribute them? Could the answer be the Pythagorean tradition? We have already learnt a considerable amount about this tradition and what we have learnt seems to fit the description of being secret and esoteric on the one hand but also unexpectedly acceptable and orthodox on the other. Simcox Lea and Bligh Bond both put forward the thesis that it is with the Pythagorean-Platonic tradition, as interpreted by

Hellenized Judaeo-Christians, that the true and acceptable gnosis can be found. The gnosis they uncovered in the text of the New Testament is an exciting sequel to what we have learnt from Simone Weil and takes us much deeper into the complex Pythagorean structure of the canonical scriptures.

9
Gematria — the Hidden Key

Let us return to the most intriguing of the questions which arose from 'the key of the knowledge' verse discussed in the last chapter. Jesus chides: 'Woe to you Lawyers, for you have taken away the key of the knowledge ... etc.' (Luke 11:52) Why did he assume that the Lawyers knew what the knowledge was and also what the key was? Why were they so blameworthy? We have already suggested that the traditional Christian interpretation, which holds that they were the guardians of the Law but had failed to understand or communicate its true nature, is sound as far as it goes but that it falls short by not explaining why the Greek text calls it specifically 'the knowledge,' not just plain 'knowledge.'

We have also proposed that the placing of the definite article in front of knowledge in this and other texts implies that Jesus was referring to a certain, recognizable corpus of knowledge which, if not actually secret, was specialist. If we add this proposition to the traditional belief that Jesus was referring to the true understanding of the Old Testament as just mentioned, we could reasonably conclude that he was talking about a specialist, secret or esoteric way of interpreting the Scriptures. Since the inclusion of the definite article *the* before 'knowledge' precludes us from agreeing with scholars who have maintained that he was ultimately talking about himself as the key, we may go on to ask: what was this specialist, secret or esoteric corpus of knowledge which held the key to a true understanding of the Law?

It would seem that the answer to this question must lie either with Gnosticism or with Pythagoreanism because these were the only two systems of specialist or secret knowledge in which the symbolism of numbers and also the concept of knowledge as initiation into spiritual mysteries, was of sufficient importance as to be regarded as central. Of these two, I believe the choice falls in favour of Pythagoreanism because it pre-dated Gnosticism by many centuries, and appears to have been the parent of the younger movement.

Thomas Simcox Lea in *Gematria*, cited in the last chapter, acknowledges that there are many links between Gnosticism, particularly in the *Pistis Sophia* and the *Books of Ieou* and the New Testament. He also asserts in *The Apostolic Gnosis* that 'the Pythagorean tradition was at the root of it,'[1] and that the *disciplina arcana* of the early Christians which flowered later in Gnosticism can be traced back to the Pythagoreans and the Essenes.[2]

Simcox Lea is well aware that there is a dubious side to a Gnostic interpretation of '*the* knowledge,' but he argues that the presence of a false gnosis must not blind us to the reality of a true one. We must be discriminating as St Paul warned Timothy (1Tim.6:20) against 'the contradictions of the pseudonymous gnosis, for by professing it some have missed the mark as regards the faith.' Perhaps we may deduce from this that already, in the second half of the first century, there were Gnostic teachings circulating which raised issues concerning the historicity of Jesus and the authority of the Apostles which were later to be at the centre of the controversy between Gnosticism and nascent orthodoxy. Perhaps we may also deduce that, because Gnosticism has sometimes been called an 'acute Hellenizing of Christianity' and 'Platonism run wild,'[3]' the true Christian gnosis was that which conformed to the Old Testament tradition of Pythagorean interpretation and was a worthy sequel to it, whereas the false gnosis was that which emphasized a higher cosmic spirituality at the expense of historic acts of salvation through Israel and the person of Jesus Christ. If there is any truth in this, then perhaps we can go on to speculate that such was the eventual hostility of the orthodox party to the Gnostic heretics that the Pauline distinction between a true and a false gnosis was lost and was superseded by a general anathematization of all gnosis, false or true. If this was the case then it would explain why later translators left out the definite article in the Greek text as outlined. It would also explain why the true *gnosis* was largely forgotten, for it would be barred along with the false. This in turn would explain why the discovery of Pythagoreanism throughout the Bible, by succeeding generations down the centuries, has been accompanied by surprise, even shock. For if the true gnosis was what we, for want of a better name, call Pythagoreanism, and Pythagoreanism had spawned the presumed false gnosis of Gnosticism, to put it very crudely, then, when the true was condemned with the false, Pythagoreanism itself would fall under the same interdict. This is the only way in which I can explain the overwhelming incidence of number symbolism in the New Testament on the one hand, and the general suspicion with which the same number symbolism has generally been treated by orthodoxy from the post-apostolic age onwards. I say this despite the testimony to the great tradition of Pythagorean biblical interpretation as outlined earlier. Great tradition though it has undoubtedly been, it has also been regarded with great suspicion by those who have constantly cried with Tertullian 'What has Jerusalem to do with Athens, the Church with the academy (Plato), the Christian with the heretic'[4] and who have neither been persuaded that the Greek tradition could be conflated with the Hebrew, nor that Plato was 'Moses Atticus.'

This suspicion has nowhere been more evident than in the general assessment of the most arcane and hidden dimension of biblical Pythagorean numerology which equates the letters of the Hebrew and Greek alphabets with numbers. So much has this been the case over the years, that generations of biblical scholars have either dismissed this dimension as worthless or not even believed it existed. The fact that it is indeed there and has by no means been considered worthless, particularly in the Judaic tradition, is attested by the lengthy entry in the *Encyclopaedia Judaica* under *Gematria*, for such is the name of this particular branch of number symbolism:

GEMATRIA (From Greek *geometria*), one of the haggadic hermeneutical rules for interpreting the Torah (Baraita of 32 Rules, no. 29). It consists of explaining a word or group of words according to the numerical value of the letters, or of substituting other letters of the alphabet for them in accordance with a set system. Whereas the word is normally employed in this sense of manipulating according to the numerical value, it is sometimes found with the meaning of 'calculations' (Avot 3:18). Similarly where the reading in present editions of the Talmud is that Johanan ben Zakkai knew 'the heavenly revolutions and *gematriot,*' in a parallel source the reading is 'the heavenly revolutions and calculations' (Suk 28a; BB 134a; Ch. Albeck, *Shishah Sidrei Mishnah*, 4 (1959), 497).[5]

There is much more detailed information in this article, some of it complex, but this is enough to attest the existence of gematria as one of the legitimate and authentic methods of interpreting the Bible.

The use of letters to signify numbers was known to the Babylonians and the Greeks. The first recorded use of it was on an inscription of Sargon II (727–707 BC) which says that the king built a famous wall 16,283 cubits long to correspond with the numerical value of his name. Gematria was recorded widely among the Magi and dream interpreters in the Hellenistic world. Likewise among the Gnostics. From our point of view it is significant that the author says that as far as it is known 'Its use was apparently introduced in Israel during the time of the Second Temple, even in the Temple itself, Greek letters being used to indicate numbers. (Shek. 3:2)'[6] In other words it postdated the time of Judah's exile in Babylon in the sixth century BC and began at about the same time as Pythagoras and the Pythagoreans first flourished in the late sixth — early fifth centuries. The use of Greek rather than Hebrew letters to indicate numbers in the Temple itself, indicates the extent of Hellenistic influence.

The origins of this numerical alphabet are evidently shrouded in the mists of antiquity. Bligh Bond and Simcox Lea after an extensive study, concluded that it first developed in Syro-Phoenicia during the fifth century BC although an earlier Eastern source could not be ruled out. They believed that both the Hebrew and the Greek alphabets derived from this area and that both show evidence of highly intelligent planning:

> Both systems attained a high degree of development about the third century BC. Both languages are constructed with great skill, and are evidently the work of highly instructed men animated by a clear purpose. Though compiled from older and far less perfect material, they represent something far more than the natural evolution of that material. They show system, but they also show peculiarities, sometimes having the appearance of intention, for which no adequate reason has yet been offered. Their alphabets, which are also numerals, exhibit unexplained features, some of which may be described as mysterious. It is scarcely reasonable to suppose that the element of chance

has in any appreciable degree entered into their framing.
And this is the more unlikely in that there is evidence of a
contrary belief among these peoples, who showed a
peculiar reverence for their alphabets, ascribing to each
letter its own mystical value, and to the whole, a body of
symbolic teaching in which the principles of Number,
Sound and also Form, which are connected with each letter,
all played their part.[7]

What Bond and Lea are saying, is that the Hebrew and Greek
alphabets as we now know them, were composed and constructed
from earlier material, along Pythagorean lines. Also, the letters are
not just linked to number, but also to Form, by which they mean
Geometry or number in space and also to Sound, that is to Music
or number in time. Later in their work they propose an Aeonial or
cosmic connection as well, thus completing the links between the
alphabets and the four Pythagorean disciplines of number, known
later to history as the Quadrivium. These are considerable claims,
and, as we shall see, they are able to substantiate them from their
extensive researches.

They conclude their historical findings by noting: 'The Greek
Alphabet was perfected in Athens about 400 BC, when several new
signs were added and older compound letters superseded. Other
old signs were retained as numerals only.'[8] Again, we may note
that this post-dates Pythagoras and coincides with the Pythagorean
and Platonic heyday.

So much for the authentication of the existence of gematria and
its historical origins in the Hebrew and Greek alphabets. Now we
can move on to other authors and identify four more important
principles regarding its use in practice. The first, as enunciated by
S.L. Mathers in his essay 'Introduction to the Zohar,' is:

Words of similar numerical values are considered to be
explanatory of each other and this theory is extended to
phrases. Thus the letter Shin, Sh is 300, and is equivalent to
the number obtained by adding up the numerical values of
the letters of the words RVCh ALHIM, Ruach Elohim, the
spirit of Elohim. For R = 200, V = 6, Ch = 8, A = 1, L = 30,
H = 5, I = 10, M = 40; Total 300. Similarly, the words
AChD, Achad meaning Unity or One, and AHBH, Ahevah

meaning love, each equal 13; for A = 1, Ch = 8, D = 4, total 13; and A = 1, H = 5, B = 2, H = 5, total 13 ... so the one is taken as symbolical of the other.[9]

This practice is still widely used in Hebrew among Israelis when composing laudatory or humorous verses at weddings and birthdays.

The second concerns the rule known as 'colel' which John Michell explains: 'By the conventions of gematria one unit, known as colel, may be added or subtracted from the value of any word without affecting its symbolic meaning. Thus *ekklesia Theou*, 778, Church of God, is equivalent by gematria to *stauros*, 777, a cross.[10] This latitude given by colel may be considered something of a fudge or even a fiddle by those not convinced that gematria is a reputable system, but it can perhaps be compared legitimately to the difference between natural tuning and equal temperament in music.

The third important principle concerns the method of counting or allocating numbers to the alphabets. There were two ways of doing this. One was with smaller numbers and the other was with larger ones. John James explains this, in his case referring to the Latin alphabet:

> There are two ways of counting in gematria. The straight-forward series of numbers from 1 to 22 applied to the Latin alphabet, known as the Lesser Canon, and another when the letters after the tenth are numbered 20, 30, and so on up to 100, and then the remainder in hundreds. This latter is known as the Greater or Greek Canon. Greek numbers had been written as letters from the sixth century before Christ. It was an adaptation of an even earlier system employed by the people of the Euphrates basin and brought westward by the Israelites after their captivity in Babylon. In the Greater Canon the first ten letters were counted in the same way as the Lesser, but thereafter the counting proceeded in tens and then hundreds.[11]

It does not appear to be generally acknowledged that there was a Lesser as well as a Greater Canon, even by eminent practitioners of gematria such as S.L. Mathers, John Michell, Bligh Bond and Simcox Lea, quoted above. However, it can be easily demonstrated

Hebrew		Lesser	Greater	Greek		
'Aleph	א	1	1	A	α	Alpha
Beth	ב	2	2	B	β	Beta
Gimel	ג	3	3	Γ	γ	Gamma
Daleth	ד	4	4	Δ	δ	Delta
He	ה	5	5	E	ε	Epsilon
Waw	ו	6	6	F	ϝ	Digamma
Zayin	ז	7	7	Z	ζ	Zeta
Heth	ח	8	8	H	η	Eta
Teth	ט	9	9	Θ	θ	Theta
Yodh	י	10	10	I	ι	Iota
Kaph	כ	11	20	K	κ	Kappa
Lamedh	ל	12	30	Λ	λ	Lambda
Mem	מ	13	40	M	μ	Mu
Nun	נ	14	50	N	ν	Nu
Samekh	ס	15	60	Ξ	ξ	Xi
`Ayin	ע	16	70	O	o	Omicron
Pe	פ	17	80	Π	π	Pi
Tzadhe	צ	18	90	Ϙ	ϙ	Quppa
Qoph	ק	19	100	P	ρ	Rho
Resh	ר	20	200	Σ	σ	Sigma
Sin, Shin	ש	21	300	T	τ	Tau
Taw	ת	22	400	Υ	υ	Upsilon
			500	Φ	φ	Phi
			600	X	χ	Chi
			700	Ψ	ψ	Psi
			800	Ω	ω	Omega

Figure 5. The Gematria of the Hebrew and Greek Alphabets.

that, as John James asserts, this was indeed the case. For instance *kithara*, which is a harp or lyre in Greek, is 51 in the Lesser Canon. The equivalent Hebrew word *kinnor* is also 51. This is surely more than a coincidence because scholars such as Alfred Sendrey in *Music in Ancient Israel* accept that the *kithara* and the *kinnor* were similar if not identical instruments.[12] Likewise *dabar*, meaning 'word' in Hebrew, is 26 in the Lesser Canon. This is the same as the number for YHWH, Yahweh, the Jewish God. In the Greater Canon this would be very different because *dabar* would be 206 and would not equal Yahweh which would still be 26. It is reasonable to assume that 'word' was supposed to equal 'God' from the verse 'and the word was God' (John 1:2) because, although it is in the Greek of the New Testament, its Old Testament Hebrew origin is implied. Accordingly the Greater and the Lesser Canon in Hebrew and Greek is given opposite and both will be used in subsequent chapters.

For the fourth and final principle we return to Bond and Lea. It is from their section 'On Geometric Truth' and concerns the link between gematria and architecture. They explain that words alone are inadequate to interpret spiritual ideas unless they have a figurative meaning. Symbolism, myth and parable have been the indispensable tools of the poet, prophet and religious teacher. This has been extended beyond words to architecture and its allied arts, through which great concepts have been communicated:

> Architecture has been the interpreter to man of the
> Universal Truths, those which express the Mind and
> Works of the Creator, for Architecture is the witness to the
> Formative principles which underline Nature, and speaks
> of the Immutable Foundations.[13]

These truths are expressed in geometric forms as they are related to measure and number. In this way architecture can be called a 'higher language' which is particularly suited for sacred purposes:

> Now in the Greek Gematria we have what may be termed
> the *Architecture of Language*, for the Gematria unites both
> elements, both modes of expression, and in a wonderful
> accord, since words are therein related in their sense to
> Number, by their Number to Geometry, and by their

Geometry again to Building. For all Building, whether of Words, Ideas, Figures or Material Forms, is founded on fixed proportionals which we have termed Aeonial, and these we study under the name Geometry.[14]

It is obvious from all this that Bond and Lea are latter day Pythagoreans. Everything they say about language in relation to number, geometry, building, architecture and the Aeonial dimension, fits a Pythagorean interpretation. Indeed all that has been said about gematria in this introduction, in the Hebrew as well as the Greek, can be seen as integral to the Pythagorean tradition. It therefore seems appropriate that we should now apply this Pythagorean key to the Scriptures to see what hidden knowledge may be revealed. However, since the Scriptures are a vast body of literature let us select certain important words for examination. Of the words which we might consider important, there could be none more so than the words 'Jesus' and 'Christ.' Since we are conducting an enquiry into the proposition that Jesus Christ might have been in some way linked to the Pythagoreans, let us submit the gematria of his names to a Pythagorean analysis.

Jesus Christ and the Fibonacci Numbers

First, let us decide whether we are going to use the Lesser or the Greater Canon for this examination. The fact that the Greek for 'Christ' contains a chi (X) indicates that we should use the Greater Canon because this letter was added later and was not part of the earlier 22 letters of the Lesser Canon. The Greek for 'Jesus' is *Iesous* and for 'Christ' is *Christos*, therefore the numbers equivalent to these letters and words are as follows:

IESOUS	CHRISTOS
I (iota) = 10	CH (chi) = 600
E (eta) = 8	R (rho) = 100
S (sigma) = 200	I (iota) = 10
O (omicron) = 70	S (sigma) = 200
U (upsilon) = 400	T (tau) = 300
S (sigma) = 200	O (omicron) = 70
This totals 888	S (sigma) = 200
	This totals 1,480.

So by gematria *Iesous* = 888 and *Christos* = 1,480. Therefore the two names together come to 888 + 1,480 = 2,368:

Jesus	Christ	Jesus Christ
888	1,480	2,368

The remarkable mathematical fact about these three numbers is that they are in a proportional relationship to each other. This becomes obvious when we divide them by their highest common factor (HCF) which is 296, for: 888 ÷ 296 = 3; 1480 ÷ 296 = 5 and 2368 ÷ 296 = 8. The proportional relationship is therefore 3 to 5 and 5 to 8. This is a geometric proportion of the type *A* is to *B* as *B* is to *C*. It has three terms of which *B*, or 5, is the mean proportional. In other words, the numerology of the names 'Jesus,' 'Christ' and 'Jesus Christ' fit the same theology of proportion which Simone Weil discovered in the Johannine sayings we looked at in the last chapter. Whether *he* realized it or not, Jesus Christ embodied in his own name and title that principle of mean proportional, or mediation, which lay at the heart of his teaching about the reciprocal relationships between himself, God and his disciples.

Surprising though it may be, this revelation or something like it, is to be expected if gematria is the authentic biblical interpretative system which it claims to be. In fact, we could go as far as to say that if we could *not* find something really special in the numerology of the names 'Jesus' and 'Christ,' then we would have every reason to doubt the validity of gematria as a hermeneutic principle. However, this is clearly not the case, so we will go on to point out that the ratios 3 to 5 and 5 to 8 not only exemplify the geometric proportion, that 'most beautiful of bonds' according to Plato, but are also part of a series of numbers known as the summation or Fibonacci series.

The summation series is so called because it is the progression of numbers in which each progressed number is the sum of the two previous ones, thus: 1 + 1 = 2, 2 + 1 = 3, 3 + 2 = 5, 5 + 3 = 8. So the series is 1, 1, 2, 3, 5, 8, 13, 21, 34, 55, 89, 144 etc. It is also called the Fibonacci series after Leonardo of Pisa, nicknamed Fibonacci, who introduced it into Europe from the Arabs of North Africa in the early thirteenth century.

The supreme importance of the Fibonacci series lies in the fact that its sequence of ratios underlies so many patterns and processes in nature that it can be considered ubiquitous. For instance, it governs the multiple reflections of light through mirrors, the gains and losses in energy radiation, the breeding patterns of rabbits, the male-female ratio of bees in hives, phyllotaxis or leaf distribution in plants, branch distribution in trees, seed distribution in daisy and sunflower heads, the proportions of animals' bodies, the proportions of the human body, the spiral growth of many shells, the growth of the foetus in animals and humans, the spirals of the inner ear, the unfolding bracken, animal horns and distant nebulae. In other words the series of ratios generated by the Fibonacci numbers lie at the heart of the growth patterns of nature and were held to be the signature of the Creator throughout Creation. In embodying the Fibonacci numbers 3, 5, and 8, the name Jesus Christ thus perfectly expresses the New Testament belief that he was Co-creator with God. As St John affirmed 'all things were made through him' (John 1:3) and St Paul echoed 'in him all things were created, in heaven and on earth.' (Col.1:16).

There are many today who have been persuaded by a number of New Testament scholars that these and other verses, which speak of Jesus as the Pantocrator or creator of all things, were later additions inserted into the text by pious hagiographers determined to divinize a man who was in essence no more than a gifted Galilean peasant,[15] a charismatic Hasid[16] or a wandering Cynic teacher.[17] Such people would probably not countenance the existence of gematria let alone the evidence which it produces. Yet, should the possibility of this exegetical method be seriously entertained, it ought at least to be conceded that if what we have uncovered is only coincidental, then the coincidences betray a remarkable consistency and congruity with each other. It should not be beyond the consideration of the reasonable critic that we may be dealing with the elements of a coherent system. If this is so, it would have to be accepted that these exaggerated claims, concerning the divinity of Jesus Christ, may have been there from earliest times and were not added later. Evidence for this becomes even stronger when we realize that the numbers 3, 5 and 8 not only identified Jesus Christ with the signature of the Creator, as expressed in the Fibonacci series, but also with the Divine Proportion to which this series approximates very closely.

The Divine Proportion or Golden Section is defined as that point

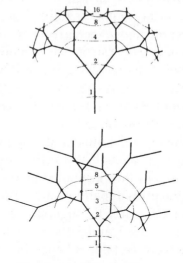

The two major branching patterns, one demonstrating the geometric progression by 2 ($\sqrt{2}$), and the other the Fibonacci Series (ϕ).

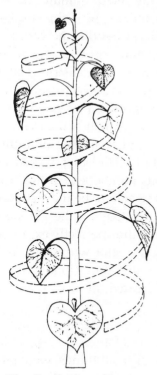

The distribution of leaves around a central stem is governed by the Fibonacci Series: 5 leaves in 3 turns, 8 leaves in 5 turns.

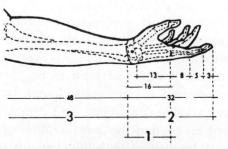

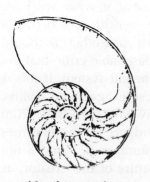

Nautilus pompilius.

The appearance of the Fibonacci Series in the relationships between the bone-lengths of the human finger, hand and arm is another instance of the numerous ϕ relationships which occur in the human body.

Figure 6. Examples of Fibonacci Numbers

on any line which divides it in such a way that the smaller part is to the larger part as the larger part is to the whole. It is an expression of the geometric proportion where *A* is to *B* as *B* is to *C*, as explained earlier. But it is a unique expression of this proportion where *C* equals *A* + *B*. In other words it only has two terms, *A* and *B*, because *C* equals *A* + *B*. It is the only proportion which has two terms and not three or four. It is thus unique and was called *he toma, the* proportion by the Greeks and was held to be miraculous. Among the early Christians it came to symbolize the doctrine of the Trinity. We have already spoken about this in relation to the geometric proportion of three terms but here we have the even more perfect expression of it in two, thus symbolizing the Three that are Two as well as the Three that are One.

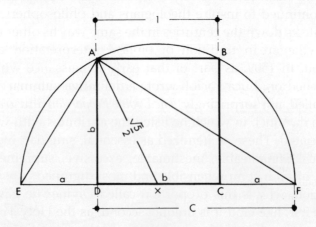

$$a:b::b:c.$$
$$c = a+b$$
$$\text{hence, } a:b::b:a+b$$

We then have the values:

side of the square $AB = b = 1$

$$XA = \frac{\sqrt{5}}{2}$$

$$ED = a = \frac{\sqrt{5}}{2} - \frac{1}{2}$$

$$DF = c = \frac{\sqrt{5}}{2} + \frac{1}{2} = \frac{\sqrt{5}+1}{2}$$

Figure 7. The Theorem of the Divine Proportion

The theorem of the Divine Proportion is proved from a square drawn inside a semi-circle and depends on Thales' law of similar triangles. It is not necessary to understand this, only to believe that it is so. Nevertheless, the demonstration from Robert Lawlor's *Sacred Geometry* is given for those who are interested. From this we learn that the Divine Proportion is $(\sqrt{5} + 1) \div 2 = 1.6180339...$, known by the Greek letter φ (phi). The Fibonacci numbers approximate closely to this, thus: $5 \div 3 = 1.6666$; $8 \div 5 = 1.6$; $13 \div 8 = 1.625$; $21 \div 13 = 1.6153$; $34 \div 21 = 1.6190$ etc. As the numbers increase, so the ratios between them become ever closer to $1.6180339...$, yet they are never exact but continue to oscillate fractionally below and above.[18]

The symbolism of the Trinity which the Divine Proportion embodied continued to inspire theologians and philosophers, artists and architects down the centuries in the same way as other aspects of the Pythagorean tradition of biblical interpretation already considered. In 1509, as part of that early Renaissance which we have touched on, Luca Pacioli wrote a definitive summary of the subject called, not surprisingly, *The Divine Proportion*, illustrated by Leonardo da Vinci, in which he listed the attributes with which it was associated. These he itemized as essential, singular, ineffable, miraculous, unnameable, inestimable, excessive, supreme, most excellent, quasi incomprehensible and most dignified. Answering the question, why is this proportion called Divine? he gave four reasons: First, like God it is unique; second, as the Holy Trinity is one substance in three persons, it is one single proportion in three terms; third, as God cannot be defined in words, it cannot be expressed by any intelligible number or rational quantity, but is always occult and secret and is called irrational by the mathematicians; fourth, like God it is always similar to itself.[19]

What we have discovered from this analysis of the numerology of the name 'Jesus Christ' is that the tradition which identified him with the Divine Proportion and the Divine Proportion with the Trinity, was not a later addition to the Gospel record born of an alien Hellenization bent on an inappropriate divinization of the man Jesus. The contrary seems to have been the case, for, as we have seen, it sprang in the first instance, from the Pythagoreanism implicit in the name 'Jesus Christ' itself. There were obviously also later influences from Hellenization in the way the doctrine of the Trinity was worked out, such as the Nicene formula 'being of one substance with the Father, by whom all things were made,' but if the testimony of gematria is worth anything, it should confirm what has been intimated in earlier chapters, that the Pythagorean paradigm was integral to the Scriptures and was not imposed later. It is of the warp and woof, the very fabric of the numero-geometric alphabets of which it is composed.

Nevertheless, it could still be argued that those who edited the New Testament material, however early, could still have imposed a Pythagorean interpretation on documents which were initially innocent of such arcane complexities. Perhaps, right from the start, the intellectuals among the earliest Christian communities were entrusted with the work of writing down the stories about Jesus, or at least of writing up those of others and in doing so recast them in the mould of their Pythagorean mindset. Perhaps they changed the grammar or the spelling of words or phrases to make them fit numerical or geometric patterns which were not initially there. Perhaps they even changed the spelling of Jesus Christ, *Iesous Christos*, to fit the Fibonacci series and the Divine Proportion.

This was certainly what Simcox Lea and Bligh Bond considered to have been the case. They believed that as a general practice, 'words would be coined to give certain numbers, in order to express associated ideas. And, more commonly, the spelling of a known word or name would be modified to give the number desired.' This, they say, began very early and was 'associated with the Pythagorean schools.'[20]

They also believed that sometimes new words would be introduced and that in the special cases of 'Iesous' and 'Christos' this is indeed what happened:

> Take the names Iesous and Christos. Both forms are
> specialized forms of more ordinary words; the first a
> common name derived from the Hebrew Joshua or Jeshua,
> and the second possibly a variant of Chrestos = good. But
> the argument for contrivance of number in the spelling of
> these names is so strong as to be irresistible.[21]

Do we therefore have to accept that the words New Testament generally and the names *Iesous* and *Christos* specifically, were manipulated by editors to fit a Pythagorean numerological mould? It would appear so and yet it is important to point out that, as regards the names *Iesous* and *Christos*, the modification of older names, or the contrivance of new ones, was *not* done by either New Testament writers or editors. Lea and Bond rightly observe that *Iesous* was the Greek translation of the Hebrew Joshua or Jeshua, but they are obviously not aware that this was the standard spelling for that name throughout the Septuagint (LXX), the third century BC translation of the Hebrew scriptures into Greek. Likewise, they do not seem to know that *Christos* was the standard Septuagint translation for *Meshiach*, Messiah or Anointed One, for example: 'The anointed, *Christou*, of the Lord,' 2Sam.1:14; 'and against his anointed, *Christou*' Ps.2:2; 'thine anointed, *Christou*,' Hab.3:13; 'my anointed, *Christo*, Isa.45:1. They imply that such contrivance was introduced through the Greek and confirm this later saying that 'the tradition can be traced back to the period at which the language of philosophic Greek was in process of formation.'[22] They do not realize that both *Iesous* and *Christos*, as spelt consistently in the New Testament, derive unaltered from the Septuagint. Thus, while the language was Greek, we may presume that those who first contrived the spellings of these names were not. They were Jewish, Greek-speaking Rabbis, reputedly 72 in number, who seemingly took 72 days to arrive at 72 identical translations of the Hebrew scriptures into Greek. Hence the name, Septuagint, the translation of the 72 or 70.

Why did the Rabbis of the Septuagint translate *Jehoshua* or *Jeshua* as *Iesous* and not *Ieosua* or *Iesua*? Why did they translate *Meshiach* as *Christos*? Were they fitting the Greek into a numero-geometric system with which they were already familiar in the Hebrew and were they thus creating a brilliant synthesis of the numbers, geometry and letters of the two languages simultaneously? The fact that the numbers 72 or 70 are central to the legend concerning their translation, is, most likely, a clue that something of this sort was going on, since 72 or 70 crop up as important symbolic numbers in a variety of sacred traditions, notably the Egyptian. If we now analyse the numbers and geometry of the Hebrew for *Iesous Christos*, that is, Joshua, *Yehoshua* and Anointed, *Meshiach*, we shall find that this was indeed the case. We shall also find ourselves entering the dimensions of architecture, cosmology, and what the Pythagoreans called the music of the spheres, at such a profound level that it may become hard to doubt that Jesus himself was party to this gnosis.

10
Joshua the Anointed One

First it must be decided whether we use the Greater or the Lesser Canon to analyse *Jehoshua ha Meshiach* and here I have to admit that I have been unable to make much sense out of the Greater Canon. However, I believe I have identified a coherent system by using the Lesser Canon. Therefore, while accepting that there may well be riches waiting to be revealed through the Greater, I will use only the Lesser.

Jeshua was a later contraction of the earlier *Yehoshua*. The Hebrew gematria of the latter in the Lesser Canon is Y = 10, H = 5, 0 (V) = 6, Sh = 21, U (V) = 6, A (Ayin) = 16. This totals 64. Likewise the word Messiah or Anointed, in Hebrew is *Meshiach* which in the Lesser Canon is M = 13, Sh = 21, I (Y) = 10, Ch = 8. This totals 52. Adding 64 and 52 we get 116. If we add the definite article, i.e. *Jehoshua ha Meshiach*, Joshua *the* Anointed or Jesus *the* Messiah, as is used today among congregations of Jewish Christians, we have to add 5 for the 'the.' This gives us 116 plus 5 which is 121.

What is special about these numbers? Not very much to the casual eye but to the Pythagorean they are all easily recognizable as either square numbers or multiples of four. *Jehoshua* is 64 which is 8^2; *Meshiach* is 52 which is 4×13; *Jehoshua Meshiach* is 116 which is 4×29 and *Jehoshua ha Meshiach* is 121 which is 11^2. What is so important about square numbers? Nothing much to the modern mind but remembering their symbolism from earlier chapters, we will be aware that for the Pythagoreans, justice was held to be equivalent to 2^2, 3^2 or any square number. As Simone Weil told us 'Among these numbers, some have a particular bond with unity. These are the numbers which are of the second power or square.' Therefore since in this system Unity or One symbolized God, we may assume that both *Jehoshua* as 8^2 and *Jehoshua ha Meshiach* as 11^2, symbolized the justice of God. This would be in addition to *Jehoshua*'s literal meaning of Saviour. Likewise *Jehoshua ha Mashiach*,

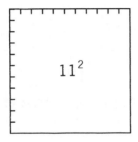

Figure 8. The Square of Eleven

as 11^2, would have been understood as God's Just or Righteous One. While this tells us nothing we didn't know before, it nevertheless helps to vindicate gematria as a reputable system and throws fresh light on the Hebraic background to the use of the term 'the just' in the New Testament Greek, as in 'your Father ... sends rain on the just and on the unjust' (Matt.5:45). It also adds an exotic exegetical flavour to 'the Just One' as applied to Jesus himself (Acts 3:14; 7:52; 22:14).

Having established the importance of square numbers in general, let us go on to explore the particular significance of 11^2, since that is the number of the complete name *Jehoshua ha Meshiach*. What was so special about this square number? As far as I can see, the answer to this question involves the acceptance of the principles of gematria as given in the last chapter, especially those which spoke of the links not only between numbers and geometry but also between music and cosmology. It appears to me that it is only when cosmology and music are added to numero-geometry, that the full significance of this sacred name is revealed. I present my theory with this presumption clearly in mind.

The square of 11 would seem to be the basic geometrical figure for expressing the harmonic relationships between the earth, the sun and the moon in simple whole number ratios. It appears to be the simplest whole number foundation for the essence of the Hebrew cosmology as expressed through the squaring of the circle or circling the square. Squaring the circle was the most powerful symbol which the ancients used to picture the sacred marriage between heaven, seen as the circle, and the earth, seen as a square of equal size. In common speech today the phrase 'squaring the circle' is used to denote an impossibility, and it is true that it cannot be drawn with complete accuracy. But a close approximation can be achieved, not in area but in perimeter, using 22/7 for the ratio between the circumference and diameter of a circle, known as Pi (π).

In order to find the diameter of a circle which has the same circumference as the perimeter of a square with sides of 11, i.e. (11 × 4), 44, we must divide by π i.e. 44 × 7/22 = 14. So 14 units will be the diameter of a circle of circumference 44. That this was taken as a model of the earth by the Hebrews is implied by the fact that the Earth, *Ha'AReTz*, in the Lesser Canon is 44. It is also implied in the word *HUG* meaning circle when referring to the earth which, in the Lesser Canon, is 14, that is, the diameter. These two words *Ha'Aretz* and *Hug* are found together in Isaiah 40:22 where it is said of God that he 'sits above the circle of the earth.'

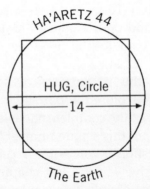

Figure 9. The Squared circle of Ha'Aretz and Hug

Now, let us add the sun to this model of the earth. A square of sides 14 is constructed so that its centre line is the diameter of the circle as already drawn. This square will have a perimeter of 14 × 4 = 56. To find the diameter of a circle with a circumference of 56 we once again divide by π. This gives us 17.818 recurring which is an irrational fraction. If however we use another ancient value for π, 16/5, we get 17.5 exactly. Strangely enough, if we accept 17.5 as our required diameter and multiply by π as 22/7 we get 55. So 17.5 × 16/5 = 56 and 17.5 × 22/7 = 55. By the principle of colel this difference of one is acceptable. Although 17.5 is not a whole number, it is a whole fraction and as 17½ is easily measured. It

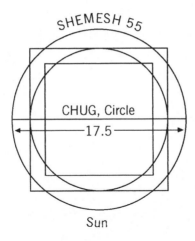

Figure 10. The Squared Circle of Shemesh and Chug

would appear that this was considered to be the diameter of the sun's circle because the number of *SheMeSh*, sun, in the Lesser Canon is 55 and the number for *ChUG*, circle, when used for the heavens is 17, as in Job 22:14 where it says of God that 'he walks on the circuit (or vault) of heaven.'

Now let us add the moon to this model of earth and the sun. The most frequent word for moon is *yareach* but there are two others also widely used, *chodesh*, a month or a new moon and *lebanah*, a white moon. Taking *ChoDeSh* and *LeBaNaH*, we find that they both have the number 33 in the Lesser Canon. Now 33 could be a circle of circumference 33 with a diameter of 10.5 sitting inside Figure 11 as drawn. If it is taken as such it completes a very beautiful figure of three concentric circles, two of them squared, which are in significant ratios to each other, namely 33:44:55. If we divide these by their Highest Common Factor (HCF) which is 11 we get 3, 4 and 5 and 3, 4 and 5 are the most important numbers in ancient geometry when recognized as the Pythagorean triangle in which the square of the hypotenuse equals the sum of the squares of the other two sides. But more than that, this famous triangle had specific harmonic connotations because it represented in its ratios the musical tones of the fourth (3:4), the major third (4:5) and the major sixth (3:5). It was thus an expression of the music of the spheres in which the ratio between the sun and earth was taken to be the major third, that between the sun and

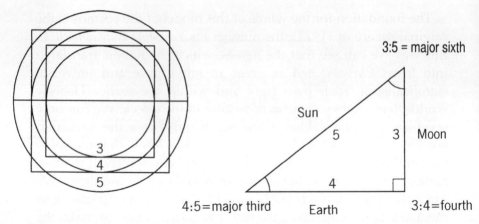

3:5 = major sixth

Sun

5   3   Moon

4

4:5=major third   Earth   3:4=fourth

Figure 11.
The Sun:Earth:Moon Ratio

Figure 12. The Pythagorean Triangle
3:4:5 and musical ratios

the moon was taken to be the major sixth and between the earth and the moon, the fourth.

Thus, this figure brings together gematria, geometry, the ratios among the earth, sun and moon, the musical tones associated with them, and the 3:4:5 Pythagorean triangle. It can also be thought of as the architecture of the macrocosm and this in turn can be seen embodied in the musical ratios of Solomon's temple. On the principle of 'as above, so below' the temple of the ancient Hebrews was considered to be a microcosm of this same macrocosmic harmony between music, geometry and architecture. It was the earthly focus of the music of the spheres.[1] Its sides were made up of 3:4:5 triangles.

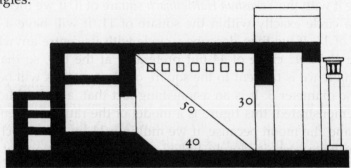

Figure 13. The 3:4:5 Triangles in the Holy Place of Solomon's Temple

The foundation for the whole of this model of the cosmos is the original square of 11; 121, the number for *Yehoshua HaMeshiach*. In this way we can see that the names, which the Rabbis translated into *Iesous Christos*, had as great an importance and universal significance in their own right and within the earlier Hebrew world-view, as they came to have later in the Greek. We can only speculate that the Rabbis of the Septuagint chose the particular spellings for *Iesous* and *Christos* because they knew that the spellings of the Hebrew names had themselves been contrived to fit an earlier synthesis of number, music, architecture and cosmology. We can only speculate that they also knew the central importance of this particular name and title and that they wanted to make the gematria in the Greek as fundamentally important as it had been in the Hebrew. It would appear that by the numbers alone, they had already anticipated in third century BC Alexandria, that the Christ would be Jesus.

The Earth:Moon Ratio

If we take 33, the moon's number, and instead of defining it as the innermost circle of our cosmogram, see its factors, 11 and 3, as describing the ratio between the earth and the moon, we arrive at a geometric construction of no less significance. The earth:moon ratio *is* 11:3 in actual fact, which is a startling reminder that the originators of the cosmic system which we are exploring were more knowledgeable and intelligent than we often think they were.

Let us go back to the *Ha'Aretz* circle of circumference 44 and square it with the *Yehoshua HaMeshiach* square of ll. If we then describe a circle exactly within the square of 11, it will have a diameter of 11. If we then describe a circle with its centre anywhere on the *Ha'Aretz* circle of 44 but preferably at the top, so that its circumference is tangent to the square of 11, its radius will be 1.5 and the diameter 3. It is an astonishing fact that, as John Michell has demonstrated, this figure is a model of the ratio between the earth and the moon because, if we multiply 11 by 720 (which, as 72, we have seen is closely linked with the translations of the Septuagint), we get 7,920 which, if taken as miles, is the mean diameter of the earth. If we then multiply 3 by 720, we get 2,160 which, in miles, is the exact diameter of the moon. As Michell says:

It is a curious fact of nature, ignored by modern cosmologists but evidently of the greatest interest to their ancient
predecessors, that the answer to the problem of squaring
the circle is presented nightly to public view, for it occurs
in the relative dimensions of the earth and the moon; and
this same source provides the sacred numbers of the canon.[2]

By 'the sacred numbers of the canon,' Michell means that this
geometrical figure is paradigmatic not only for the earth-moon
ratio but for the great cosmological traditions of the ancient world.
He has traced its recurring pattern of numbers and geometry and
has found it to be as central for the Greeks and the Egyptians, as
we have found it to be for the Hebrews. The squaring of the circle,
the symbol of the marriage of heaven and earth seems to have
been the most important way in which these civilizations pictured
their desire to achieve a harmony between the spiritual and
material worlds.

Squaring the Circle at the Great Pyramid

Using the measurements of the Egyptian Government survey
where the square base of the Great Pyramid is given as equivalent
to 1,760 royal cubits and the height 280, Michell notes that a circle
with radius 280 has a circumference of 1,760. 'The perimeters of
square and circle in Figure 15 are therefore equal.'

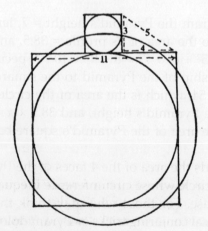

Figure 14. Squared Circles of Earth and Moon

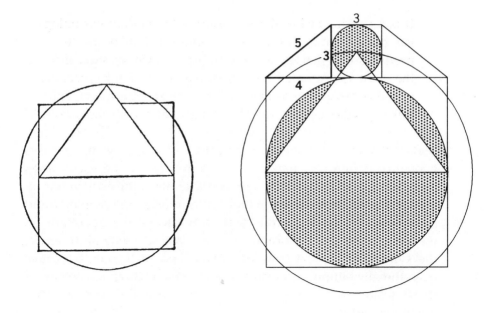

Figure 15.   Figure 16.

He develops this model in Figure 16 so that it resembles the earth-moon ratio of the squared circle as already demonstrated, only this time he adds the profile of the Pyramid. It is constructed via the 3:4:5 triangle and, as before, the height is 7 units and the length of base 11. Once again, the area of the base of this model is 11^2 or 121. This is our *Jehoshua HaMeshiach* square. Michell makes another interesting observation about this connection:

> In this diagram the Pyramid's height = 7, length of base = 11 so the area of its profile = 38.5, and $385 = 1^2 + 2^2 + 3^2 + 4^2 + 5^2 + 6^2 + 7^2 + 8^2 + 9^2 + 10^2$. A peculiar feature of the relationship of the Pyramid to the squared circle is that $38.5 \times 4 = 154$, which is the area of the circle of radius equal to the Pyramid's height, and $38.5 \times \pi = 121$ or 11^2, which is the area of the Pyramid's square base.[3]

In other words the area of the 4 faces of the Pyramid is equal to the area of the circle whose circumference is equal to the perimeter of its square base. For those who may think that Michell verges here on numerical conjuring tricks or Pyramidology, it is important to point out that he is merely emphasizing one of the many geometrical peculiarities which make the Great Pyramid unique in the world's store of ancient monuments. All that he states is in complete agreement with the secrets which Heroditus learnt from the priests in Egypt as early as the fifth century BC. In particular, that a square on the Pyramid's height is equal to the area of each of its four faces. This is confirmed by Peter Tompkins with reference to the Divine Proportion or Phi (φ) as explained in the last chapter:

> In the Great Pyramid the φ relation is found in the triangle formed by the height, the half base, and the apothem; that is to say, in the basic cross section of the structure (Figure 17a). 'These proportions create a relation between the sides of the triangle such that if the half base is 1, the apothem is φ and the height is $\sqrt{\varphi}$ (Figure 17b). This relation shows Heroditus' report to be indeed correct, in that the square on the height of the Pyramid is $\sqrt{\varphi} \times \sqrt{\varphi} = \varphi$, and the areas of the face $1 \times \varphi = \varphi$.[4]

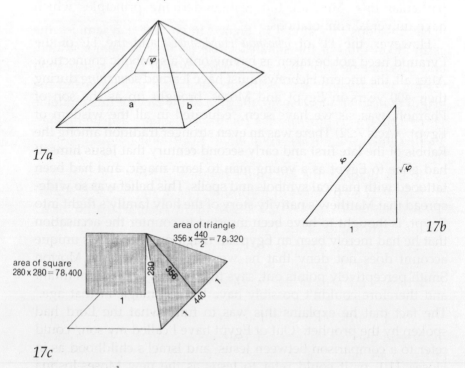

Figure 17. The Phi proportions in the Great Pyramid

It is pertinent to note that the proof of this theorem assumes that the base of the Pyramid is a square of 2 and 2^2, as mentioned, symbolized justice *par excellence* for Plato. (Perimeter of square $= 2 \times 4 = 8$; circumference of circle with height of Pyramid as radius ($\sqrt{\varphi}$ or 1.272) $= 1.272 \times 2 \times 22/7 = 7.99$).

From the point of view of our study, it is sufficient to note that 11^2 is completely central to all Pyramid calculations. Does this therefore mean that, by the dubious logic of numerology, *our* 11^2, i.e. *Jehoshua HaMeshiach*, can be thought of as the square base of the Great Pyramid? Obviously the answer is 'no' if it is taken literally but if it is taken symbolically then why not? It has been shown that the names *Jehoshua HaMeshiach* were themselves tailored to fit a pre-conceived cosmology of the earth, sun and moon, which was similar if not identical to that which Michell has proposed for the Pyramid. If these names were chosen in the first place because of their cosmic significance, then wherever that same cosmology appears, the same cosmic names could be said to apply. We are dealing not just with a particular person, Joshua or a particular title, Messiah, but with underlying principles which have universal connotations.

However, the 11^2 of *Jehoshua HaMeshiach* and the 11^2 of the Pyramid need not be taken as having only a symbolic connection. After all, the ancient Hebrews must have learned *something* during their 400 years in Egypt and Moses, brought up as the son of Pharaoh, was, as we have seen, 'educated in all the wisdom of Egypt.' (Acts 7:22) There was an even stronger tradition among the Rabbis of the late first and early second century that Jesus himself had gone to Egypt as a young man to learn magic, and had been tattooed with magical symbols and spells. This belief was so widespread that Matthew's nativity story of the holy family's flight into Egypt, is thought to have been inserted to counter the accusation that he had merely been an Egyptian magician. Matthew's unique account does not deny that he went to Egypt, but, as Morton Smith perceptively points out, says that he only went as an infant and therefore couldn't possibly have learned magic at that age.[5] The fact that he explains this was to fulfil what the Lord had spoken by the prophet: 'Out of Egypt have I called my son,' could refer to a comparison between Jesus' and Israel's childhood as in Hosea 11:1, or it could refer to Jesus as the new Moses-Joshua leading the new Israel out of the bondage of sin. Either way, there is more than a hint of Jesus recapitulating the history of the Old Testament with regard to Egypt.

We are used to thinking this way because that is how the Gospel writers want us to think. We do not find it hard to make this metaphorical connection with Egypt. Why then should we find it so hard to imagine that there might have been some element of literal truth in it? After all, no one knows where Jesus went during the silent years of his youth and early manhood. Perhaps he *did* go to Egypt to learn not magic but also wisdom as Moses had done, and that this was only called magic by his enemies. When he returned to Nazareth, they asked 'Where did he get all this wisdom?' Christians have usually thought that he got it straight from God because he was the Son of God. But this is a simplistic explanation which implies that his humanity was not at all like ours. It is much more convincing to think of him as really human and, to a degree at least, having had to learn wisdom. There is absolutely no reason why he should not have spent a considerable amount of time in Egypt. It is obvious from the Gospel narratives that he was capable of walking enormous distances. Egypt is not far from Palestine. Jesus could easily have walked to Egypt. This hypothesis would be entirely consistent with the tradition, described earlier, in which Plato was believed to be Moses Atticus and both were thought to have derived their wisdom from ancient Egypt.

Did Jesus know about the Numbers of his Name?

All that has been proposed above as an explanation of the importance of the number 121 has seemed reasonable to me, in terms of gematria and its associated disciplines of geometry, music, architecture and cosmology. I have kept well within the bounds of the principles of procedure laid down for this ancient exegetical method. Yet I am conscious that even so, I may have strayed beyond the bounds of reason for some, and been guilty of having seen patterns where there are none, and designs where there are only coincidences. So be it. I cannot apologize for my own belief that gematria is real and genuinely present in the biblical text, and that it can help to illuminate dimensions of meaning which otherwise might remain hidden. As regards the accuracy of my own speculations above, I would concede that a measure of doubt is legitimate. Nevertheless, I would contend that if a statistical analysis was made of my findings, it would show that the congruence of the numbers with geometry, music, architecture and cosmology, indicates a coherent system and not the randomness of chance.

The question to which I now want to return is that which was touched on in relation to Simone Weil's assertion that Jesus knew himself to be the incarnation of 'the mean proportional' of Greek geometrical theology, as much as the Isaianic 'man of sorrows.' I said then that we would need more evidence than that which Weil presented, before we could begin to speculate on this most intractable subject. I now believe that the extra evidence necessary to do this has been offered in the shape of my findings above. Exciting though her revelations were, especially of the pattern of geometric proportions in certain Johannine sayings, I considered that they were not systematic enough to form the basis from which to assess the vexed question of Jesus' consciousness of himself. However, I would contend that gematria, properly understood, with its related disciplines, does provide us with a sufficiently sys-tematic basis, as exemplified in the gematria of the name and title Jesus Christ as *Iesous Christos* in the Greek, and *Jehoshua ha Meshiach* in the Hebrew. I believe that all which has been put forward in this connection justifies us looking into the question of Jesus' self-perception from the point of view of a very specific question, namely: did he know about the numbers of his name? Was he aware of the link between letters, numbers, geometry, music, architecture and the cosmos? If the answer is 'no,' then we must assume that all that has been said about the gematria of *Iesous* and *Christos* in the Greek, was unknown to him and was only known to those scholarly editors, who later imposed a Pythagorean interpretation on what became the New Testament material. If this was so, then presumably the spelling of his name would not have mattered. If he ever had to spell his name in Greek then he might have spelt it Iesus or Esus, because he was ignorant of the gematria of *Iesous*. Similarly, if he ever thought of himself as Messiah or had to use the Greek equivalent, he might have pronounced or spelt it *Chrestus* like Pliny, or *Christus* like Tacitus. What mattered was his office, not how it was spelt. In saying this I am aware that many scholars believe that Jesus only spoke Aramaic and Hebrew, but I maintain that in so doing, they have underestimated the pervasive Hellenization of Judea, the importance of the Septuagint and the intelligence of Jesus himself. In Israel today many of the indigenous population are trilingual.

It would be easier to accept this position if we hadn't already found out that both *Iesous* and *Christos* in the New Testament were identical to the translation of *Jehoshua* and *Meshiach* in the Septuagint. However, this being so, it can be assumed that Pliny, Tacitus and other early commentators unfamiliar with the Septuagint and its Hebrew source, might get the spelling wrong, but that those who knew Hebrew as well as Greek would not. Thus, when the angel appeared to Joseph saying that Mary would have a child 'and you shall call his name Jesus,' (Matt.1:21; Luke 1:31) it had to be spelt *Iesous*, because this was the standard Septuagint translation of *Yehoshua*. This is obviously what is being referred to because the angel goes on to say 'for he shall save his people from their sins,' which is the spiritual interpretation of the original Hebrew name. Both the Greek of the Septuagint and the Hebrew scriptures lie behind this particular spelling of this uniquely appropriate name. It is thus hard to believe that Jesus was unaware of the existence and importance of gematria when it was obviously so much part of the tradition of the Hebrew scriptures and their Greek translation, out of which he came.

So if the answer is 'yes,' he did know about the link between letters, numbers, and the architecture of language, then this means that he must have been party to the interpretation which the Gospel writers are usually thought to have imposed on him later. He must have belonged to that same tradition which had constructed the Hebrew scriptures, which had produced the Septuagint and which was about to perform a similar feat of numero-geometric synthesis in what was to emerge as the New Testament. This would explain the overt numerical symbolism in the record of his public ministry. It has generally been held that through his use of number symbolism, for example, the calling of 12 Apostles, spending 40 days in the wilderness and commissioning 72 disciples, he was either recapitulating the 12 tribes, the 40 years in the desert and the 72 Mosaic elders of the Old Testament, or his interpreters were imposing this on him. While the former and indeed the latter might still to some extent be the case, it is now possible to see that if he was aware of how much this dimension was part of his heritage, he would appropriate it not just so that the scriptures might be fulfilled in some symbolic way, but because he also recognized it as an essential part of himself and indeed, of the whole of creation. For these overt numbers like all the others which he used, such as 3, 7, 10 and 153, were part of the same system as that which we have identified in the gematria of his own name and title and were, in turn, as we have seen, of universal significance.

Whether obvious or hidden, exoteric or esoteric, these numbers pointed beyond themselves to the things they symbolized. It would seem from our examinations that the things they signified were ultimately all the different aspects, principles and powers of the universe, which, as we saw earlier, were known to the Greeks as the *archai*. It was the whole cosmos, no less, which was the great reality behind, as well as *in*, the appearances of all things. It was this cosmic dimension which was believed to be made in the image and likeness of the Creator, and to express his character. It is in this sense that the gematria of the Bible and its related disciplines can be said to constitute the substance of a coherent, but covert, sacred cosmology of which the overt numbers and their symbolism are the outward visible expression.

In appropriating this for himself, Jesus would have been entering into his own cosmic personhood, moving through the symbols to the thing symbolized. The eastern mystical doctrine of *Tat Tvam Asi*, 'I am that,' or the Celtic bardic teaching of 'I have been that,' would perhaps be the easiest way of describing his identification with this dimension. The architecture of language leads from *Jehoshua HaMeshiach* to the squared circles of earth, sun and moon. It leads from *Iesous Christos* through the Fibonacci numbers to the Divine Proportion throughout the universe. This is all as it should be if Jesus Christ is who he was believed to be, the Lord of All, the Pantocrator 'the first-born of all creation.' (Col.1:15). But those titles imply an observer looking at his creation, an inventor watching his invention. What is implied in gematria and the architecture of language, is a Life Force which stands inside as well as outside creation. It implies an intrinsic, as well as an extrinsic, relationship between Creator and Creation. The names *Yehoshua HaMeshiach* and *Iesous Christos* are made up of the same ratios, harmonies, and geometries as the cosmos itself. They are thus not only pointing to lordship and rule, they are expressing intimate participation. The name *Yehoshua HaMeshiach* not only speaks of the harmonies of earth, sun and moon as 'I am Lord of all that,' but also 'I am *in* all that' and 'I *am* that.' Likewise the name and title *Iesous Christos* not only says 'I am the Pantocrator,' but also 'I am the essence of all things.' It was in this sense that *Iesous Christos* was understood to be the creative Word or Logos, the one in whom 'all things hold together,' (Col.1:17) the one who says 'I have been that; I *am* that.' Without the assumption that the Scriptures are talking primarily about intimations of macrocosmic reality impinging on the microcosmic world of finite appearances, gematria with its attendant geometry, music, architecture and cosmology is a meaningless irrelevance. However, once this basic assumption is accepted, it becomes a key to unlock a chest full of forgotten treasures, a lamp that leads into a cave of wonders, a magic carpet that can fly us to the stars.

We may thus conclude that Simone Weil was in all probability entirely correct when she claimed that Jesus recognized himself as 'that mean proportional of which the Greeks had for centuries been thinking so intensely.' We may also conclude that he entered into the whole of the universal gnosis which this implied, as into his own cosmic personhood; in mystical Oneness with the All.

Let us now go on to examine his occupation, the trade which he was said to have plied, to see if we can find out whether he had any actual Pythagorean connections.

11
The Master Builder at Sepphoris

Can all this cosmology help us to understand why Jesus was called a carpenter? Not if by 'carpenter' we only mean someone who worked in a joiner's shop, which is the picture we have inherited from popular piety throughout the centuries. The Greek word *tektōn* (Mark 6:3 and Matt.13:55) can be applied to workers in stone or metal as well as wood, so it could mean that he might as easily have been a mason or a smith as a joiner.[1] The controversy over his possible occupation goes back to Justin in the second century who claimed that he made ploughs, yokes and farm implements,[2] and to Origen in the third century who denied all woodworking associations, saying that no gospel text supported them.[3] Modern scholarship divides along similar lines with those favouring Origen's position maintaining that if the reference is to be taken as literal and genuine, then Jesus could just as well have been a smith or a stone mason.[4]

George Wesley Buchanan in *Jesus, the King and His Kingdom* develops this broader interpretation of 'carpenter' in a most impressive way, putting it in the context of related words:

> The Greek word that is translated 'carpenter' is *tektōn*. This has the basic meaning of one who scrapes, planes, hews, or builds. Words closely related to *tektōn* are *teknadzo*, which means to employ, contrive, use cunning or practice; and *tekne* which means a way, means or manner whereby a thing is gained. It is an art, system, set of rules of making or doing; *technema* is a work of art or treatise; and a *technites* is a skilled workman in some special area, such as war, religious practices, theatrical art, or trickery. This is the term used to describe God who is the builder of the city which had foundations[5] (Heb.11:10).

Buchanan's reference to the link between *tektōn*, understood as 'builder,' and *technites* as used in the letter to the Hebrews where Abraham 'looked forward to the city which has foundations, whose builder and maker is God,' takes our inquiry to an altogether higher level. He shows that the word can be used to describe God's handiwork as well as man's and that if we were to take it literally *and* metaphorically and apply it to Jesus, we could assume an implied comparison between his human and divine activities. If in fact, as Buchanan goes on to claim, Jesus was a builder who was not so much a labourer as someone who got things built, like a site manager, then his earthly profession would have been an exact counterpart of his role as the one through whom God had created all things. The description of him as a *tektōn* could therefore be seen as code for master mason on earth and architect (*architektōn*) of the heavens. Buchanan's conclusion that he 'had once been a businessman but later joined a sect and became a scholar' would concur on the one hand with Geza Vermes' assertion that 'carpenter' stands for 'scholar' in certain Talmudic sayings,[6] and on the other with the possibility that the Gospel writers knew that he had trained and worked as a master builder or architect. Such knowledge would have been a closely guarded secret, just as it would in masonic circles today. So Jesus would have been understood to have been a carpenter, and the son of a carpenter, by those who were satisfied with the simple message that the son of God became a poor workman and a humble labourer. But, by those who knew how to interpret *tektōn* in its more profound meaning, he would also have been understood to have been the earthly counterpart of the Maker of the Universe. This is the conclusion which Bligh Bond and Simcox Lea come to. They say:

> ... that He was trained as a Carpenter or Builder ... suggests
> that behind this natural and outward fact there lies a
> mystery, namely that He, in His Divine Personality, was
> the Builder of the Aeons (Heb.1:2) and that the Knowledge
> which He gave His Church was the knowledge of those
> principles by which the worlds were made (Heb.11:3).[7]

This cosmic or Aeonial interpretation may also be implied in the gematria of *tektōn*. Strictly speaking, because of the omega, it should only be counted in the Greater Canon, in which it totals 1,475. This breaks down to 5 × 5 × 59 which is not obviously symbolic. If however we count in the Lesser Canon, replacing the omega with omicron, we get 88. This gives us an immediately recognizable number which takes us straight back to the geometric figure of squaring the circle. The square of eleven units was *Yehoshua HaMeshiach*, Joshua the Messiah, and the circle of circumference 44 was *Ha'Aretz*, the earth. In John Michell's variation of this, the square of 11 enclosed the circle of the earth, while the circle with circumference 44 was associated with the centre of the moon's diameter. Either way, 88 symbolizes the squaring of the circle; the circling of the square which we have discovered to be paradigmatic and foundational to Hebrew cosmology. Bearing in mind the secrecy which surrounded all esoteric teaching, it perhaps should not surprise us that this important number lies hidden within this keyword and is only revealed to those who have discovered the cosmic significance of *tektōn*, hence the real occupation and identity of the earthly Jesus.

It is intriguing that in the development of this 'tektōnic' interpretation, from carpenter's shop to cosmos, the letter to the Hebrews has been quoted three times, once by Buchanan and twice by Bond and Lea. This would suggest that the writer, in claiming that Jesus was the Builder of the Aeons, would have been appealing to a cosmic dimension already familiar to his Hebrew readers, and that something of what has been discussed above might have been known to them.

It seems as though once again we are confronted by the symbol

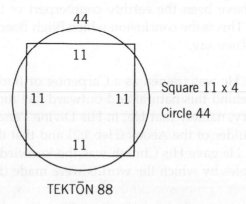

Figure 18. Squaring the Circle: Tektōn

of squaring the circle. Maybe this is because we are reading far too much into the text, seeing numerical coincidences where there are none and forcing things to fit. That is a distinct possibility. Nevertheless, it is impossible not to notice the strong likeness which 88 has to 888, *Jesous*. Is that pure coincidence? And is it just by chance that, according to the Lesser Canon, *arithmos*, the Greek word for number, counting and arithmetic, just happens to be 88? Is it also coincidental that, according to Simone Weil, *arithmos* was believed to be synonymous with *Logos*, the Word that was with God, through whom all things were made? Not if there is any truth in the precept of gematria that 'Words of similar numerical values are considered to be explanatory of each other ... the one is taken as symbolical of the other.' It is just possible that these coincidences are not the product of randomness but are something to do with what Michell calls 'the secrets of the canon.' He refers of course, to the canon of the Pythagorean number system, but perhaps we have reached the point where we can apply it also to the canon of the Scriptures.

The Suburban Sepphorite

The interpretation of *tektōn* as applied to Jesus, is strengthened enormously by the realization that the little village of Nazareth was situated only four miles away from Sepphoris, the biggest city in Judea outside Jerusalem and the capital of Galilee. It was therefore not a sleepy and remote hamlet as it has been portrayed, but the suburb of a great metropolis. This single fact has such an important bearing on our understanding of the youth and early manhood of Jesus, that it is relevant to describe the city's history in some detail.

Four miles north of Nazareth, the modern Israeli settlement of Zippori lies at the foot of the hill on which the old city of Sepphoris stood. Herod the Great had made it his Galilean capital and his son Herod Antipas did the same, but not without a great deal of trouble. The story is dramatic. On his deathbed, Herod commanded his three sons to go to Rome to get their successions ratified by the Emperor. While they were away, in 4 BC, the rebel leader Judas, attacked Sepphoris, arming his men with weapons taken from the arsenal. The rebellion spread and the population of the city, although they didn't fight with Judas, sympathized with him because his main grievance was about Roman taxation. The rebellion was soon crushed ruthlessly by the Roman legions. The city was burned and its inhabitants sold into slavery.

When Antipas returned as Tetrarch, he decided, in spite of the destruction, to rebuild the city and keep it as his capital. He initiated an enormous building programme which was to last for over twenty years until he moved to his new fortress at Tiberias in AD 26. By the time he had finished all the splendid public buildings, the mosaic tiling and the huge theatre he had, in Josephus' words, made Sepphoris 'the ornament of all Galilee.'

When Josephus, the leader of the Jewish revolt against the Romans in AD 66, came to Sepphoris looking for military support, the elders refused even to let him in. They remembered only too well what had happened when they had supported Judas in 4 BC and they feared it could happen again. Once Josephus knew that he couldn't win over such an important strategic centre, he began to accept that his cause was futile. This process of disillusionment eventually led him to change sides, a betrayal for which he is still largely unforgiven.

Standing among the recently excavated remains of the city, looking south, it is easy to see the silhouette of the sprawling city of modern Nazareth on the horizon. Today, the roles are reversed for it is Sepphoris which is the village, but the proximity is still as striking. It isn't hard to realize that if the young Jesus lived so near, he could have walked to this major centre of Greco-Roman culture in an hour. More importantly, it isn't hard to speculate that if he was a builder, as has been suggested, and there were massive building works going on there from approximately the time of his birth until he was in his twenties, he most probably did his apprenticeship and found his first employment there. Easy though it is to speculate, it would mean that we would have to make a radical reassessment of our image of Jesus' youth and early manhood, similar to that which we have carried out on the word *tektōn* and consistent with it. Having discovered his most likely occupation, we have now discovered the most probable context and location for it.

The implications of this proposed link between Jesus and Sepphoris have been developed by Shirley Jackson Case and Richard Patey. Writing in *The Journal of Biblical Literature* in 1926, in an article 'Jesus and Sepphoris,' Shirley Jackson Case noted: 'The proximity of Nazareth to Sepphoris suggests the possibility of important social contacts for Jesus during his youth and early manhood.' She then drew out the possible results of this contact, the first being his spirit of tolerance:

> The unconventionality of Jesus in mingling freely with the common people, his generosity towards the stranger and outcast, and his conviction of the equality of all classes before God, perhaps owe their origin in no slight degree to the proximity of Nazareth to Sepphoris. Had Jesus spent his youth in a remote village, amid strictly Jewish surroundings, he would have been less likely to acquire these generous attitudes which afterwards characterized his public career.[8]

The second Sepphorite characteristic Shirley Case put forward was that it made Jesus less separatist in his religious outlook:

> Still another distinctive feature about the career of Jesus was his method of effecting reform. He quite reversed the programme of the contemporary Jewish reformer, such as one meets in the Zadokite sectary, the Essene, a Bannus, or a John the Baptist. The representatives of these movements summoned people to separate themselves from the customary pursuits as a condition for realizing a better righteousness. In his new religion was something that could function to the full while people were engaged in their normal activities.[9]

Shirley Case then concluded with the third possible influence of Sepphorite attitudes on Jesus, that is, with regard to the Romans. She recounted the sad story of the destruction of the city in 4 BC and the fact that they had learnt their lesson. During the Jewish revolt of AD 66 to 70, they not only failed to support Josephus and the rebels but earned the title, minted on their coins, of 'Eirenopolis' the city of peace: 'That shortly before the year AD 30 a carpenter from the neighbouring village of Nazareth should have had his own attitude towards the Roman government influenced by this characteristic psychology of the people of Sepphoris is, of course, only a conjecture.' Nevertheless it is a strange coincidence that 'Throughout his career Jesus maintained this attitude of non-resistance toward Rome.'[10]

The most pertinent aspect of Case's article and one which comes very close to what we have already suggested, was that Jesus had not merely been influenced socially, culturally and spiritually by the proximity of Sepphoris to Nazareth, but that he had actually worked as a tradesman on the reconstruction of the city:

> That a vigorous building enterprise was in progress at
> Sepphoris while Jesus was still a youth, and at the same
> time the main support of a family of at least six younger
> children and a widowed mother, compels one to ask
> whether Jesus himself may not have sought an opportunity
> to ply his carpenter's trade in the city. It has been
> maintained with a high degree of probability that
> 'carpenter' as applied to Jesus meant not simply a worker
> in wood but one who worked at the building trade in
> general, and it requires no very daring flight of the
> imagination to picture the youthful Jesus seeking and
> finding employment at Sepphoris.[11]

This point was taken up and developed by Richard Patey in two articles in *New Testament Studies* in 1984, the first of which was called 'Is not this the Carpenter?' This was based on his first-hand experience as administrative director of James Strange's excavations there in 1983. He first queried Case's theory asking why, if Sepphoris was so important to the early life of Jesus, was it never mentioned in the Gospels and why did he never go back? His answers were that the Gospels were not written as biography and also, after Herod Antipas had beheaded John the Baptist, Jesus' own life was in danger through guilt by association, and that he would have therefore avoided going near Herodian strongholds. This would have applied equally to Tiberias, much nearer to his base at Capernaum, but apparently also never visited.

Patey then went on to enlarge on the Sepphorite attitudes traceable in Jesus' ministry, as already outlined by Case, making more perceptive observations, such as Jesus' famous answer to the question 'Is it lawful to pay taxes to Caesar or not?' sounds as though 'it came from Sepphoris rather than from the rebellious Galileans;'

that archaeological evidence from local tombs would suggest that Jesus, like other workers in Sepphoris, probably spoke Greek as well as Aramaic and Hebrew; and that there is considerable tragic irony in the presumption that although Antipas only finally met Jesus at his trial where he mocked and his prisoner remained silent, there was a poignancy between the two men 'who for some time had known each other by reputation, even although they had lived just six kilometres apart most of their lives.'[12]

Patey concluded that although the reconstruction of Sepphoris was in a Hellenistic style and had a considerable Greco-Roman culture, the fact that its residents were predominantly Jewish incomers with a strong priestly link with Jerusalem, meant that there was:

> ... no apparent reason for a young man from Nazareth to avoid this city. It is entirely possible that Jesus and Joseph worked on the construction projects. But, if they did not, they had knowledge of the work in progress and were acquainted with the workers. These contacts helped to shape the world in which Jesus grew up and his understanding of it.[13]

All this mainly amplified Shirley Jackson Case, but it is in his second article of 1984 that Patey propounds a theory of his own whose implications are very important and far-reaching.

Jesus and the Theatre

In 'Jesus and the Theatre' Patey presents a hypothesis that Jesus not only knew about the theatre at Sepphoris but attended it and learnt from it. This thesis centres round Jesus' frequent use of the word hypocrites, which is recorded seventeen times in the Gospels. The word *hupocrites*, comes uniquely from the Greek, there are no Hebrew or Aramaic equivalents, and it means a stage actor. It was used consistently by Jesus to characterize, caricature and castigate the Scribes and the Pharisees who made an outward show of their piety but whose hearts were far from God. They were *hupocrites*, because they were like actors, performing a staged, insincere religion. Patey makes a particularly telling point when he says that because many orthodox Jews held the Hellenistic theatre and actors in contempt, they would have found Jesus' comparison especially offensive. If he and they were unaware of the actors' profession, this comparison would have been meaningless.[14]

Patey then goes on to address the question: did Jesus attend the theatre at Sepphoris? While he admits that no certain answer can be given, he speculates in a most intriguing way:

> Antipas would have used his theatre for dramatic productions. His education in Rome probably gave him an appreciation for the stage. Jesus' references to actors who painted their faces to appear sad and dismal, indicates that he had viewed tragic actors. If Jesus had seen a tragic hero, like Oedipus, pursue his identity and destiny against all counsel to the contrary, what impression could this have made on his understanding of his own life and ministry? Could the roles of the prophet and Suffering Servant from Jewish tradition have been reinforced and shaped by the tragic hero?[15]

These arresting questions , in their own way so reminiscent of Simone Weil, must be answered in the affirmative, if we accept that the geography and circumstances of Jesus' youth were chosen so that he might grow to the realization that his mission was to incarnate the wisdom of the Gentiles, as well as that of the Jews. Patey's thesis gives us firm grounds for the assumption that Jesus was effectively a Jew *and* a Greek or Greco-Roman, that he was Jewish by race and background but was Hellenized to the point where it was indeed possible for him to see himself as fulfilling the role of the Greek tragic heroes as well as the mean proportional as outlined above. And yet to say he was Hellenized or Greco-Roman perhaps misses the even deeper point; that he had come to embody truth, which was ultimately not Jewish, Greek or Roman, although these all contained profound aspects of it. Patey's conjectures strengthen the case for believing what has already been proposed, that the concept of Jesus as Pantocrator, the Lord of All, did not first emerge during the later Hellenization of the Gospel, but was there from the beginning in Jesus' own consciousness of his universal, not just Jewish, identity and mission. Sepphoris was the unique setting where this consciousness could grow to fruition.

There is another section in Patey's article which is even more arresting and pertinent to our theme. This concerns the style of the theatre which Antipas built at Sepphoris. He shows that it conformed to the recently formulated architectural principles of Vitruvius, the most famous and influential of all Roman architects.

In order to please Augustus, Herod the Great sent his son Antipas to Rome in 8 or 7 BC to be educated. He stayed there until his father's health declined in 5 or early 4 BC. Herod had built theatres in Judea and Antipas was probably going to do the same. In Rome the magnificent theatre of Marcellus, begun by Julius Caesar, had recently been completed by Augustus in 11 BC. This theatre, a beautiful three-storied structure with Doric, Ionic and Corinthian columns and all the latest acoustical devices, became a model for a number of other theatres. It was built according to principles laid out in Book V of *The Ten Books on Architecture* by Marcus Vitruvius Pollio, known to history as Vitruvius. When Antipas returned home and built the theatre at Sepphoris, it was the Vitruvian style of design and technical skill which he used, as Patey explains: 'The design of the stage in the theatre at Sepphoris follows Vitruvius' basic blueprint!'[16]

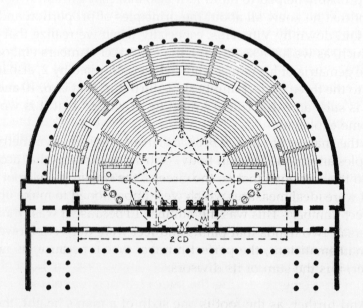

Figure 19. Vitruvian Theatre

This brings the Greco-Roman world so close to the world of Jesus that the two begin to merge together, and a composite figure who is as much Greek and Roman as Jewish begins to stand before us. It has already been established that he was not a carpenter but a master builder along masonic lines. But even if we were to backtrack on that and reassert that he was indeed only a carpenter, we would still have to change our perception of the *kind* of carpentry he did, in the light of Patey's hypothesis. If he did work at Sepphoris as seems likely, he would have probably made wooden templates for the stone masons, as well as tables and chairs for the furnishings. In other words, even as a mere carpenter, he would have been involved in the actual building, for until early modern times, the details of the construction of buildings were measured and built to the moulds of wooden templates. So, even the most conservative interpretation of Jesus' trade still points towards him having been a builder and thus preserves the proposition that his earthly profession was an image and embodiment of his divine activity.

If we accept Patey's hypothesis, then it is reasonable to assume that Jesus not only went to the theatre at Sepphoris but that he also probably helped to build it. It also makes it extremely hard to doubt that he knew all about the principles of proportion and design laid down by Vitruvius, especially when we realize that 3, 5, 8, which, as we have seen, were the Fibonacci numbers embodied in the gematria of his name, were, when multiplied by 2, also identical to the three perfect numbers of Vitruvius, that is, 6, 10 and 16. This is such an extraordinary meeting of worlds that it is worthy of some explanation.

In the chapter of *The Ten Books on Architecture* 'On Symmetry: In Temples and in the Human Body,' Vitruvius explains that according to the Ancients, that is, the Greeks, the finger, palm, foot and cubit were ideal measures which were apportioned to make up the 'perfect number.' This was the number 10 because it was from the fingers of two hands that palms and feet were derived. However, for mathematicians, the perfect number was 6 because, as noted earlier, it is the sum of its divisors:

And further, as the foot is one sixth of a man's height, the height of the body as expressed in number of feet being limited to six, they held that this was the perfect number, and observed that the cubit consisted of six palms or of twenty-four fingers. This principle seems to have been followed by the states of Greece.[17]

Later, he says that because they considered both 10 and 6 to be perfect numbers, they added the two together and made 16 the most perfect number. Therefore they held 6, 10 and 16 all to be perfect.

If we divide these by their Highest Common Factor, 2, we get 3, 5, 8. These, as we have seen, are Fibonacci numbers approximating very closely to the Divine Proportion, and are the proportional relationships in the gematria of *Iesous Christos*!

In the same chapter, Vitruvius shows that ancient temples were modelled on the proportions of these perfect numbers as expressed in the human body. He concludes with praise saying '... we can have nothing but respect for those who, in constructing temples of the immortal gods, have so arranged the members of the works that both the separate parts and the whole design may harmonize in their proportions and symmetry.'[18] He goes on to classify the various types of temple, giving many examples. György Doczi in *The Power of Limits* has analysed some of these of which Labianda and Priene are two striking examples:[19]

On the basis of this remarkable identity of proportional theory, we may say that Jesus was the embodiment of Vitruvian man, the perfect *Anthropos* of the Greeks. Far-fetched though this might seem at first, it is really no more than another way of describing him as a Pythagorean for Vitruvius, whether he knew it or not, wrote consistently as if he were a Pythagorean, on all matters concerning architectural proportion, design and mathematics. It is also another way of making a direct connection between the Pythagorean tradition of biblical interpretation as outlined above, and its flowering in the early Renaissance. This concept of the ideal Vitruvian man was at the heart of Alberti's notion of *concinnitas*, that harmonious blend of number, measure, proportion and arrangement, which became the norm for Renaissance artists, sculptors and architects. The proportions of the ideal man from which all other proportions were taken, were such, according to Vitruvius, that a circle and a square which exactly enclosed him, had its

Figure 20. Types of Vitruvian Temple: Labianda.

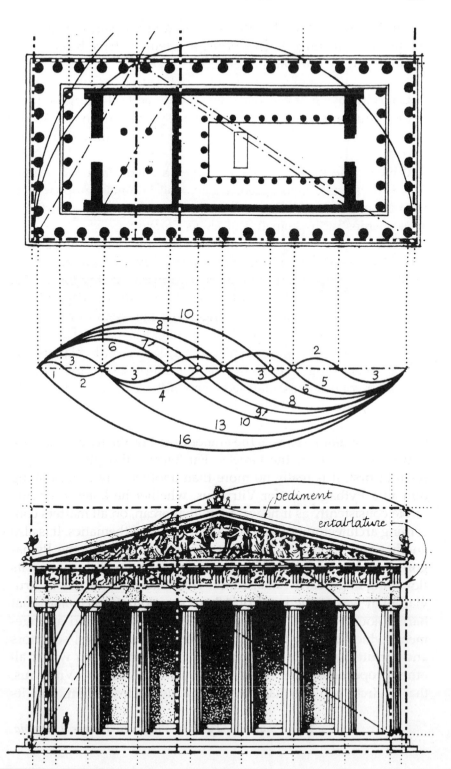

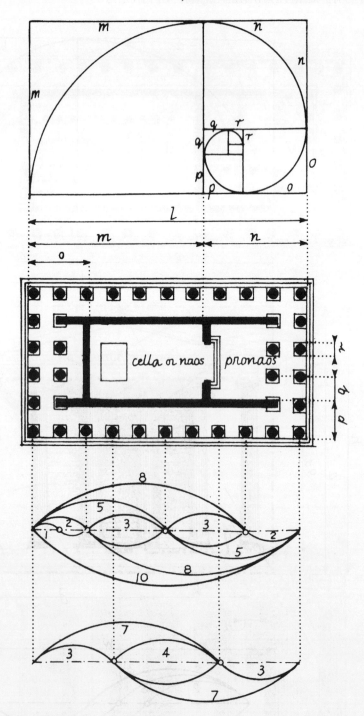

Figure 21. Types of Vitruvian Temple: Priene. Plan (above), elevation (right).

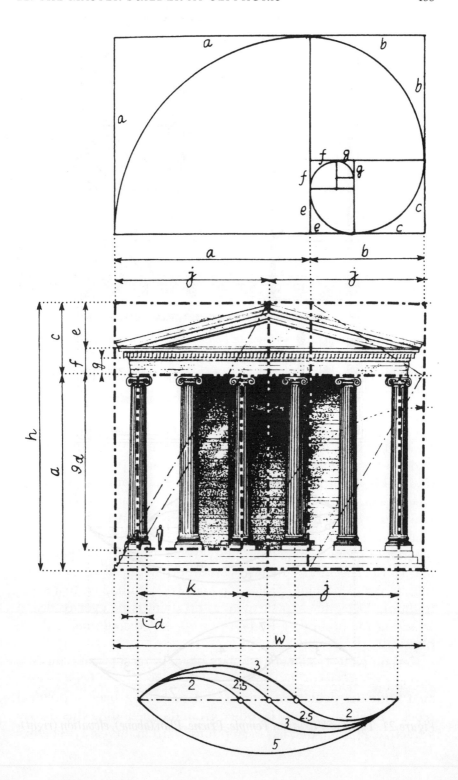

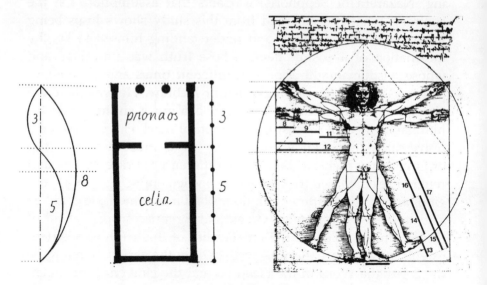

Figure 22. Vitruvius' proportions of temple construction and ideal man.

centre at his navel. Alberti changed this centre to the base of the
pelvis which is more accurate. But he also used the perfect
numbers 6 and 10 to define the ratios of head to navel and navel
to foot. In this he was correct because the navel is usually taken to
divide the human body into the Divine Proportion, and 6 to 10
divided by 2 equals 3 to 5, a whole number approximation to φ
(Phi). This Albertism obsessed the Renaissance mind and was, to
a large extent, the paradigm for the unitary theory of knowledge
which produced the archetype of the Renaissance or Universal
man. It is well known that its roots lay, via Vitruvius, in Greek
theories of proportion and harmony. What is not so well known is
that it was specifically Pythagorean in origin and that Jesus himself, in name, teaching, profession and work, embodied that same
tradition. Does this explain why at no point is he ever recorded
attacking the occupying Roman powers or Greco-Roman culture
physically or verbally?

Certain New Testament scholars have, in recent years, made a
strong case for Jesus, to some extent at least, having been associated with the Zealot movement and to having been a political
rebel.[20] While there may be other grounds for finding this theory
attractive, nothing that has been put forward in this essay whether

from gematria, geometry, architecture, cosmology, carpentry, building, Nazareth or Sepphoris, warrants that assumption. On the contrary, what has emerged from this study shows Jesus being understood to have been, and understanding himself to be, the incarnation of a cosmic being whose truth was universal, and whose wisdom might appear at different times and in different places as Greek, Roman, Egyptian or Hebrew. He was therefore above the patriotic battles, and there is a much stronger case for him having been a pacifist than a political rebel. He represented a universal system of knowledge which was as much Roman, Greek or Egyptian as Hebrew. Behind the differences of race, culture and religion he embodied truth which reconciled opposing factions and emphasized what different traditions had in common. He could be said to be Jewish, Roman, Greek and Egyptian insofar as all of these cultures accepted the universality of this truth to a certain extent. In this sense, he was perceived by the early Church to be the *Logos,* the Word of the Hebrews and the Universal Intelligent Principle of the Greeks.[21]

It is quite extraordinary, yet also entirely appropriate that he should fit the Vitruvian model as well as the Hebrew and Egyptian ones already examined, for if his earthly profession as *tektōn* reflected his divine personality as Builder of the Aeons and Architect of the Universe, then he would be predisposed towards architecture in general and the Vitruvian tradition in particular, because it embodied the three perfect numbers of his own names.

The Monument to the Ideal Vitruvian Man

In their article 'Sepphoris Ornament of All Galilee' in *The Biblical Archaeologist,* of March 1986, Eric and Carol Meyers and Ehud Netzer describe the discovery of the theatre in 1931 by the expedition from the University of Michigan led by Leroy Waterman: 'Their most notable contribution was the discovery and excavation of a Roman theater dug into the sharp north-eastern slope. Although badly disturbed, the theatre's proportions and character were established by the Michigan team. It is a semi-circular building with a diameter of 74 metres and a seating capacity of 4,000 to 5,000 people.'[22]

It was a huge auditorium, bigger than almost all modern theatres. Was it built purely for prestige or did a vast number of people attend performances? If they did then many of them would presumably have been Jewish because, as we have seen, the majority of the city's population was Jewish. Amongst them would have been the young Jesus who had probably helped to build it. Perhaps he, as a master builder or architect conversant with Vitruvian principles, had also helped to plan it. What justification would there be for this last suggestion? None at all, except that it is curious that Meyers and Netzer give the diameter of the theatre as exactly 74 metres. They do not tell us whether this is the outside, inside or centre wall measurement so we cannot tell exactly what they mean. Nevertheless, the measurement they give is exact in metres, and although most authorities would not accept that metres or their equivalent were used before the early nineteenth century, it is odd that the number 74 is given, because 74 is a factor of 2,368, *Iesous Christos* (74 × 32 = 2,368) and, if it is multiplied by π as 16/5, becomes a circle with circumference 236.8! This of course is just chance and mustn't be taken seriously, but it is, nevertheless, a very curious coincidence in the light of all that has been discussed. If we were to be responsible in our calculations, we would convert the 74 metres into Roman feet (i.e. × 3.2808333 English feet ÷ 6.8 Greek fathoms × 7). This would give us 249.92229 which can be taken as 250 Roman feet. If we multiply this by π as 16/5 we get 800 for the circumference. This, according to the Greek Greater Canon is the number for *Kurios* meaning Lord which in the New Testament is the appellation often given to Jesus. It is the word which the 72 authors of the Septuagint used to translate Adonai which itself was the pronounceable name of the unpronounceable God, YHWH, usually translated into English as either Jehovah or Yahweh. Thus 800, known as the Dominical number throughout the Christian era, is one of the most important in the Canon. It may therefore, also be significant that although Vitruvius specifies that his theatre plan should be divided up into 12 segments, as illustrated, Sepphoris is in fact divided not into 12 but 8 segments.

We don't know what value they were using for π. Neither do we know how accurately the archaeologists measured the diameter of the theatre. Nevertheless, to get the number for Jesus Christ when 74 metres are used and the number for Lord when 250

Roman feet are used for the diameter, makes the circumference of this theatre look very special. Coincidence or not, you could hardly do better than the numerical symbolism for 'Lord Jesus Christ.' Perhaps after all it was his theatre, his monument to the genuine *hupocrites* and the ideal Vitruvian *Anthropos*!

12
The Essene Connection

Even if only half of the evidence presented in the last four chapters has the semblance of possibility rather than wild speculation, it would still be enough on which to base the proposition that Jesus was in all probability a Pythagorean. This became increasingly clear during the last chapter and yet we are still left without any evidence whatsoever that he had any actual contacts with contemporary Pythagoreans. If, as seems possible from all that has been put forward, he was one himself, then what was his context or did he stand alone? The latter is unlikely because, as has often been pointed out, no matter what theory is being presented, there was most likely some tradition, sect or group in which he was nurtured and out of which he came, however difficult it might be to identify. This being so, did he pick up his Pythagoreanism in the Greco-Roman setting of his work at Sepphoris? If this was to some extent the case, we would still have to find a specifically Jewish Pythagorean context to complete a convincing picture. After all, as has been shown, his Greek names came directly from the Hebrew and, as shown earlier, the Hebrew scriptures were also clearly Pythagorean. So who were the heirs of this Hebrew Pythagoreanism, and who were the successors of the Septuagint cosmologists? Where could Jesus have found out about Jewish, as distinct from Greco-Roman, Pythagoreanism? Surely there must have been some Jewish Pythagorean group out of which not only he, but also the Gospel editors, could have come.

There was indeed one Jewish group, contemporaneous with Jesus which, according to a tradition going back to Pliny, Philo and Josephus, was reputed to have been Pythagorean. This was the Essenes. Since the discovery of the Dead Sea Scrolls, there has been a great deal written about this mysterious sect, but very little of it has mentioned their Pythagoreanism. The most eminent exception to this is Martin Hengel who, in his magisterial study *Judaism and Hellenism*, provides enough evidence to show that the Essenes could have been the channel whereby Jesus could have come into contact with Jewish Pythagoreanism, and through whom he could have found a Jewish Pythagorean context.

Martin Hengel and the Pythagorean Essenes

A straightforward reading of the Bible from Old Testament to New, does not reveal the great amount of Greek thought which came into Palestine during what is called the Inter-Testamental Period. This was the 300 years following Alexander the Great's conquest of the Middle East between 336 and 323 BC. Since most of the sacred literature of that era has not generally been regarded as canonical, there has tended to be an ignorance about the extent to which Judea became Hellenized.

Judea became part of Alexander's empire in 333 BC. After that, for over a hundred years, there was a time of cultural exchange between the Greeks and the Jews, with mutual respect between them. Hengel says: 'The positive verdict of the Greeks on the Jews in this early period corresponds to the still open attitude of the latter ... There was a close conjunction of Palestinian wisdom and Greek philosophy in the Jewish wisdom schools of Alexandria.' Sophia — wisdom — became hypostatized. 'Wisdom,' 'Logos' and the number seven were 'equally holy to the Pythagoreans and the Jews' and 'became the principle of the spiritual ordering of the world and at the same time the basis of the knowledge and moral will of the individual.'[1] The Hasidim or 'Pious ones' developed apocalyptic ideas as in Daniel and First Enoch, while the Greeks developed 'higher wisdom through revelation' in dreams, visions, revelations, astral journeys and ecstatic experiences. This was the expression of a revival of popular piety throughout the Greek world after two centuries of scepticism, and the collapse of traditional forms of religion in the fourth and third centuries. 'The revival of Neo-Pythagoreanism in the first century BC and the success of the mystery religions are to be explained in the light of these tendencies.'[2] Thus Hengel gives us the historical context for the pervasiveness of Hellenistic thought in Judea and of Pythagoreanism in particular during this period.

However, in 169–168 BC this changed. The Greek Seleucid Emperor Antiochus IV sacked Jerusalem and raided the temple in order to reinstate his puppet High Priest Menelaus and the Jewish Hellenistic party. Jerusalem became like a Greek *polis*. When he then attempted to exterminate the Jewish religion, setting up 'the abomination of desolation' (Daniel 11:31, 12:11) in the temple, an armed rebellion broke out. This was led by a family of priests called Maccabees and the Hasidim. Under Judas Maccabaeus they were victorious, recapturing the temple in 164 BC and achieving almost complete independence from their Greek oppressors by 142 BC. It was at this time that the Essene community began.

There are different theories about the details, but it is usually thought that the Essenes were founded by a mysterious person called the Teacher of Righteousness who was probably a Zadokite priest, who led a splinter group of Hasidim out of Jerusalem into the desert sometime between 152 and 143 BC. He set up an ascetic monastic community with a rigorous rule which was meant to restore a true Torah-based life free from alien Hellenistic influences, and from corrupt Maccabean power politics. He saw his new community as a faithful remnant, the only true spiritual heir of Israel, who expected the imminent arrival of 'the time of salvation.' The paradox is that while they could be described as a bunch of rabid, extreme, fanatical, separatist, schematic ascetics, they were strangely open to certain new developments and Hellenistic influences.

In the section 'New Spiritual Developments and Foreign Influences among the Essenes.'[3] Hengel itemizes a very un-Jewish list of foreign influences under seven headings. Reading between the lines, it is easy to see that most of these could equally well be subsumed under the broad title of Pythagoreanism:

1. An almost gnostic concept of 'saving knowledge'; an 'eschatological knowledge of salvation,' for the individual and the community. This had much in common with Hellenistic 'wisdom through revelation.' Knowledge is illumination. 'Jewish apocalyptic, above all in its Essene form, influenced the development of later Jewish-Christian gnosticism.'[4]

2. Dualism and double predestination: The two spirits, one of light and one of darkness moving inexorably towards an imminent end-time as in Zoroastrianism.

3. God's predetermined ordering of the world along Platonic lines: 'In striving for a more rational version of the event of creation, Essene theology — like late wisdom of Palestine and Alexandria generally — adopts notions which have contacts with the ideas of Greek philosophy.'[5]

4. Angelology: They swore 'to preserve the names of the angels.' Gabriel, Michael etc. were taken from Hasidim (Daniel and I Enoch). There were good and evil or fallen angels. The workings of nature were explained by various angels, the lowest classes 'represented little more than personified natural forces.' There were also stars or 'heavenly watchers': 'The Essenes also shared with apocalyptic and the whole Hellenistic environment the widespread conception of a *sympatheia* between earthly and heavenly events.'[6] The stars were thought of as living beings and the angels were essentially foreign gods stripped of their power. They became intermediaries for a distant god, and were most influential. Jewish and Hellenistic views could easily be combined.

5. The Stars and the Sun: Their precise movements symbolized god's perfection. They regulated everything including epochs in history as in jubilees and weeks of years. They adopted a solar calendar (the Jewish was lunisolar). Thus the festivals were on the same day each year. This was an Egyptian-Hellenistic model, but not directly Pythagorean, although we find it in Pythagoras, Plato, Eudoxus of Cnidus and Aristotle. The perfect ordering of the stars was held to be a kind of proof of the existence of God. This god of heaven was later associated with Helios. Sun symbolism for the Essenes was central.

6. Astrology: 'After the end of the third century it (astrology) became more and more the spiritually dominant force among the educated. The collapse of old Greek religion in the fifth and fourth centuries BC, and its relegation to a mere belief in fate had inevitably to culminate in astrology.'[7] The Essenes seem to have adopted astrological knowledge from their foundation. Parts of a horoscope for a messianic personality were found in Cave IV. Other texts confirm the significance of zodiacal knowledge, for example I and II Enoch. 'The significance attached in

Qumran to these esoteric astrological doctrines is shown by the fact that they were partly written in cryptic writing ... Thus astrological secret doctrines of this kind, alien to the Old Testament were traced back to Moses ... It is remarkable that views of this kind from the Hellenistic environment penetrated the Essene community.[8] They were part of the general move away from the sceptical century after Alexander towards new religious feeling.

7. Manticism and Magic: Daniel (an Essene document) was the overseer of all the magicians of Babylon. Josephus says the Essenes had fortune-tellers who had astrological-mantic writings similar to Hellenistic manticism and dream interpretation. The Essene mantis Judas, foretold the exact time and place of Hasmonean Antigonus' death. A similar story is told of one Simon, regarding the dream of Archelaus' banishment. Mantic-magic medicine using the occult properties of roots, plants and stones, was also practised. 'Thus even Essenism will have had its share in the development of Jewish magic in antiquity. The prohibition against giving away 'the books of the community and the names of the angels' was meant to prevent a magical misuse of their own secret knowledge. Jewish magic was one of those phenomena in Judaism in which non-Jewish observers were most interested ... Its roots go well back into the pre-Christian Hellenistic period.[9]

This is a truly remarkable account of an almost unbelievably eclectic range of thought. It is one which would normally be considered antithetical to the usual perception of the narrow Jewish mind set. How did the Essenes manage to get over the problem that all these themes could be said to have been taken from heathen wisdom which they officially abhorred? According to Hengel they did it by maintaining that 'counter-revelations' had been given to their own *kosher* patriarchs, Enoch, Noah and Abraham, which were similar but superior in certain subtle ways:

When the Essenes were occupied with astrology and iatromantics they believed this to be something fundamentally different from what was happening outside the community in the same area ... They wanted to set against the 'demonic' Chaldean, Egyptian or Greek 'wisdom,' a more comprehensive, genuine wisdom of their own, encompassing the cosmos and history, and founded on revelation and not on betrayal. It is not to no purpose that the groups of concepts relating to knowledge and understanding lie at the centre of Essene theology. In this sense one could speak of a Hasidic-Essene 'gnosticism' comparable to the Wisdom of Solomon, where Wisdom teaches 'the varieties of plants and the virtues of roots.[10]

Whatever we may think of this questionable way of legitimizing Gentile wisdom, it is interesting how close this list of Essene foreign influences is to that given above by Clement of Alexandria, for the origins of philosophy among the barbarians, and also to the countries visited by Pythagoras according to his later biographers. The whole tone of Hengel's description is also reminiscent of the syncretism of the Renaissance humanists who assimilated the same range of ancient knowledge. This theme keeps recurring in the course of our enquiries and can no longer be considered to be marginal.

It is also intriguing to note that the Pythagorean-Druid connection also mentioned by Clement recurs elsewhere in Hengel. When describing the revival of Pythagoreanism in relation to Hasidic Judaism in the first century BC, he refers to Heraclides Ponticus, a pupil of Plato, who spawned a tradition which featured a Pythagorean link with Abaris from Hyperborea, who other sources say specifically was a Druid magician.[11] This will be explored in Part III.

Applying this Essene method of making Gentile wisdom *kosher* to Jesus, we can see how it would have been possible for him to have been exposed to Chaldean, Egyptian, Greek and indeed almost any other *gnosis*, without the accusation of betrayal, such was the extent of acceptable pluralism within the sect.

As if the list of new and foreign Essene developments was not Pythagorean enough, Hengel goes on to make another very strong comparison between the two movements. This he bases on recent scholarship regarding the Greek law concerning *private religious associations*. He says that the *form* of the Essene community was 'new and underivable from the Old Testament Jewish tradition ...

It can only be understood in the light of the spirit of a new time.'[12] All family ties had to be broken off with a decisive conversion to the community of salvation. The nearest parallels to this are to be found in 'the law of associations in the Hellenistic period.' The Essene community was designated as *hayyahad* which is equivalent to the Greek common-law term *to koinon*. The Jewish synagogues of the Diaspora had the same legal form and they 'imitated this form of alliance.' The Essenes were thus the earliest known private Jewish association in Palestine, whose features included: 1. Honour to the founder; 2. Rules for precedence, full assembly and officials; 3. Tests, oaths, common meals, finance; 4. Ethics, punishments, exclusion and burial. It was a 'towering example of the appropriation of Hellenistic community thought with all its legal consequences by the Jewish spirit of the second century BC,' which, because of its doctrine of eschatological immanence and certainty that they alone represented the true Israel, 'produced a self-estimation which is almost without analogy in the Hellenistic world.'[13] They didn't necessarily know that the form of their community was not in the Old Testament 'but the very confidence with which they could take over alien forms of organization shows how strongly Hellenistic law and, in conjunction with it, Hellenistic thought-forms, had found their way into Palestinian Judaism.' Hengel goes on to state that, in this respect, the Essenes can only be compared to the Pythagoreans:

> The only religious or philosophical movement whose strict organization and heightened self-estimation corresponded in any way to the Essene community was that of the Pythagoreans ... The close affinity between the two groups was already often assumed in the eighteenth and nineteenth centuries on the basis of the tradition of Josephus, Philo and Pliny ... In this century, too, significant scholars ... have conjectured Pythagorean influence; I. Levy has even devoted a monograph to the relationship between Pythagoreanism and Judaism. After the discovery of the Qumran texts, which shattered all previous views, Dupont-Sommer in particular, and T.F. Glasson, more cautiously, have once again put forward the Pythagorean hypothesis.[14]

Aristobulus, the Jewish early second century BC Alexandrian philosopher, taught that Pythagoras and Orpheus learnt from Moses and followed both traditions in speculation regarding the number seven. Other sources, for example, Hermippus' *Life of Pythagoras*, indicate that the founder of the Essenes could have known Pythagorean doctrines. 'Nevertheless, direct dependence is improbable.' Hengel is critical of those who have pressed for Pythagorean dependence. Some err and others neglect the obvious origins in the Hasidic *kosher* teaching. We must adopt a balanced position. There is much influence on the Essenes from Hellenism, Babylonia, Iran and Egypt: 'But they are not typical Pythagoreans. Even the doctrine of the immortality of the soul merely corresponded to a widespread religious opinion in their Hellenistic environment.'[15]

Hengel then concludes: 'If we consider the Essene community against its environment, the essential thing is not the supposed "Pythagorean" influences, but the fact that Hellenistic observers like Josephus — or Nicolaus of Damascus — could present them as Jewish "Pythagoreans".' As ancient reporters tell us, they were philosophers: they belonged to that widespread ideal of wisdom with a religious basis which ... was typical of the 'prophets of the Orient.' In one sense the 'Hellenized' interpretation of the Essene order by the various ancient writers was not completely mistaken, for precisely in Essenism, Judaism points beyond the narrow context of Palestine; the retreat into the solitariness of the desert unleashed great religious consequences which had their effects on primitive Christianity, the baptist movements in Transjordania and early gnosticism ... The very features which disturb us and seem strange to us, like the dualistic doctrine of two spirits, their determinism, the hierarchical angelology, astrology, manticism and magic, aroused attention within and outside Palestine through their speculative scientific character, and in conjunction with the ascetic life of the community, occasioned the supposition that the Essenes were Jewish 'friends of god' (i.e. Pythagoreans) on Palestinian soil.[16]

It is clear from this précis, that Martin Hengel, for all his scholarly caution, believes that the Essenes were Jewish Pythagoreans and that Josephus was right when he described them as a 'Jewish pendant to the Greek Pythagoreans.'

Essenes and Christians — Cheek by Jowl

The point of citing Hengel *in extenso* is to make it abundantly clear
that Jesus could have been introduced to Pythagorean thought in
Judea through the Essenes. Without answering the question as to
whether or not he was actually an Essene, Hengel has shown without any shadow of doubt, that the Essenes could have provided
him with a Pythagorean context, either at Qumran or any of the
towns round the country which Josephus also says had groups.
Thus we now have enough evidence to conclude that he could
very easily have been a Jewish Pythagorean.

While there is therefore no reason to doubt that the conduit of
transmission for Jesus' Pythagoreanism could have been the
Essenes, the question remains: is there any evidence to show that
this might actually have been the case? Are there any similarities
between his teachings and those of the Essenes which might point
in this direction? Well, of course, the general answer to this is: yes,
there definitely are, for although scholars have differed over details, the consensus has never seriously held this question in doubt.
Indeed, the extent to which this is so has been such an important
issue for so long, that it must be examined in some detail. As we
do so, it will become obvious that the connections between the
Essenes and the Jesus of the Gospels, were probably very close
indeed.

In fact, if we were to agree with André Dupont-Sommer, the
most prominent of the early Dead Sea Scrolls scholars, we would
conclude that the connections were so close as to amount to an
identification between Jesus and the Teacher of Righteousness who
founded the Essenes:

> The Galilean Master, as He is presented to us in the
> writings of the New Testament, appears in many respects
> as an astonishing reincarnation of the Teacher. Like the
> latter, he preached penitence, poverty, humility, love of
> one's neighbour, chastity. Like him, He prescribed the
> observance of the Law of Moses, the whole Law, but the
> Law finished and perfected, thanks to His own revelations.
> Like him He was the Elect and the Messiah of God, the
> Messiah, redeemer of the world. Like him, He was the

object of the hostility of the priests ... Like him, He was
condemned and put to death. Like him, He pronounced
Judgement on Jerusalem. Like him, at the end of time, He
will be the supreme judge. Like him, He founded a Church
whose adherents fervently awaited His glorious return.[17]

The majority of scholars have disagreed with this identification
because it is unlikely that the sect held the Teacher to be the
Messiah. It is also doubtful whether he was executed. Furthermore,
the Scrolls nowhere suggest that he would be the supreme judge
at the end of time, nor that he would make a glorious return.
Edward Cook assessing this in *Solving the Mysteries of the Dead Sea
Scrolls* concludes: 'Most scholars were content to follow Dupont-
Sommer's more justifiable suggestion about the Essene origin of
the Dead Sea Scrolls and to leave his Christological speculations to
one side.'[18]

Despite all the criticism of Dupont-Sommer, it is important to
notice that it was only his Christological speculations which were
rejected. This has also been the fate of others who have been
similarly speculative. His suggestion that the Scrolls had an Essene
origin has not. It has been widely believed by scholars from
Dupont-Sommer's time to this, as Geza Vermes, the leading contemporary authority states: 'With negligible exceptions, scholarly
opinion recognized already in the 1950s that the Scrolls found in
the caves and the nearby ruined settlement were related ... the
Essene identity of the ancient inhabitants of Qumran gained
general acceptance.'[19]

Vermes says that although some still question the Essene theory,
it remains the best option:

Indeed, it accounts best for such striking peculiarities as
common ownership of property and the lack of reference to
women in the Community Rule; the probable co-existence
of celibate and married sectaries (in accordance with
Flavius Josephus' account of two kinds of Essenes), and the
remarkable coincidence between the geographical setting of
Qumran and Pliny the Elder's description of an Essene
establishment near the Dead Sea between Jericho and
Engedi ... since none of the competing theories associating
the Qumran group with Pharisees, Sadducees, Zealots or

Jewish-Christians can withstand critical scrutiny, I believe my statement formulated in 1977 is still valid; 'The final verdict must ... be that of the proposed solutions, the Essene theory is relatively the soundest. It is even safe to say that it possesses a high degree of intrinsic probability.'[20]

Likewise James VanderKam, a member of the International Team of Dead Sea Scroll translators, in his overview of opinions on the question, comes to the same conclusions as Vermes: 'The upshot of the whole investigation is that many strong arguments point to the residents of Qumran being Essenes and no certain points tell against the identification.'[21]

VanderKam accepts the general criticism of Dupont-Sommer mentioned above: 'Some of his claims rested on serious misreadings of texts.'[22] He is also dismissive of others who have been too quick to 'draw Christianity and the Scrolls into much closer proximity than the mainline view allows.' Nevertheless, he endorses the research of the majority of scholars who 'have quietly, patiently engaged in the work of establishing precisely the points of contact and the differences between the two literatures and how one might explain their interrelations.'[23] Notable amongst these was Millar Burrows of Yale who saw similarities between John the Baptist and the covenanters and Jesus and the Teacher, and their respective messages:

> But he (Burrows) thought that the more convincing resemblances were to be seen in matters such as communal structure (12 non-priests in the Qumran council parallel the 12 apostles), forms of worship (baptism, meals), practices (community of goods), doctrines (dualism of light and darkness, a righteousness conferred by grace), and interpretation of scripture (without a fixed notion of what constituted the Bible.)

The sorts of kinship noted by Burrows (and a few other parallel items such as eschatology) have remained the areas in which scholars have perceived the greatest likeness between the two communities and what they wrote. The simple fact of a substantial list of parallels between them showed, if it needed showing, that

Christianity in many ways emerged from Judaism and borrowed much of Judaism's heritage in shaping its own life and doctrine.[24]

From this it is clear that VanderKam is as positive about the many similarities between the Qumran community and Christianity as he is about those between the Dead Sea Scrolls and the Essenes. Although there are slight differences between the conclusions of both of these surveys and Dupont-Sommer's earlier position, it is fairly obvious to the untrained layman that the scholarly consensus today agrees substantially with those who have held the Essene and Christian hypotheses in the Scrolls' scholarship over the last forty years.

In *Jesus, Qumran and the Vatican*, two Tübingen scholars Otto Betz and Rainer Riesner set out successfully to demolish the maverick hypothesis put forward by Michael Baigent and Richard Leigh in *The Dead Sea Scrolls Deception* as developed from Robert Eisenman's theory that Jesus, Qumran and the Essenes were all Zealots.[25] Their book, however, is much more than a blow-by-blow destruction of Baigent, Leigh and Eisenman and takes us step-by-step towards some very unexpected propositions regarding the close links between the early Christians and the Essenes.

They agree with the authorities quoted above that the Essenes and the Qumran community are best seen as identical. Even the majority of non-biblical Qumran texts should be regarded as Essene. This identification is 'almost indisputable.' They quote Frank M. Gross:

> The scholar who wants to 'exercise caution' over identifying the Qumran group with the Essenes finds himself in an amazing position. He must in all seriousness propose that two major groups of religious communities founded settlements in the same region of the Dead Sea and in fact lived in the same two centuries, shared the same sometimes bizarre views and performed similar or the same purification, ritual meals and ceremonies. Furthermore the scholar must assume that a community described so precisely in the ancient sources simply disappeared without leaving the remains of buildings or even potsherds behind. By contrast, the other community, which is completely ignored by the classical sources, left behind extensive ruins and even a library.[26]

Betz and Riesner claim that, among many striking similarities, the concept of service on the model of Jesus (Mark 10:45; John 13) can also be found at Qumran. This was characteristic of Mary, Martha and Lazarus at Bethany who were all unmarried 'perhaps they originally belonged to the "second order" of Essenes living outside the monastery.' They gave Jesus hospitality:

> According to Josephus, such hospitality was characteristic of the Essenes: 'When adherents arrive from elsewhere, all local resources are put at their disposal as if they were their own, and men they have never seen before entertain them like old friends.' (*Jewish War II*, 124) Jesus, too, approached this family in the same matter-of-fact way. The figures depicted by Luke in his infancy story, Zechariah and Elizabeth, Joseph and Mary, Simeon and Anna, have the piety of the humble or the poor *(anawim)* which characterized the Essenes.[27]

They were looking for the consolation of Israel. Likewise the family of Jesus might have come from 'the wider circle of the Hasidic movement':

> The language in the birth stories in Luke 1–2 and in the Lucan special tradition generally has a kind of Hebrew stamp and comes close to linguistic forms and notions which have their closest parallels in the Qumran writings. The expression 'man in whom (God) is well pleased' (Luke 2:14) is only the most famous example of that (cf. IQH 4.32f; 11.9). An old problem of textual criticism here could be resolved by the Qumran text.[28]

Betz and Riesner then go on to present their most arresting and from our point of view, most pertinent, theories. They say that while some Pharisees became Christian, most notably Paul, probably 'a great many of the priests became obedient to the faith' (Acts 6:7) refers to the conversion of Essenes. They suggest that these may have been members of the earliest church and that they may have lived in the Essene Quarter in Jerusalem. This Essene Quarter was located, according to recent excavations by Fr Bargil Pixner and his team of archaeologists, in the area of Mount Zion,

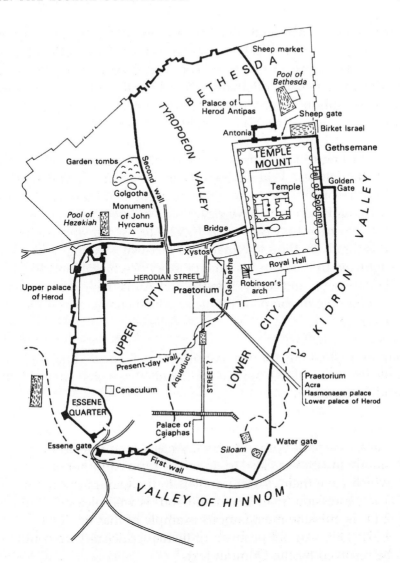

Figure 23. The Essene Quarter and Gate

the south-west corner of the city. Local tradition has identified this
area as that of the Christian community's first meeting place, particularly with regard to the room of the Last Supper. As this tradition can be traced back to the early second century, it is probably
reliable.

According to Bargil Pixner it can be traced back to the actual
record of the Last Supper for the word *katalyma*, guest house, in
'The Teacher asks: where is my guest house where I may eat the

Passover' (Mark 14:14), is only used in one other context, the inn at Bethlehem (Luke 2:7). Pixner maintains that it refers to the Essene guest house, adjacent to the Essene Quarter, which was rented out to friends or acquaintances who wished to celebrate one of the feasts of the Essenes.[29] Pixner strengthens this assertion with a detailed and most convincing analysis of the chronology of the events leading up to the death of Jesus, based on the assumption that he and his disciples observed an Essene Passover meal which was on the Tuesday evening, not on the Thursday as traditionally maintained.[30]

Further down Mount Zion, at the southern extremity of the hill, Fr Pixner's team excavated a gate dating from New Testament times which is in all probability the one which Josephus called the 'Essene Gate.' For many years scholars have suggested that the gate's name is derived from an Essene settlement in Jerusalem. Very large ritual baths, Mikweh, comparable only to those at Qumran and Bethany (where it is thought there was another Essene group), have also been discovered in that area, which would tend to confirm this supposition.

This Essene Quarter would probably have been formed after the earthquake at Qumran around 31 BC. According to Josephus, Herod the Great (37–4 BC) was well disposed towards the Essenes at this time because they are reputed to have used their mantic or prophetic skills in his favour. After the destruction at Qumran, he offered them quarters in the city and when the time came to return, only a few did so.[31]

Bargil Pixner, in With Jesus in Jerusalem, gives a full account[32] of all this, showing that during the lifetime of Jesus, most of the Essenes were therefore not at Qumran any longer, but in the Essene Quarter of Jerusalem. This radically changes the traditional picture of the Essenes from being geographically remote to being very close to the heart of New Testament action.

Betz and Riesner use Pixner's work to propose that the Essenes and Christians lived next door to each other. They say that evidence for this is found in a possible Essene interpretation of 'pious men dwelling in Jerusalem' (Acts 2:5) in the story of Pentecost, because Eulabes, the Greek word for pious, is hase in Aramaic. This word is probably the root for the Greek Essenos. Two other observations support this Essene link with Pentecost. First, the obvious Sinai comparison with Pentecost has parallels in

Qumran texts. Second, the sharing of all possessions, which is a marked feature of the early Church (Acts 2:44–45; 4:32–35) is the same as the normal practice of the Essenes. They also think that if the earliest Christian community developed in, or adjacent to, the Essene Quarter, it would explain how 'the first Christians could remain in the Holy City, though it was dominated by the enemies who had executed their master.'[33]

This argument in favour of the first Christian Pentecost having taken place within an Essene environment, is strengthened by Yigael Yadin in *The Temple Scroll* who shows how celebrating the feast of Pentecost was far more important to the Essenes than it was to mainstream Judaism.[34] It also strengthens the connection between Qumran and the Jerusalem Essenes because the Temple Scroll, which stresses Pentecost, was found in Qumran.

This further literary link between the Scrolls and the Essenes, leads on to the observation that the Essenes were prolific writers. This very obvious fact should not blind us from observing the truism that the New Testament writers were also prolific. Putting these two observations together an equally obvious question emerges: were they connected? If the two communities, the Essenes and the Christians, lived cheek by jowl; if many practices and teachings of the former were adopted by the latter, and if the Last Supper and the first Christian Pentecost took place in the Essene guest house, then it would be reasonable to assume that there might also have been some literary overlap.

Betz and Riesner think this assumption would be justified. The Scrolls tell us that the study of the Scriptures was most important to the Essenes. The Community Rule devoted a quarter of the working day to it. Their writing came out of their study and 'It is quite striking how often the Essenes and the earliest Christians refer to a quite specific group of Old Testament texts.'[35] So, did Essene Christians play a part in the writing or editing of what became the Gospel narratives? The main objection to this possibility would be that biblical scholars believe that most of the New Testament material was written much later, towards the end of the first century. But this consensus is not as united as it was. Some scholars such as Rudolf Pesch, Gerd Theissen, Carsten Peter Thiede and Matthew D'Ancona contend that there are good grounds for accepting an earlier dating.[36] One of the reasons for holding to later dating has been that it has been difficult to believe that the scholarly sophistication and theological profundity which is manifest throughout, came from the eyewitness accounts of supposedly simple fishermen and not from a lengthy process of mature reflection. However, if it was members of the Essene scriptorium in Jerusalem who, when converted to Jesus as Messiah, brought their literary and theological expertise to the writing or editing of the stories about Jesus, then this objection to an early dating would be overruled. This is what Betz and Riesner conclude:

> So we may reckon that a whole group of Essenes were converted to Jesus as the Messiah. These converted Essenes formed a body of theologians who were highly qualified for their time. They were capable of working out at a deep intellectual level who Jesus was and how he had brought salvation. A comparison with the Qumran texts shows that New Testament expressions and notions which many people regarded as Greek and late are, rather, Palestinian and early. That applies to such disputed parts of the New Testament as the Gospel of John and the first chapter of Acts.[37]

In this conclusion, Betz and Riesner provide the missing link between Martin Hengel on the one hand, who gave extensive evidence that the Essenes were Pythagoreans and the New Testament writings on the other which, we have demonstrated to be permeated with Pythagorean number symbolism and cosmology from an unknown source. Although they never mention the Pythagorean dimension of Essene thought, they nevertheless answer the question posed earlier: how did Pythagoreanism get into the New Testament? They have told us in a most convincing way how in all probability it could have come from the Essenes. If many of the early Christians in Jerusalem were converted Essenes, steeped in the Old Testament and Inter-Testamental literature, with all the eclectic Pythagorean skills listed by Hengel, then they would have been perfectly equipped to produce Pythagorean editions of the Gospel narratives in which the Greek number symbolism, gematria and cosmology, would have been cleverly matched to the Hebrew, for they would have been equally proficient in both. Here at last we may have identified the inspired scholars who hid the precious Pythagorean treasure in the foundations of the linguistic structure of the New Testament, which has been dug up, identified and valued by Simcox Lea, Bligh Bond, Simone Weil and others.

Bearing in mind the conclusion from the section 'Did Jesus know about the Numbers of his Name?' — that he not only knew about them but entered into the cosmology they implied, as into the cosmic extension of his own person — it is difficult to doubt that he was so deeply involved with the first Essene converts as to have been himself the agent of their conversion. Without pressing the matter too closely, it is also reasonable to infer that all the close Essene-Christian connections which have been discovered, whether geographical, doctrinal, practical, experiential or scriptural, would have been initiated in the first place by Jesus himself. The disciples were not greater than their Master. This was most probably *his* Pythagorean context, just as much as theirs.

PART III

WISDOM IN THE NORTH

13
Wisdom is Universal

Is there any other word in the Bible whose meaning is the same as *tektōn*, or any other concept equivalent to master craftsman, builder or architect? Is *tektōn*, as applied to Jesus, unique or is there a similar descriptive term which could confirm and enhance what has already been put forward?

There is one other word, and only one. It can be found in Prov.8:30 where it says that Wisdom was beside God at Creation like a master craftsman:

> I was by his side, a master craftsman
> delighting him day by day
> ever at play in his presence. (JB)

The Hebrew word translated 'master craftsman' is *'amon* but there is a textual problem here. In the original Hebrew, the vowels were left out, so *'amon* could have been *'amun* meaning 'pet' or 'darling child.' This translation is favoured by the New English Bible and also by Gerhard von Rad who reads the verse:

> ... then I was beside him as his favourite,
> and I was daily his delight,
> playing in front of him all the time.[1]

There have been others over the centuries, cited by von Rad, who agree that the concept of wisdom as the 'darling child' fits in with other metaphors in this seminal passage such as her being 'brought forth' (v.24) and 'at play' (v.30). However, most disagree, and like Derek Kidner, contend that such an infantile interpretation 'makes wisdom's role completely irresponsible.'[2] Of this majority opinion, one of the most authoritative has been W.O.E. Oesterley,[3] who has been followed by others such as A. Cohen[4] and Edgar Jones.[5] His belief, that *'amon* means 'master workman,' is based on ancient rabbinical tradition. He cites particularly Rabbi Hoshajah in the third century AD who was accustomed to open his lectures on wisdom by quoting this verse, explaining that the word 'amon was equivalent to 'uman, 'architect.' This interpretation can be traced back to the Septuagint in the third century BC which translated 'amon as harmozousa, 'the bringer into harmony.' From this came the Latin Vulgate's componens, a similar concept. Following this, among recent commentators, R.B.Y. Scott[6] has proposed that amon should really read omen, an active participle, meaning one who unites or binds together. 'Thus,' as Kathleen Farmer points out 'Scott translates v.30a, "Then I was beside him binding [all] together".'[7]

If we accept this majority opinion, then we are led back through the rabbinical tradition to the Septuagint's translation of amon as harmozousa. Picking up this theme, Martin Hengel says that this approximates to the Stoic concept: 'wisdom accommodates, brings into harmony.'[8] He points out that throughout the whole of Prov.8:22–31, there are significant deviations from the Hebrew in the Greek translation which make him think that wisdom is being consciously likened to a kind of 'world soul' as in Plato's Timaeus. He itemizes passages describing the world soul which he finds strikingly similar to that of Wisdom:[9]

1. The world soul, like wisdom, appears as the first and most excellent creation of the demiurge which permeates the universe: 'So he established a single spherical universe in circular motion, alone, but because of its excellence needing no company other than itself and satisfied to be its own acquaintance and friend.' (Timaeus, 34b)

2. Like wisdom, the world soul surrounds the seen world as a rational and harmonious unseen mediatrix: 'the soul ... provided a divine source of unending and rational life for all time. The body of the heaven is visible, but the soul invisible and endowed with reason and harmony, being the best creation of the best of intelligible and eternal things.' (Timaeus, 36c–37a)

3. The divine father also delighted in the perfection of the world soul which he had created: 'When the father who had begotten it perceived that the universe was alive and in motion, a shrine for the eternal gods, he was glad, and in his delight planned to

make it still more like its pattern; and as this pattern is an eternal Living Being, he set out to make the universe resemble it in this way too as far as was possible.' (*Timaeus*, 37c)

4. The world soul like wisdom was begotten by the father as a blessed divine being: 'His creation, then, for all these reasons, was a blessed god.' (*Timaeus*, 34b)

5. The world created by the demiurge through the world soul is beautiful, harmonious and good: 'The divine form he made mostly of fire so that it should be as bright and beautiful to look at as possible; and he made it spherical like the universe and set it to follow the movement of the highest intelligence, distributing it round the circle of the heaven to be a kind of universal, cosmic embroidery.' (*Timaeus*, 40a)

The full text of Prov.8:22–31 to which Hengel compares wisdom in these passages, is as follows:

> Yahweh created me when his purpose first unfolded,
>   before the oldest of his works.
> From everlasting I was firmly set,
>   from the beginning, before earth came into being.
> The deep was not, when I was born,
>   there were no springs to gush with water.
> Before the mountains were settled,
>   before the hills, I came to birth;
> before he made the earth, the countryside,
>   or the first grains of the world's dust.
> When he fixed the heavens firm, I was there,
>   when he drew a ring on the surface of the deep,
> when he thickened the clouds above,
>   when he fixed fast the springs of the deep,
> when he assigned the sea its boundaries
>   — and the waters will not invade the shore —
> when he laid down the foundations of the earth,
> I was by his side, a master craftsman,
>   delighting him day by day,
>   ever at play in his presence,
> at play everywhere in his world,
>   delighting to be with the sons of man. (JB)

Hengel tells us that the unknown author of Proverbs was probably a near contemporary of Aristobulus, the first known Jewish philosopher of religion, around 170 BC. Aristobulus himself tells us that Plato knew Moses' account of creation. He, Aristobulus, will therefore probably have been familiar with the *Timaeus* which has very close links with the Septuagint translation of the Genesis creation story. It is hard to tell 'whether and how far the translator of Proverbs knew the *Timaeus*,' and we mustn't jump to the conclusion that the former actually borrowed from the latter; 'nevertheless,' Hengel concludes, 'we can see how Jewish wisdom speculation and the doctrine of creation grew increasingly close to analogous Greek conceptions.'[10]

From this survey of the scholarly interpretations of Prov.8:30, it would appear that *amon* or *uman* could very reasonably be understood to mean master craftsman, builder or architect. As such it complements exactly the meaning of *tektōn* when seen as the earthly counterpart of the heavenly architect, and 'Builder of the Aeons' as applied to Jesus the 'carpenter.' By analogy, it therefore takes us from a concept which is not overtly biblical, namely Jesus the Pythagorean, to one that is, namely Jesus as the incarnation of divine Wisdom, for, as St Paul affirms 'he is the power and the wisdom of God' (1Cor.1:25). Nevertheless, even though we have moved from an implicit to an explicit concept, we do not seem to have changed our *locus classicus*, namely Plato's *Timaeus*. However deeply we might have plunged into the Old Testament, we have quickly surfaced again in familiar Platonic waters. For it was Christopher Butler who first told us that many Christian thinkers did not find it hard to associate the *Timaeus* with *Genesis*, and to accept the concept of God as a master craftsman. It was Simone Weil who used part of the same section from the *Timaeus*, quoted by Hengel above, to point us towards the presence of the geometric proportion 'the most beautiful of bonds' in the structure of some important Johannine sayings of Jesus.

However, although it could be implied, at least as far as this initial comparison is concerned, that the Pythagorean and the wisdom traditions were therefore synonymous, it is still important to have moved from what seemed to be a relatively unknown, esoteric tradition to a very well-known one. The wisdom tradition, unlike the Pythagorean, is acknowledged in the Old Testament in the wisdom literature not only of Proverbs but also of Psalms, Job,

Ecclesiastes, the Song of Solomon and the Wisdom of Solomon, and in the New Testament, for instance, where St Paul clearly refers to the wisdom passage we have been discussing, when he says of Jesus:

> He is the image of the unseen God
> and the first-born of all creation,
> for in him were created
> all things in heaven and on earth:
> everything visible and everything invisible,
> Thrones, Dominions, Sovereignties, Powers —
> all things were created through him and for him.
> Before anything was created, he existed,
> and he holds all things in unity. (Col.1:15–17, JB)

Furthermore, what we have discovered about wisdom or *amon* or *uman*, the master craftsman, implies that the wisdom tradition itself was Pythagorean, at least to a certain degree. This is exemplified in Philo, the first century Jewish Platonist quoted earlier when he lists the subjects which Moses was supposed to have learnt from the Egyptians. He is commenting on the text we have come to know well 'Moses was educated in all the wisdom of Egypt,' and states:

> Arithmetic, geometry, the love of metre, rhythm and harmony, and the whole subject of music as shown by the use of instruments or in textbooks and treatises of a more special character, were imparted to him by learned Egyptians. These further instructed him in the philosophy conveyed in symbols, as displayed in the so-called holy inscriptions and in the regard paid to animals, to which they even pay divine honours. He had Greeks to teach him the rest of the regular school course, and the inhabitants of the neighbouring countries for Assyrian letters and the Chaldean science of the heavenly bodies. This he also acquired from the Egyptians, who give special attention to astrology.[11]

This description so closely resembles Pythagorean education in general and the Quadrivium in particular, as to be indistinguishable from it.

It would thus appear that what we call Pythagoreanism was in fact subsumed within a very old wisdom tradition which was prevalent throughout the ancient world. As we have already seen, it might have had minor variations of emphasis in different cultures, but was substantially the same in Egypt, Assyria, Chaldea and Israel.

The universality of this wisdom tradition, if not the Pythagoreanism or proto-Pythagoreanism within it, has been accepted in recent years by most scholars who have come to agree with W. Baumgartner that 'from the Nile to the Tigris an essentially similar wisdom literature came into existence and was cultivated.'[12] In so doing, modern scholarship has confirmed and validated the opinion of the early Church fathers of Alexandria, in particular Clement, who, as quoted earlier, held that philosophy, properly understood as the love of wisdom, had a universal provenance in the ancient world long before the Greeks.

For Clement, the philosophies of ancient Egypt, Assyria, Gaul, Bactria, the Celts and Persia were so similar that they could all be lumped together and put on a par with the philosophy of Greece which they preceded. He implies that the Egyptian prophets, the Chaldeans, Druids, Samanaeans, Keltic philosophers and Magi, could all have had good relations with each other and with Greek philosophers. This is echoed by a similar passage from Diogenes Laertius:

> Some say that the study of philosophy was of barbarian origin. For the Persians had their *Magi*, the Babylonians or the Assyrians the *Chaldeans*, the Indians their *Gymnosophists*, while the Kelts and the Galatae had seers called *Druids* and *Semnotheoi*, or so Aristotle says in the 'Magic,' and Sotian in the twenty-third book of his 'Succession of Philosophers.'[13]

This is the passage referred to by Simone Weil when she was discussing the origins of the Pythagorean doctrine. She assumed that there was a link between the origin of the philosophy-wisdom tradition and that of Pythagoreanism. This assumption is also apparent in another passage from Clement:

> Alexander, in his book 'On the Pythagorean Symbols,' relates that Pythagoras was a pupil of Nazaratus the

> Assyrian ... and will have it that, in addition to these,
> Pythagoras was a hearer of the Galatae and the Brahmins.[14]

Although these texts have all been mentioned before, their theme has now become so central to this enquiry that they can legitimately be used again to make the further point that the Pythagorean tradition was part of the philosophy-wisdom tradition As such it was derived from all the known civilizations of the ancient world including the Brahmins and Gymnosophists of India, and the Druids and philosophers of the Gauls and Celts.

Was this the 'secret and hidden wisdom' which St Paul was referring to when he said 'Yet among the mature we do impart wisdom' (1Cor.2:6)? We have already shown that there is a strong case for linking the Pauline concepts of 'secret wisdom' and 'the knowledge' to Pythagoreanism in general, and gematria in particular. The case is even stronger now that we have established that Pythagoreanism was part of the philosophy-wisdom tradition. Perhaps we are in a position to put this question another way: was the secret wisdom secret, not only because it was Pythagorean but because it was universal and had therefore come to be viewed with suspicion by Zealot authorities? Had Jesus come to liberate men and women from a narrow sectarianism in which wisdom effectively meant Law, into the freedom of an ancient internationalism which meant universal truth? Was this at the heart of his battles with the Scribes and Pharisees, the lawyers and the Chief Priests? If these questions can be answered in the affirmative then it would certainly be a legitimate way of understanding his provocative invective in at least one of the passages in which he castigates his opponents:

> And he said, 'Woe to you lawyers also! for you load men
> with burdens hard to bear, and you yourselves do not
> touch the burdens with one of your fingers. Woe to you!
> for you build the tombs of the prophets whom your fathers
> killed. So you are witnesses and consent to the deeds of
> your fathers; for they killed them, and you build their
> tombs. Therefore also the wisdom of God said, "I will send
> them prophets and apostles, some of whom they will kill
> and persecute," that the blood of all the prophets, shed
> from the foundation of the world, may be required of this

generation, from the blood of Abel to the blood of
Zechariah, who perished between the altar and the
sanctuary.' (Luke 11:46–51)

The Pharisees had turned wisdom into Law, legalism and an
outward show of religion. They had become *hupocrites*, actors.
Likewise the lawyers had forgotten the ethical precepts of the wisdom tradition. They had forgotten the basis of what we would call
natural law and natural justice. Jesus, in the next verse, makes a
crucial link between this betrayal of wisdom with its dire consequences, and the removal of the key of 'the knowledge' which
was discussed earlier. This is the context in which he goes on to
say:

Woe to you lawyers! for you have taken away the key of
the knowledge; you did not enter yourselves and you
hindered those who were entering. (Luke 11:52).

We can thus legitimately conclude from this that the wisdom
which had been rejected was associated with 'the knowledge'
which had been suppressed; that this was Pythagorean and
universal in character and that Jesus saw it as his mission to
represent and restore it; to *be* it, as *amon* or *uman* as much as *tektōn*,
for the master builder at Sepphoris was also the initiate of
universal wisdom.

When, in the early days of his ministry, he had returned to his
home town and taught in the synagogue on the sabbath, many in
the congregation were so impressed with his teaching that they
were genuinely perplexed. They said to each other 'Where did this
man get all this? What is the wisdom given to him?' They knew
his family well enough to know he couldn't have got it from them.
Did they know that he had been away for years? The question
'isn't this the carpenter?' could be taken to mean that they weren't
entirely sure who he was because they hadn't seen him for a long
time, during which he had changed. It could imply that they
needed reassurance concerning his identity, not just that they were
incredulous that such a gifted young man should come from such
an ordinary family.

If there is any validity in interpreting the question in this way,
then we can assume that the true answer was a closely guarded

secret. For if he had become an initiate in the tradition of universal philosophy-wisdom of which Pythagoreanism was an important, integral part, then after completing studies in Jewish Pythagoreanism with the Essenes, he could have embarked on a lengthy course of intellectual and spiritual studies in which he would have imbibed the best of the wisdom of Egypt, Assyria, Persia, India, Bactria, Gaul and the Celts. Whether he actually went to all these lands or studied them from a special centre, for instance the monastery of the Therapeutae outside Alexandria, is perhaps taking speculation a little too far. But to doubt that he *knew* the essence of all these philosophies would be to doubt his standing as a Pythagorean, for, as we have seen, they were all closely related. And to doubt that the wisdom which had been given him was related to the universal wisdom, would be to fly in the face of all the evidence put forward above.

Whether he went to these lands in person or only learnt about their wisdom, we cannot say. What we can say is that in principle there is no reason why he should not have gone to all of them. The Gospels are completely silent about his activities from the age of 12 to 30, so there would have been plenty of time to have been a builder at Sepphoris and to have travelled to all the wisdom centres of the known world. Judging by the speed with which he travelled round Judea during his public ministry, there are strong grounds for regarding him as a compulsive and inveterate walker. If Alexander's troops could footslog to the Pyramids and the Indus, why couldn't he? If the Roman legions could reach Gaul or Britain why couldn't he? There is absolutely no reason why he couldn't have done so. The only thing that stops us accepting this possibility is that we have been brought up with an inadequate conceptual model of who Jesus was. We have also failed to grasp the international, universal nature of the wisdom which he embodied. Only when we extend our conceptual model from a narrow Judaic to a broad international one, are we able to do justice to the close connection which Jesus had to this cosmopolitan tradition of philosophy-wisdom. This will become clearer when we analyse the numerology of *Chokmah*, the most widely used Hebrew word for wisdom, and then compare it with that of Jesus Christ, as examined earlier, for it will take us on an international journey to unexpectedly familiar places.

14

Wisdom goes North

In 1984, in a hitherto unpublished paper 'The Cracking of a Unique Code,' Vernon Jenkins, then of the Department of Computer Science at Cardiff University, presented the results of his independent research into the gematria of the first verse in the Bible.[1] He had discovered by computer analysis, that Genesis 1:1 contained regular patterns of numbers and geometry which were so clearly beyond the product of chance that he had become convinced that they proved the divine authorship of Scripture.

He had begun by finding out the gematria of the seven Hebrew words which are translated 'In the beginning God created the heavens and the earth.'

90 200 1 5	400 1 6	40 10 40 300 5	400 1	40 10 5 30 1	1 200 2	400 10 300 1 200 2
296	407	395	401	86	203	913

בראשית ברא אלהים את השמים ואת הארץ

| earth the | — and | heavens the | — | God | created | beginning the In |

Figure 24. The Numerology of Genesis 1:1

As can be seen, the numbers are: In the Beginning, 913; Created, 203; God, 86; Eth (untranslatable), 401; The Heavens, 395; And, 407; The Earth, 296. At first glance, no simple number or pattern is evident, but when they are all added together, they come to 2701 which is 37 × 73. Likewise, if the sixth and seventh words, which are, 'And,' 407, and 'The Earth,' 296, are added together the result is 703 which is 37 × 19. Curiously, 2701 is the 73rd triangular number, and 703 is the 37th triangular number.

There were other equally arresting geometric figures coming out of these numbers which indicated that the number 37, as well as being the root prime for the whole verse (2701 = 37 × 73), had a disproportionately high rate of incidence throughout. Vernon Jenkins therefore decided to do a factor analysis of all seven word-

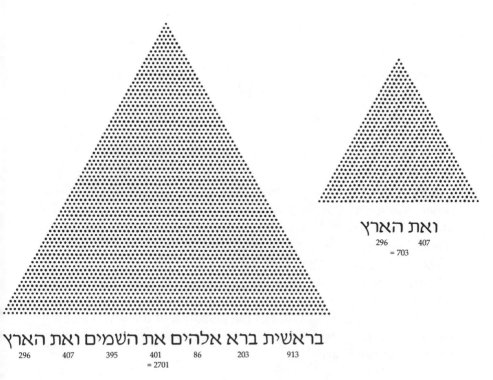

ואת הארץ
296   407
= 703

בראשית ברא אלהים את השמים ואת הארץ
296   407   395   401   86   203   913
= 2701

Figure 25. The Triangular Numbers of Genesis 1:1

number combinations. He found that 23 out of a possible 127 were multiples of 37. This surprised him because, according to statistical probability, this was over six times more than expected.

He then went on to discover some more remarkable attributes of these numbers, of which the most outstanding was that 37 and 73 were not only linked to the triangular numbers 2701 and 703 as illustrated above, but were also linked to each other as a compatible figurate hexagon-hexagram pair. The unexpected appearance of the star of David in this context, was also intriguing:

He then discovered that the hexagon of 37 is not only compatible with the hexagram of 73 but also has another unusual property; it is the only number, except 1261, which is both a hexagon and a hexagram. Insofar as it occurs as a hexagon (the fourth) and a hexagram (the third) in successive members of the series, 37 is thus unique (see Figure 26).

For Vernon Jenkins, all these revelations confirmed the evangelical doctrine of the divine inspiration of the Scriptures, but for more pedestrian souls who remember the early history of mathematics,

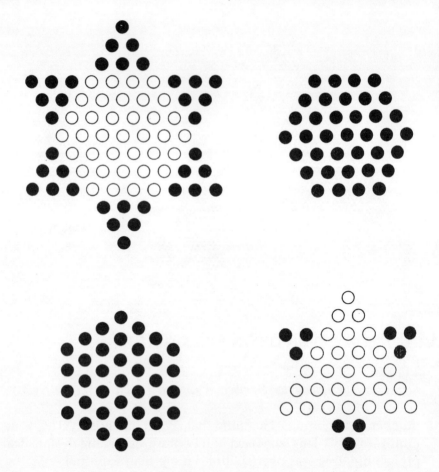

Figure 26. Star of David and Hexagon of 37

there is evidence of a more earthly hand at work. The clue to the
identity of this is Jenkins' discovery of the prevalence of figurate
numbers. The use of these was attributed to the Pythagoreans.
Boyer and Mercbach confirm this in *A History of Mathematics*: 'The
thoroughness with which the Pythagoreans wove number into
their thought is well illustrated by their concern for figurate
numbers.'[2] It would therefore appear that the divine inspiration for
this extraordinarily complex numerological jigsaw puzzle, was
mediated through the Pythagoreans and their obsession with the
numero-geometric alphabet. The so-called 'Priestly' authors of
Genesis 1:1, must have been skilled Pythagoreans and as such may
have come from the same tradition of Hebrew scholarship as those

who constructed the numerology of *Jehoshua haMeshiach*, and its Septuagint translation *Iesous Christos*, as examined earlier.

But what has all this got to do with wisdom? How precisely does it relate to *chokmah*, the word which is almost always used for wisdom throughout the Old Testament? Everything, it would seem, because the gematria for *chokmah* in the Lesser Canon is Ch = 8, K = 11, M = 13, H = 5, which totals 37 and in the Greater Canon it is Ch = 8, K = 20, M = 40, H = 5, which totals 73. There are very few Hebrew words of importance which total 37 and even less which total 73. *chokmah* is the only one which totals both these unusual prime numbers. This is really remarkable and yet it is also highly appropriate because scholars generally maintain that 'wisdom theology is creation theology' and 'the influence of wisdom is sometimes found in Genesis 1.'[3] This is borne out by the fact that the first, or Priestly, Creation story of Genesis 1 probably follows a schematic structure which is itself based on a hexagon in which each point represents one of the six days, with the sabbath in the centre. This is implied by St Augustine, following Philo, who, in the famous passage quoted earlier, said that 'God created all things in six days because the number is perfect and it would have been perfect even if the work of six days did not exist.'

It is intriguing to speculate that if we enlarge this hexagon from seven to 37 units, we may well have uncovered the basic paradigm of creation in the Hebrew wisdom tradition, because the third hexagon has 12 units round its perimeter which could symbolize the 12 tribes and the zodiac, and the fourth has 18, which could

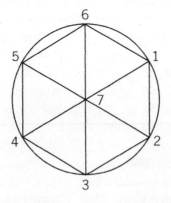

Figure 27. The Seven Days of Creation

Figure 28. Foundations by Ya'acov Kaszemacher

represent all life, because Life, *Chi* = 18. This has been proposed by
the orthodox Jewish artist Ya'acov Kaszemacher.

This may well have been the numero-geometric model of wisdom as Creator, which was used by the Priestly Pythagoreans to
structure their literary composition and encode their belief that
God had created all things through wisdom his master craftsman.

The likelihood that this was indeed the case is increased considerably by the fact that in the Greek of the New Testament, the
name of Jesus Christ, *Iesous Christos*, which we have already analysed in relation to the Fibonacci numbers 3, 5, 8, can also be
factorized in relation to 37, the number for wisdom. As we have
already noted, only the Greater Canon may be used for his full
name which for *Iesous* is: I = 10, E = 8, S = 200, O = 70, U = 400,
S = 200, which totals 888. This breaks down into 37 × 24. For
Christos we get: CH = 600, R = 100, I = 10, S = 200, T = 300,
O = 70, S = 200, which totals 1480. This breaks down into 37 × 40.
So 37 is the prime number for *Iesous Christos*. Since primes are
foundation numbers in gematria, we may say that *Iesous Christos*

is built on the number 37 and shares the attributes and symbolic meanings of that number. Since it symbolizes wisdom, we may therefore say that as far as gematria is concerned, Jesus Christ is wisdom and shares wisdom's attributes.

However, this tells us nothing new. It is something we have already established. So can the testimony of gematria add anything to what we already know? I believe that it can, if we turn once more to the work of Bligh Bond and Simcox Lea, who have written extensively on this subject. They observe that taken together, *Iesous* as 37 × 24 and *Christos* as 37 × 40 total 37 × 64 which is 2368. They go on to point out that the number 37 can be seen figuratively as a cube as well as a hexagon if imagined in three dimensions. If it is viewed as a cube, as in the illustration of Kaszemacher's picture above, it is made up of 64 sub-cubes of which only 37 are visible. Thus the cube of 4 (4 × 4 × 4 = 64), when viewed at a 45° angle, is exactly the same as a hexagon displaying 37 sub-cubes. In this strange and not altogether logical way, the numbers 37 and 64 are linked. Since *Iesous Christos* totals 37 × 64, Bond and Lea propose that the cube of 4, seen as a hexagon, is the numero-geometric expression of Jesus Christ. They back this up by showing that because the Greek word for Truth, *Aletheia*, is 64 in the Greater Canon, the cube of 4 can be called 'the cube of Truth.' This symbolizes Jesus Christ as the Truth. It is 'the Cube Symbol of the Lord'[4] in which the 37 units which can be seen, symbolize the human Jesus and the 27 which are unseen represent his divinity.

All this may seem highly arbitrary and could perhaps be dismissed as fanciful speculation but for the fact that, as is obvious from the illustration, they are proposing exactly the same

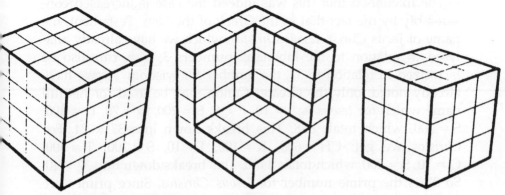

Figure 29. The Cube Symbol of the Lord

geometrical figure which leapt out of Genesis 1:1 in the researches of Vernon Jenkins and which we have identified as being the numero-geometrical expression of *chokmah*, wisdom. Since we have seen that the Hebrew of Genesis 1:1 and the Greek of *Iesous Christos* are linked to wisdom through the foundation prime of 37, it is not so easy to attribute this coincidence, however strange, to the randomness of chance. The possibility that we may be uncovering a mosaic of intentional interconnection, may have to be entertained, particularly when Bond and Lea claim that their interpretation is not original but is based on certain writings of the early Church fathers, principally Clement of Rome in his Seventeenth Homily, written about the year 100 AD.

In this little-known but influential tract, Clement, purporting to speak for St Peter, claimed that when the apostle was challenged to name the place where God is to be found, he said that it was at '*to mè on*,' literally 'the place that is not.' This is described as the meeting place of the Six Boundless Lines:

> Who, wheresoever He be, is as it were, in the middle of a
> boundless space being the terminal of the All. Taking their
> origin therefore from Him, the six extensions have the
> nature of unlimited things ... For at Him the six boundless
> lines do terminate and from Him they take their boundless
> extensions.[5]

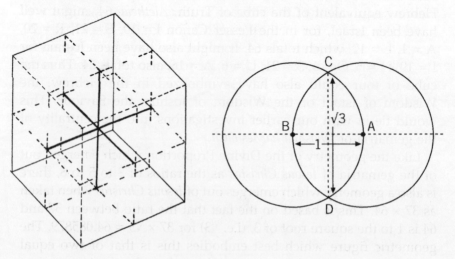

Figure 30. Six Boundless Lines   *Figure 31. The ratio of 37 to 64 (or √3)*

If Clement had any justification whatsoever in attributing such an abstruse philosophical description to St Peter, the simple Galilean fisherman, then we could not have clearer evidence that Pythagorean geometrical symbolism lies near the heart of the Christian revelation. For these Six Boundless Lines are the axes of a cubic structure which expands from one point to infinity. Today they would be called the Cartesian Coordinates. This cubic nature of Truth and its identification with Jesus Christ, is confirmed for Bond and Lea by the gematria of KUBOS KURIOU, the Cube of the Lord (692 + 1000), which is the same as that of OCTO KUBOI, the Cube of Eight (1190 + 502).[6]

However tenuous the links in this chain of coincidences may seem to be, it is, nevertheless, most extraordinary that Vernon Jenkins found the same geometric figure in the Hebrew of Genesis 1:1 as Bond and Lea had found in the Greek of *Iesous Christos*, without any knowledge of the earlier scholars' work. It is likewise very strange that neither Jenkins, Bond nor Lea had any idea that this figure was linked to that of wisdom. What has emerged clearly is that the cube of 4, the cube of Truth, the 'cube symbol of the Lord' is not just 'the image of the form of God' but is also the image of the form of wisdom, and indeed of the Creation which wisdom brought forth from God. It is wisdom that seems to have been the underlying, secret presence throughout. If Jenkins had seen this he would no doubt have wanted to point out that the Hebrew equivalent of the cube of Truth, *Aletheia*, 64, might well have been Israel, for in the Lesser Canon I = 10, S = 21, R = 20, A = 1, L = 12, which totals 64. It might also have been Joshua for I = 10, H = 5, O = 6, S = 21, U = 6, A = 16, also totals 64. Thus the cube of four could also have symbolized in the Hebrew, the Wisdom of Israel or the Wisdom of Joshua, the Saviour. This would tie in with our earlier investigations into the centrality of the gematria of *Jehoshua haMeshiach*.

Like the geometry of the Divine Proportion which emerged out of the gematria of *Iesous Christos* as the ratios of 3 to 5 to 8, there is also a geometry which emerges out of *Iesous Christos* when taken as 37 × 64. This is based on the fact that the ratio between 37 and 64 is 1 to the square root of 3, (i.e. $\sqrt{3}$) for 37 × $\sqrt{3}$ = 64.085879. The geometric figure which best embodies this is that of two equal circles whose circumferences pass through each other's centres:

This figure was known to the Pythagoreans as Potential Logos

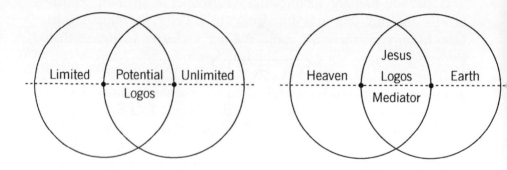

Figure 32. Potential Logos and Vesica Piscis

because it symbolized the Dyad, or twoness becoming the Triad, threeness, harmony or the Logos. It is the property of the overlapping lozenge shape in the middle, that the ratio between its short axis AB and its long axis CD, is 1 to √3. Since *Iesous Christos* could also be expressed geometrically as 1 to √3, it was appropriated by the early Christians and called the vesica Piscis, the womb of the Fish. Jesus became known as the Great Fish of the Piscean Age and the earliest creed was the acrostic *Iesous Christos, Theou Uios, Soter*, Jesus Christ, Son of God, Saviour, which spelt ICHTHUS, the Greek for Fish.

That which had symbolized the Limited, the Unlimited and the potentiality of Logos, came to represent Christ as the Logos, the Mediator between heaven and earth, light and darkness. This is another clear example of how Pythagorean geometrical concepts were integral to the nascent Christian mindset.[7]

Like the Fibonacci numbers, the vesica piscis has universal connotations, not in the organic world of growth, but in the world of geometric forms itself, for, as Robert Lawlor explains, the vesica is a 'form generator' because 'all the regular polygons can be said to arise from the succession of vesica constructions.'[8]

In the smaller illustration it is possible to see more easily what he means. Out of three circles that all intersect to make vesicae with each another, an equilateral triangle, then a square and then a pentagon can be constructed. In the larger illustration this figure is enlarged so that an octagon, decagon and dodecagon can also be constructed. In this way all the polygons can be said to have been born out of the womb of the Fish. In the same way Jesus Christ

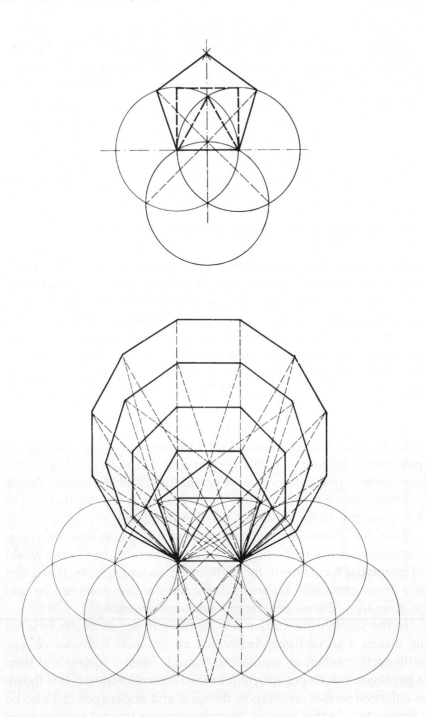

Figure 33. Vesica Piscis as Form Generator

can be seen as the 'form generator' of the polygonal 'world.' Though not so obviously important to the natural world as the Divine Proportion, the vesica pisciswas central to geometry and proved to be just as important in the sacred architecture of the Western world.

If the geometry of the Fibonacci numbers led us into the architecture of the classical tradition as represented by Greek temples, Vitruvius and Alberti, then the geometry of the vesica leads us just as surely into that of the Gothic. As Lawlor says, it has been 'the major thematic source for the cosmic temples of this age in the west, the Gothic cathedrals.'[9] This is also the opinion of architectural historians such as Claude Bragdon, who links the vesica to the aureole or mandorla around medieval sculptures of Christ:

> The *vesica piscis*, which in so many cases seems to have
> determined the main proportion of a cathedral plan — the
> interior length and width across the transepts — appears
> as an aureole around the figure of Christ in early
> representations, a fact which certainly points to a relation
> between the two.[10]

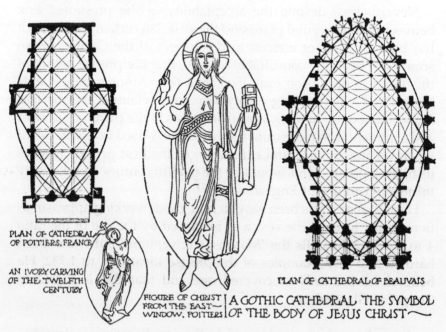

PLAN OF CATHEDRAL OF POITIERS, FRANCE

AN IVORY CARVING OF THE TWELFTH CENTURY

FIGURE OF CHRIST FROM THE EAST WINDOW, POITIERS

PLAN OF CATHEDRAL OF BEAUVAIS

A GOTHIC CATHEDRAL THE SYMBOL OF THE BODY OF JESUS CHRIST

Figure 34. Vesica Piscis in Gothic Cathedrals

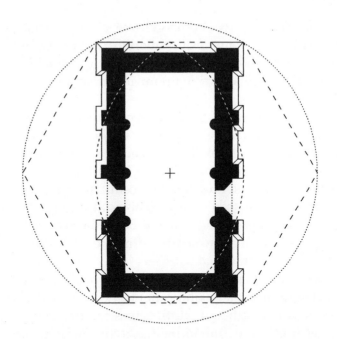

Figure 35. Vesica Piscis in the Lady Chapel at Glastonbury

Nevertheless, despite the acceptability of the presumed link between Gothic ground plans and the vesica in certain circles, such has been the lack of interest in this aspect of the Gothic and so scant have been the consultable sources, that the precise nature of this link has only been examined by a few. Among these stands Bligh Bond who, writing eighty years ago, claimed that he had found it not only 'in many approximations in the plans of our own and continental churches, but it is notoriously used in Gothic detail wherever the architectural expression of the best periods reaches its highest point ... This would be the twelfth century and the early thirteenth century of English work.'[11]

He says that it has been easy to find good, working approximations to the ideal of the vesica as instanced by the use of the ratio 4 to 7 which he calls the 'Masons' Convention,' but it has been hard to find any examples of the precise ideal of 1 to 1.732. He believes he has only discovered one and that this is the Lady Chapel at Glastonbury.

It has been the writer's good fortune to discover an almost perfect example of such a principle in the Lady Chapel of

Glastonbury Abbey, a structure whose history would be all in favour of a perfect symbolic expression, since the extreme and scrupulous care used by its builders in designing it on ancient lines, is on record.[12]

He then gives the details of how he arrived at what he believes to be a very accurate assessment of the outer and inner measurements. He observes that if the builders had used the Masons' Convention that is, the ratio 7:4, to lay out the plan, it would have been either slightly longer or wider than it in fact is. On the inside he measured exactly 37 feet in breadth. By the 'Masons' Convention' the length would therefore have been $37 \times 7 \div 4$, that is, 64 feet 9 inches. But in reality it was shorter, being almost exactly the perfect √3 ratio, which is 64 feet.

It is indeed very strange to have arrived at an architectural embodiment of Jesus Christ as the *vesica* ratio, which is as precise as any noted earlier in relation to the Vitruvian perfect ratios of 3, 5 and 8 or 6, 10 and 16. It is equally odd that of all the vesica ratios claimed for the Gothic, the only one which has been found to be exact rather than an approximation, appears to be the Lady Chapel at Glastonbury. What is even more peculiar is that this exactness is embodied not just in a perfect vesica but in the actual numbers associated with Jesus Christ, namely 37 and 64, expressed in English feet. Is it just a coincidence that the only perfect Gothic vesica has been discovered at Glastonbury? Was Bligh Bond, as the architect at the Abbey during those years, predisposed towards finding what he wanted to find? I confess that I am not in a position to judge but all I can say is that architectural historians who have since given the matter their attention, such as Keith Critchlow, John Michell and Robert Lawlor, have all accepted the accuracy of Bligh Bond's calculations.

This being so, we may therefore assume that there was an esoteric tradition of sacred architecture which knew not only that Jesus Christ, as the Great Fish of the Piscean Age, was associated with the √3 ratio of the vesica, but also that the numerology of his name could be expressed uniquely as 37 in relation to 64. We may also speculate that if it was more than a coincidence that this unique 37 to 64 ratio was embodied at Glastonbury in the early Middle Ages, it might have been because Glastonbury was a very ancient sacred site which, from the dawn of the Christian era, had been associated with esoteric mysteries, not least of which was the persistent legend that Jesus himself had come to Glastonbury during his silent years and had actually founded the church there.

By a long and circuitous route, we have arrived back at the heart of the geographical location and historical speculation which was discussed at length in Part I of this study. The wheel has come full circle. In the meantime we have presented a strong case for Jesus having been a Pythagorean and a master builder. In Chapter 11, 'The Master Builder at Sepphoris' we established the possibility that his professional title *tektōn*, could be taken to mean the earthly counterpart of his divine role as Heavenly Builder. This was argued with enough plausibility to substantiate the claim made in Chapter 4, that when St Augustine told Pope Gregory that the Old Church at Glastonbury was reputed to have been built by 'God himself' or, in another version, 'by the hands of Christ himself,' he may have been referring to a tradition which was based on actual historical fact. Furthermore, the appellation 'the heavenly Builder,' *Coelorum Fabricator*, which he used of Jesus Christ in that context, is so similar to the divine counterpart of *tektōn* to justify the assumption that all that was claimed for him in connection with the rebuilding of Sepphoris, can now be claimed for him regarding the Old Church at Glastonbury.

We have thus arrived at a position from which we may legitimately contend that the *Domus Dei*, the House of God, which, according to the Domesday Book, was called 'the Secret of the Lord' in the great monastery of Glastonbury, was none other than a church built by Jesus the *tektōn*. It was a secret in the same way as the true meaning of *tektōn* was a secret, hidden behind the veil of 'carpenter.' Both these secrets were examples of the secrecy associated with the Pythagoreans. This interpretation would appear to be confirmed by William of Malmesbury's cryptic reference to 'some holy secret' encoded in the floor patterns of the Old Church. Round the altar he says 'we may note in the triangles or squares and sealed with lead; beneath which, if I believe some holy secret to be held, I am doing no harm to religion.' However speculative the identification of this holy secret must remain, it should be conceded that the mention of triangular and square patterns, strongly suggest a Pythagorean provenance which, in the light of all that has been adduced above, could well have been that of Jesus the Pythagorean himself.

15

From Glastonbury to Stonehenge

In Part II it was proposed that Jesus not only had Pythagorean connections, but that he could very well have been one himself via the Essenes. Now that the locus of this study has returned to Glastonbury, identification of Jesus as a probable Pythagorean has strengthened the case for him having built the *Vetusta Ecclesia* enormously. However, the emphasis of the argument has now shifted from the Pythagorean tradition as such, to the wisdom tradition within which Pythagoreanism played such a significant part. It is Wisdom herself, *chokmah* and the Pythagorean interpretation of her number, 37, which has led us north and back to Glastonbury. Let us therefore continue to pursue this avenue of enquiry and see where wisdom will lead us, particularly in relation to Gothic architecture and the *vesica piscis*.

If we look again at the plan of a Gothic cathedral, we can see that the two equilateral triangles lying base to base and thus forming a rhombus, have the same ratio of axes as the vesica which encloses them, that is, 1 to √3. For the purposes of architecture the rhombus, being angular, is an easier figure to work with than the vesica and so came to represent it for practical purposes. It was this rhombic figure which formed the basis of the building principle *ad triangulam*, which, together with the principle *ad quadratum*, lay at the heart of medieval ecclesiastical architecture.

So we find that the New Testament symbol of 'the image of the form of God,' 'the cube symbol of the Lord,' re-emerges on a massive scale in the Middle Ages as the *vesica piscis*, representing Jesus Christ as ICHTHUS, the Great Fish of the Piscean Age. But what precisely is the link between the cube-as-hexagon and the vesica? If we look again at Bligh Bond's illustration of the Lady Chapel at Glastonbury we can see how the plan is contained within a circle around a hexagon (Figure 35).

We have seen how the ratio of the vesica's axes is 1 to √3. Now we can see that a rectangle drawn round the vesica and therefore

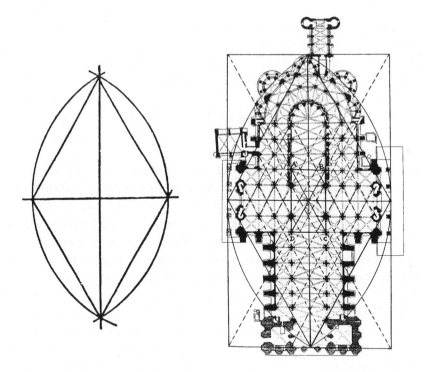

Figure 36. The Vesica and Plan of Chartres

having sides of 1 and √3, is equal to one constructed on the sides and long axes of the hexagon. This 1 to √3 ratio is the geometric property of any hexagon. It can therefore be seen how easily the New Testament cube-as-hexagon could have been transformed into the √3 rectangles of the Gothic age, for it is merely the architectural expression of the same geometric figure. Although documentary evidence for the continuity of this esoteric tradition is lacking, the evidence from the measurements of actual Gothic plans testify to all that has been discovered by Vernon Jenkins, Bligh Bond and Simcox Lea.

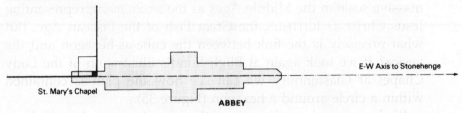

Figure 37. East-West Axis of Glastonbury Abbey

Further authentication of the architectural importance of the cube-as-hexagon, vesica-rhombic figure comes from an even more unexpected quarter and has been proposed by John Michell in *The View Over Atlantis*. It is based on his observation that the main axis of Glastonbury Abbey runs due west-east and is part of an alignment of a number of significant landmarks and Ley lines. He noticed that this axis, if extended east, goes straight to Stonehenge.[1] More evidence confirming this orientation has since come independently from Kenneth Knight, Donald Cyr and Nigel Pennick.[2]

An axis linking Glastonbury Abbey to Stonehenge, would not in itself be enough to justify a comparison between the two buildings, separated as they are by over 3,000 years, and yet, weird though it may seem, Michell demonstrates that the construction of Stonehenge contains the same geometric principle as the Gothic, namely, the vesica. If we follow his analysis and construct his plan for Stonehenge III (*c*.2200–1600 BC), this will become clear.[3]

First draw an ordinary vesica and then a third equal circle, with centre at the centre of the vesica *O*, which cuts the horizontal axis

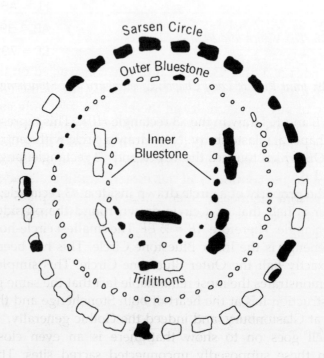

Figure 38. Plan of Stonehenge

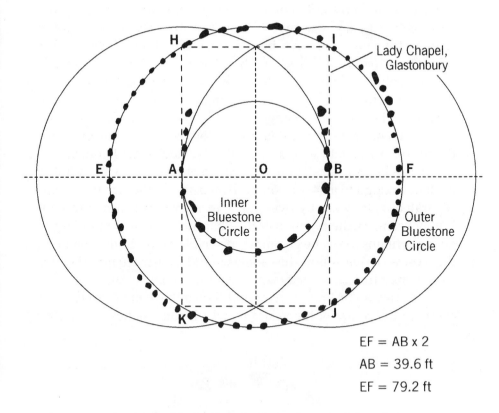

EF = AB x 2
AB = 39.6 ft
EF = 79.2 ft

Figure 39. Joint Plan of Lady Chapel, Glastonbury and Stonehenge

AOB at *E* and F. Draw in the √3 rectangle *HIJK*. This represents the Lady Chapel at Glastonbury. Now draw a circle with centre *O* and radius *OB* which touches the vesica and √3 rectangle tangentially at *A* and *B*.

It is the property of a circle drawn inside a √3 rectangle, that its diameter is half that of a circle drawn round the outside of the same rectangle. Therefore *AB* = ½ *EF*. The smallest circle-horseshoe at Stonehenge is the Inner Bluestone Circle. This has been found to be exactly half the Outer Bluestone Circle. This simple figure thus demonstrates the most remarkable fact that the same geometric construction lies at the heart of both Stonehenge and the Lady Chapel at Glastonbury, and indeed the Gothic generally.

Michell goes on to show that there is an even closer link between these supposedly unconnected sacred sites. This concerns their measurements. We have already noted Bligh Bond's

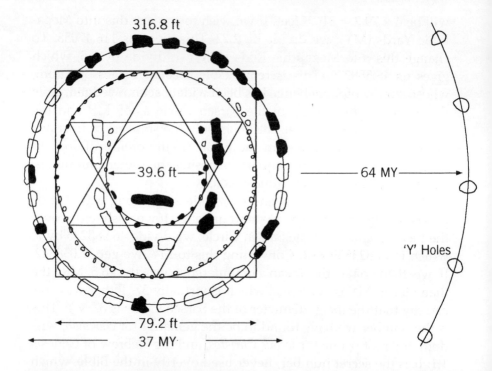

Figure 40. The Squared Circles at Stonehenge

discovery that, not only did St Mary's Chapel embody the √3 vesica ratio, but that the measurements were exactly 37 and 64, the precise numbers for Jesus Christ. But these were the *inside* measurements, as he told us. He also told us that the *outside* measurements were 40 by 69.5 feet. But Michell has found that the *outside* breadth varies slightly and that its mean average can be taken as 39.6 feet. Whether he is bending the figures a little is impossible to say without conducting an independent survey, but what he contends is that this measurement is the same as the diameter of the Inner Bluestone Circle at Stonehenge. However suspicious we may be of such remarkable coincidence, let us suspend our judgement meanwhile and examine his geometry in greater detail.

If we accept Michell's measurement for the diameter of the Inner Bluestone Circle as 39.6 feet, then the diameter of the Outer Bluestone Circle, as demonstrated, will be 2 × 39.6 = 79.2 feet. If we want to enclose this circle in a square, the perimeter of that square

will be 4 × 79.2 = 316.8 feet. If we wish to convert this into Megalithic Yards (MY), we divide by 2.72. This gives us 116.47058. To
change this into Megalithic Rods (MR) we divide by 2.5, which
gives us 46.588235. This is remarkable because Professor Thom,
whose survey of Stonehenge has been widely acknowledged, gave
the inside circumference of the Sarsen Circle as 45 MR and the
outside as 48 MR. Thus 46.588235 is only the smallest of fractions
(0.088 MR or 7 inches) from the mean circumference of 46.5. In
other words our notional square enclosing the Outer Bluestones,
squares the Sarsen Circle almost exactly.

However, this is not the end of wonders by a long way. Let us
proceed with a mixture of awe and unbelief. If we wish to discover
the mean diameter of the Sarsen Circle, we divide 46.588235 by π,
which is 14.823539 MR. Converting this to MY, we get 37.058822.
If we then make the mean circumference exactly 46.5 MR, the
diameter in MY is 36.988632 which is virtually 37. Either way, we
can say that the mean diameter of the Sarsen Circle is 37 MY. This
is the number we have found to be the gematria for *chokmah*, wisdom, the root prime for *Iesous Christos*, and the Hebrew of Genesis
1:1. It is the secret number, never used overtly in the Bible, which
has haunted our studies. And here it is again, just as secret but just
as definitely there and just as crucial, built into the most imposing
and accurately measurable feature of Stonehenge around 2000 BC.

Michell continues to astound by pointing out that if a vesica is
constructed on the Sarsen diameter of 37, then the longer axis of
64 MY, if drawn as a circle from point *O*, will pass through the
circle of the 'Y' holes, the mysterious remains of earlier Bluestone
Circles, erected and then taken down again between circa 1900 and
1700 BC.[4]

This seems almost too pat but Michell believes that this
calculation is most likely to be accurate because it coincides with
certain words from the Greek of the New Testament. Once 64 MY
is converted into feet (64 × 2.72 = 174.59), and if 174.59 is rounded
off to 174.6 or 1,746 we get a most important number about which
he has written in *City of Revelation*.[5] This is called the number of
fusion because it is the sum of 666, the masculine number of fire,
derived from the magic square of the sun, and 1,080, the feminine
number of water associated with the moon. Thus 666 plus
1,080 = 1,746. 666 will be recognized as the number of the beast in
Revelation and 1,080 is the gematria of *to hagion pneuma*, the Holy

Spirit, the feminine person of the Trinity. 1,746 itself is *kokkos sinapeos*, a grain of mustard seed which, for Jesus, symbolized the Kingdom of Heaven. (Luke 13:14)

However difficult it may be to take these numerical conjuring tricks seriously, there is one which Michell produces which may not be quite so easy to dismiss. It is that the circumference of the Sarsen Circle, which he has taken as 316.8 feet, if seen as 3168, is the gematria for Lord Jesus Christ, for *Kurios*, Lord = 800, *Iesous* = 888 and *Christos* = 1,480 — total 3,168.[6] This is an extraordinary coincidence and is immediately reminiscent of the theatre at Sepphoris whose diameter, if taken as 250 Roman feet, had a circumference of 800, i.e. *Kurios*, Lord, and if taken as 74 metres had a circumference of 236.8, i.e. *Iesous Christos*.

Perhaps such a comparison with Sepphoris might only serve to weaken credibility still further. However, before scepticism takes over altogether, let us recall one or two other peculiar numbers which may be more convincing. These were connected with our examination of Joshua the Anointed One or Messiah which in the Hebrew is *Yehoshua haMeshiach*. Much was then made of the fact that the total gematria in the Lesser Canon came to 121 or 11^2. It has since been mentioned that because *Yehoshua* is 64 and *chokmah* is 37, the two numbers together could be interpreted as the wisdom of Joshua the Saviour. What has not been given any significance is that *Yehoshua Meshiach*, Joshua Anointed or Messiah, which strictly speaking would be the exact equivalent of Jesus Christ, has the number 116. This is a multiple of four since 4 × 29 = 116.

The strange thing is that 116 is very close to 116.47058 which, according to John Michell, is the mean circumference of the Sarsen Circle in MY. In addition, 29 is uncannily close to 29.117647 which is Michell's diameter of the Outer Bluestone Circle. In fact they are so close that if the megalithic builders were using MY and preferred to use whole numbers rather than irrational fractions, which would seem to be a reasonable supposition, then we might almost suspect that 116 MY and 29 MY were the exact measurements they were using. A circumference of exactly 116 would give a diameter of 36.9 which would still be close enough to 37 for the symbolism to be maintained.

If we did make this small adjustment from 116.47058 to 116, what difference would it make? Obviously in terms of geometry,

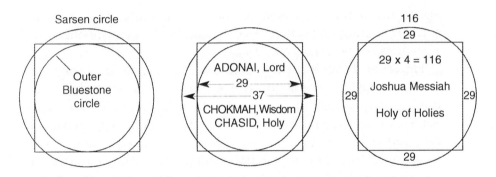

Figure 41. Number Symbolism of Sarsen and Outer Bluestone Circles

none to speak of, but in terms of symbolism it would mean that we would lose Lord Jesus Christ because 316.79997, which Michell rounds off to 316.8 would become 315.52, which, as 3,155, would miss the mark by 13. But we would gain *Yehoshua Meshiach*, Joshua Messiah, which, as we have seen, has exactly the same meaning as Jesus Christ in Hebrew.

By changing from Greek into Hebrew we would also gain some confirmation that the squared circle of 116 was indeed a very sacred space, because this is also the gematria of *Kadosh haKadoshim*, the Holy of Holies, the most holy sanctuary in the Temple of Solomon. We might therefore say that it could be called the Holy of Holies of Joshua Messiah. Likewise we would gain confirmation of the importance of the number 37 because this is also the gematria for *Chasid* meaning Holy or kind, the primary attribute of divinity. What could be more fitting than the diameter of the squared circle of the Holy of Holies of Joshua Messiah being sacred to the wisdom which is Holy; Holy Wisdom. And what about 29, the diameter of the Outer Bluestone? Is that number also associated with a divinity? Curiously enough there *is* a Hebraic divine name for this as well. It is *Adonai*. This, as noted in 'The Master Builder at Sepphoris,' was the pronounceable name of the unpronounceable *Yahweh*, YHWH, which the 72 rabbis of the Septuagint translated *Kurios*, Lord. Thus, having lost *Kurios Iesous Christos*, Lord Jesus Christ, in the Greek, we have gained the complete equivalent in the Hebrew *Adonai Yehoshua Meshiach*, Lord Joshua Messiah!

It is very odd, almost uncanny, that, having changed from the Greek of the Greater Canon to the Hebrew of the Lesser Canon, an identical match of divine names should fit the Pythagorean axiom that 'the Gods are numbers.' On balance it would appear that the Hebrew fits better than the Greek. For a start, it is all in whole numbers whereas John Michell uses irrational fractions and decimal points. Then 116 is Joshua Messiah *and*, as 4 × 29, the Holy of Holies; 37 is Holy as well as wisdom and 29 is *Adonai*, Lord. The Greek by comparison seems rather contrived. 316.8, taken as 3168, may be convincing for Lord Jesus Christ, but 174.59 rounded off to 174.6 to become the number of fusion, may be a little forced, particularly since 64 × 2.72 is 174.08, not 174.59. My own feeling is that it is better to use whole numbers wherever possible.

Nevertheless, having said that, one must concede that there is yet another dimension to John Michell's numbers, for in choosing 39.6 feet for the Lady Chapel and the Inner Bluestone and 79.2 feet for the Outer Bluestone Circle, he is also making a cosmic connection. Both these measurements are related to a model of the earth, for 39.6 feet, as 3,960 miles is the mean radius of the earth and 79.2 as 7,920 miles is its mean diameter.

If we now divide 7,920 by 720, we get exactly 11, which brings us back mysteriously to the very same square of 11 or 11^2 which was the foundation geometry for *Yehoshua haMeshiach*, and which

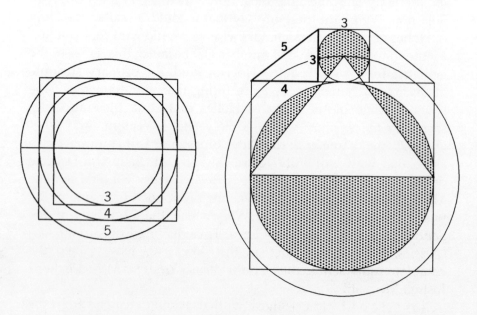

Figure 42. The Moon:Earth:Sun 3:4:5 ratio and outline of the Great Pyramid

led us on to the ratio 3:4:5 between the moon, earth and sun, and also to the earth:moon ratio paradigm and the outline geometry of the Great Pyramid:

It seems as though John Michell's model of squaring the circle can after all be applied to Stonehenge and that the slight discrepancies noted between 116 and 116.47058, and between 29 and 29.117647, are not in themselves enough to weaken his case for the cosmic connections implied there, as in these other examples which we have already examined. If this is indeed the case, then all that was then proposed cosmologically with regard to *Yehoshua ha-Meshiach*, Joshua the Anointed, can now be regarded as applicable to the holy Hebrew names which seem to be encoded in the most important measurements of Stonehenge.

16
Pythagorean Stone Circles

Quite apart from the possibility that the link between the Lady
Chapel at Glastonbury and the Inner Bluestone Horseshoe at
Stonehenge might be highly tenuous, there are three other serious
questions which arise out of the last chapter. First, is the geometry
accurate and can it be considered Pythagorean, or rather proto-
Pythagorean? Second, is there the remotest possibility of there
having been any ancient links between the builders of Stonehenge
and the later Greek Pythagoreans? Third, were there likewise any
connections at all with the Semitic world of the Hebrews? Since
these are all big questions, they will be answered one at a time for
the next three chapters, starting with the geometry.

The first objection to the geometrical method used, is that it is
chronologically anachronistic because the Sarsen Circle pre-dated
the Outer and Inner Bluestones.

The Sarsen Circle belongs to the phase of building known as
Stonehenge IIIa and dates from around 2000 BC while the Outer
and Inner Bluestones belong to IIIc and date from 1650 and 1250
BC. So there could have been over 500 years between the two,
which is a long time to take to square the circle. Nevertheless, the
geometry *could* have been done backwards and since at Stonehenge

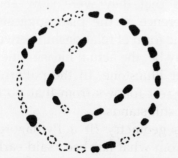 

Figure 43. Stonehenge IIIa and IIIc

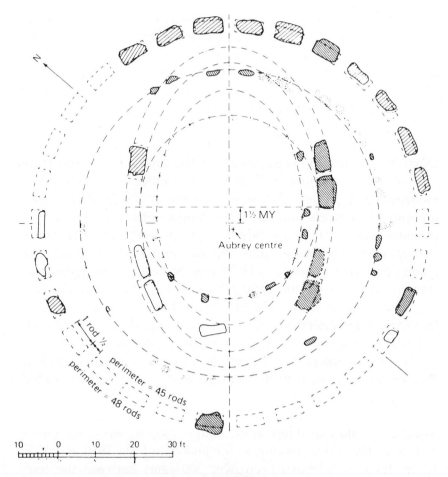

Figure 44. Alexander Thom's Plan of Stonehenge

we are dealing with a building programme which lasted over 1,500 years altogether, it could be said that they were slow about everything. Also, the overall coherence of the plan suggests a continuity of tradition and thus some form of relationship between phases. Speculative though this may be, the actual measurements of the Sarsen Circle and the Outer Bluestone, fit the pattern of squaring the circle exactly and the rest follows from that, so the argument from the geometry itself still stands.

The next question is: does this geometry fit a Pythagorean interpretation? Well it is obvious from what has been said earlier about the squaring of the circle and its symbolism, that it probably does, but there are other aspects of the plan, not mentioned so far, which strengthen this supposition. The first is the Pythagorean triangle which Professor Thom identified in the construction of the Sarsen Trilithons. He found that these, the largest stones of all, were perfectly arranged between two ellipses of 30 × 20 MY and 27 × 17 MY. The inner of these is based on a near perfect Pythagorean triangle whose square of hypotenuse is 729 and the sum of other two squares is 730:[1]

Confirmation that we are indeed dealing with a continuous tradition of proto-Pythagorean geometry, comes from the earliest building phase known as Stonehenge I which is usually dated around 3000 to 2000 BC. Pythagorean triangles of 5:12:13 have been identified in what is known as the station stone rectangle.

Thom gives the circumference of the Aubrey Holes Circle as 'almost precisely 131 Megalithic Rods.'[2] This means that the diameter is almost precisely 104 Megalithic Yards. Since the four station stones are on the Aubrey Circle, the diagonal of the rectangle they form, will be 104 MY. It has been generally accepted that the short sides of this rectangle are 40 MY and the long sides are 96 MY. Since 40^2 (1,600) + 96^2 (9,216) = 104^2 (10,816), this rectangle is made up of two perfect 5:12:13 Pythagorean triangles.[3] This being so, it is difficult to doubt that what was later called Pythagorean geometry was known and practised from the earliest phase of Stonehenge and that it continued to be used throughout its long and slow development.

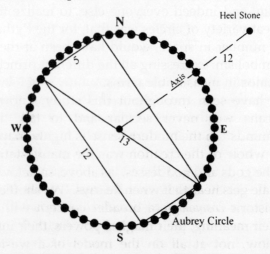

Figure 45. Pythagorean Triangle formed from a diagonal of the Station Stone Rectangle

Corroborative evidence indicating that not just Stonehenge, but the stone circles of Megalithic Britain generally, were expressions of proto-Pythagorean geometry, comes from a closer examination of the work of Alexander Thom.

In all of his extensive work on the geometry of the stone circles, Professor Thom never seems to have seriously entertained the possibility that one of the main purposes of the builders might have been to express a system of symbolic or sacred geometry. He believed that trained scientific minds, particularly astronomers, had built them to chart the solar and lunar year and predict lunar tides, eclipses and periods of maximum light. But although he identified Pythagorean triangles in what he called egg-shaped and elliptical circles, he never suspected that they might actually have been built by proto-Pythagoreans. Had he done so, he would have had an interpretative model which would have been no less scientific but would also have been symbolic, for, as we have seen, the Pythagoreans had a theory of knowledge which included the symbolic and the sacred. This would have enabled him to find a more satisfactory reason than ease of measurement for what he believed to be an obsession with trying to achieve whole number ratios for π in egg-shaped and flattened circles. If, as Pythagoreans, the builders believed that 'all things are numbers,' and 'the gods are numbers,' then each number they used, as integers, would have had an important symbolic meaning. This would also have helped him, and indeed everyone else, to realize that the reason for the great variety of circles was that, for the Pythagoreans, geometry, as number in space, would have been at the heart of their mystic symbolism, expressing all the different principles, or *archai*, of the cosmos in measurable terms.

As we have seen throughout this study, knowledge for the Pythagoreans was never secular and to talk about 'trained scientific minds'[4] in the modern sense is highly inappropriate. For them, the whole of the creation was the manifestation of the character of the gods and goddesses, 'as above, so below.' Christopher Chippindale gets near to it when he says: 'We should think instead of a prehistoric *cosmology*, a broader concern with the heavenly bodies, their meaning, their magical powers, their influence on our world below, not at all on the model of a western analytical science.'[5]

The Pythagoreans' theory of knowledge, as already stated,

centred on their fourfold understanding of number. Number as such was arithmetic. Number in space was geometry. Number in time was musical harmonics. Number in space-time was astronomy-astrology. These together made up a system of knowledge in which correspondences were seen between the different disciplines, humankind and the cosmos. The cosmos above was the macrocosmic universe. The cosmos below was the microcosmic individual. Between these was the mesocosm, the middle world, the third term, the mean proportional, spatially understood. This was the sacred space, the *temenos*, the temple, the special site where the macrocosmic energies could be focused and mediated to microcosmic men and women, tuning them to the divine.

Understood according to this cosmology, the stone circles would have been centres where these divine energies could have been experienced. They would have been the prototypes of the traditional magic circles, where every number and geometric shape would have corresponded to a divine principle, active in the macrocosm and accessible in these sacred enclosures, so long as they exactly embodied the right numbers and shapes. These principles were held to be the basis of music, the music of the heavenly spheres and human music as its earthly counterpart. Thus the astronomical alignments which Thom and others have proposed, together with the precise geometrical designs, would not only have been used for seasonal farming, fishing and sailing purposes. They would also have been considered as alignments to, and transmitters of, the energies of the gods and goddesses who were themselves often identified with the heavenly bodies. It was thus of the utmost importance to keep in tune with them in order to predict what fate they had in store.

Applying all this to what we may have uncovered at Stonehenge, we could say that the divine principles which it may have embodied and whose energies it may have mediated were those associated with Joshua Messiah, of whose cult the Sarsen Circle was the Holy of Holies, with Holy Wisdom the diameter as consort, so that the full divine attribution could perhaps be said to have been: 'the Holy Wisdom of Joshua Messiah.' Likewise, the Outer Bluestone Circle could have been associated with the divine energies of *Adonai*, Lord. This has not yet been proved and we will return to this later but, in theory, this is how the system would have worked.

This should not seem strange to us if we compare it with the dedication of churches to Saints, members of the Christian Holy Family, Mary or even St Saviour himself. Likewise the symbolic system of numbers should not seem strange because it is merely an earlier form of what we have already shown expressed in the Greek temples, Vitruvian theatres, Alberti's churches and Gothic cathedrals. The only surprise is to discover that the same numerical cosmology was in operation in megalithic Britain by at least 3000 BC.

Alexander Thom's originality was to make the daring and unprecedented assumption that our prehistoric ancestors were as intelligent as we are. He applied the sciences of engineering and astronomy to a field which hitherto, with a few exceptions, had been the sole province of archaeologists who had never questioned the presupposition that the megalith builders were primitive and savage. He proved them to have been wrong but it was not his purpose to show that he had uncovered a proto-Pythagorean civilization. As his son, the late Dr Archie Thom, says in his biography of his father *Walking in all of the Squares*, thinking in these terms 'never entered his head.'[6] It is therefore all the more remarkable that he did in fact reveal number and geometry, and indeed astronomy, which fit a Pythagorean interpretation. It is all the more convincing insofar as he found what he was not looking for and what he did not recognize and what it has taken others to identify, using the results of his objective and disinterested research in an unaltered and unadjusted form.

It is my contention, based on Thom's work, that just because the builders of the stone circles knew their astronomy and geometry to an advanced degree, does not mean that their ultimate reasons for hauling all those huge stones around were scientific in the modern sense, any more than it does for the builders of the Great Pyramid, the Greek temples, or Glastonbury Abbey. In other words, I believe that the best way of understanding our megalithic heritage is to see it as the earliest example in Europe, and one of the earliest examples in the world, of the tradition of sacred architecture which is associated in the west with the names of Pythagoras and Plato.

Many examples could be given of this symbolic use of number and geometry in the stone circles, but the most obvious and pertinent for our purposes, come from the only instances where Thom

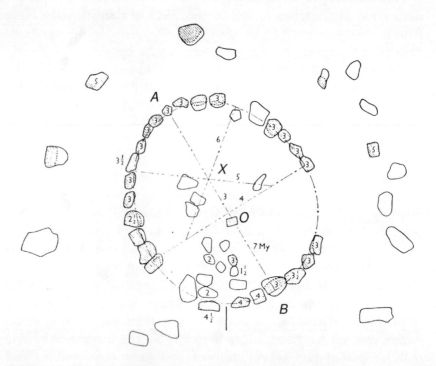

Figure 46. Druid Temple

does give the geometrical construction as he believed it to be. These are the egg-shaped circles which, as mentioned, he thought were constructed round Pythagorean triangles. Let us submit them to a Pythagorean interpretation.

Thom demonstrated that there are three types of egg-shaped circles: those constructed round two triangles whose short sides are adjacent, such as Druid Temple near Inverness; those whose triangles have their heights adjacent, such as Allan Water in the Scottish Borders, and those which have their triangles with hypotenuses adjacent, such as Borrowston Rig near Lauder.[7] What did they symbolize?

In ancient symbolism the egg universally represented the origin from which all life came; the germ and potentiality of creation and the womb of all existence. A modern example of this is the Easter egg.

Pythagorean triangles themselves, according to J.C. Cooper in

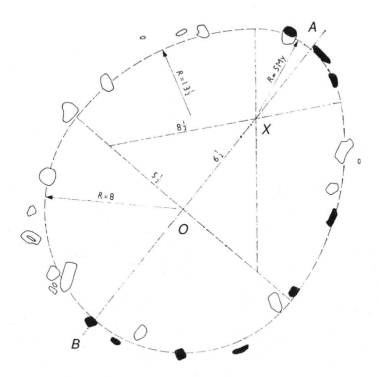

Figure 47. Allan Water

An Illustrated Encyclopaedia of Traditional Symbolism, symbolized body, mind and spirit in tune with the cosmos.[8] This interpretation is perfectly expressed by the numbers and ratios in Thom's constructions. In Druid Temple, the major axis *AB* is made up of *AX* = 6 MY, *XO* = 3 MY, *OB* = 7 MY, so the total length is 16 MY. If we divide it at X we get two parts *AX* = 6 and *XB* = 10. Therefore the ratios can be said to be 6 to 10 to 16. These are instantly recognizable as the ratios of the three numbers which Vitruvius told us were held to be most perfect among the ancients. If we now divide by 2 we get 3, 5 and 8 which are immediately identifiable as the Fibonacci numbers implicit in the gematria of *Iesous Christos.* It will be recalled that *Iesous* was 888 which is 3 × 296, *Christos,* was 1480 which is 5 × 296 and *Iesous Christos* was 2368 which is 8 × 296. Does this mean that in some extraordinary way, we are back in the world charted for us earlier by Christopher Butler, Simone Weil, Vernon Jenkins, Bligh Bond,

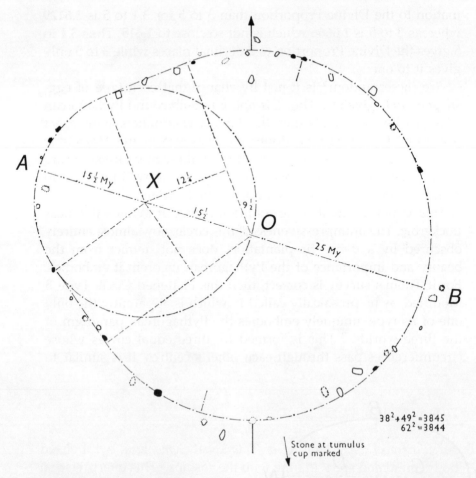

$$38^2 + 49^2 = 3845$$
$$62^2 = 3844$$

Stone at tumulus
cup marked

Figure 48. Borrowston Rig

Simcox Lea and John Michell? An examination of the other circles would indicate that we are.

Turning to Allan Water, the three radii used to mark out the ring, are given by Thom as 5 MY, 8 MY and 13.5 MY. It seems extraordinary that he didn't notice that 5, 8 and 13 are also numbers in the Fibonacci series and 'never identified Phi in megalithic geometry,'[9] but he didn't. It is the same in his plan for Borrowston Rig where radius *AX* = 15.5 MY and radius *OB* = 25 MY. Divide by 5 and the Fibonacci 5 and 8 appear, or very nearly. The fact that the ratio is not 3:5 precisely but 3.1 to 5 suggests some doubt about a Fibonacci interpretation. Nevertheless, it is extraordinary that the ratio 3.1 to 5 gives a more accurate approximation to the Divine Proportion than 3 to 5 for 3.1 to 5 is 1.6129 whereas 3 to 5 is 1.6666 which is not so close to 1.618. Thus 3.1 to 5 gives the Divine Proportion to 2 decimal places while 3 to 5 only gives it to one.

Are these random? Is it just by chance that each type of egg-shaped circle given by Thom, is not only built round Pythagorean triangles but also embodies the Fibonacci numbers with exact precision? For those who doubt the existence of the Megalithic Yard, the answer must be yes. But I think these measurements are too precise and fit a symbolic interpretation too well for there to be much doubt about the intention of the builders.

This is borne out if we examine the ring at Whitcastles near Lockerbie. The unimpressiveness of this circle, now almost entirely obscured by a dense fir plantation, does not detract from the beauty and importance of the Pythagorean theorem it embodies. For if Thom's survey is correct, then this Flattened Circle Type B Modified, as he prosaically called it, which is apparently the only one of its type, uniquely embodies the Pythagorean paradigm of the three worlds.[10] This is formed by three equal circles whose circumferences pass through each other's centres. It is similar to

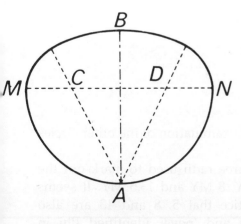

Figure 49.
Flattened Circle, Type B Modified.
MC/MN = ¼
AB/MN = 0.8091
perimeter/MN = 2.8746

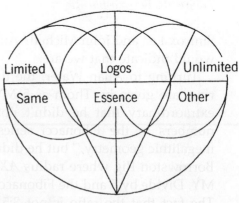

Figure 50. Logos-Essence Symbolism.

the construction drawn in the last chapter to show the connection between the Lady Chapel at Glastonbury and the Bluestone Circles at Stonehenge, except that here the three circles are equally spaced. It is moreover similar to the *vesica piscis* and can be called the double vesica. Like the vesica it represents the Logos in relation to the Limited and Unlimited but in this case the Logos, the third term, is not potential, it is fully realized. It therefore represents the Triad, which was also called *Harmonia*, Harmony. Its three terms for the Pythagoreans were called the Limited, the Unlimited and the Logos while for Plato they were the Same, the Other and the Essence.

Whitcastles is one of the many rings for which Thom did not give the actual geometric construction. It was left to my colleague Colin Forsyth to deduce from Thom's calculations that if $AB/MN = 0.8091$ when $MN = 1$, then when $MN = 2$, $AB = 2 \times 0.8091 = 1.6182$ which equals the Divine Proportion to three places of decimals! He was also the one who deduced that it could be constructed round three equal circles, from Thom's calculation that $MC/MN = \frac{1}{4}$. The spectacular accuracy of this is confirmed from

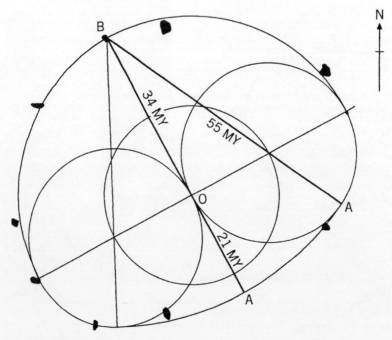

Figure 51. Whitcastles

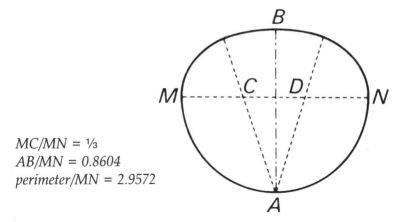

MC/MN = ⅓
AB/MN = 0.8604
$perimeter/MN$ = 2.9572

Figure 52. Flattened Circle, Type B

Thom's site plan, where he gives *BO* as 34 MY. This means that
OA = 21 MY and *BA* = 55 MY.[11] But 21, 34 and 55 are also Fibonacci numbers. Thus Whitcastles, like Druid Temple, Allan Water
and Borrowston Rig, embodies the Divine Proportion. The symbolism could not be clearer, more consistent or more crucial. It is
difficult not to conclude that it was also consciously planned.

Turning from Thom's Flattened Circle Type B Modified to what
he called merely Flattened Circle Type B, an equally arresting yet
familiar figure emerges for, as Keith Critchlow in *Time Stands Still*
and John Michell in *Old Stones of Land's End* both point out, this is
constructed round a *vesica piscis*.[12] Once again Thom does not show
how it was constructed geometrically but gives the necessary clue
by telling us that *MC/MN* = ⅓. From this it can be deduced that *C*
and *D* are the centres of two equal circles whose circumferences
pass through each others centres. Furthermore, Thom gives the
ratio of axes *MN/AB* as 1 to 0.8604. If *MN* is taken as 2, then
AB = 1.72 which is close enough to 1.732 or √3.[13] Critchlow's analysis of Long Meg in Cumbria is an example of this.[14]

Thus once again we find ourselves back in the familiar world of
the Pythagorean paradigm of Potential Logos, the *vesica piscis*, the
√3 ratio in the 37 × 64 of *Iesous Christos* and the Gothic plan. The
only difference is that we have discovered it to be embodied in the
Flattened Type B circles of megalithic Britain. Does this make it
easier to believe that there might possibly have been a connection between the notional vesica within which the Inner Bluestone

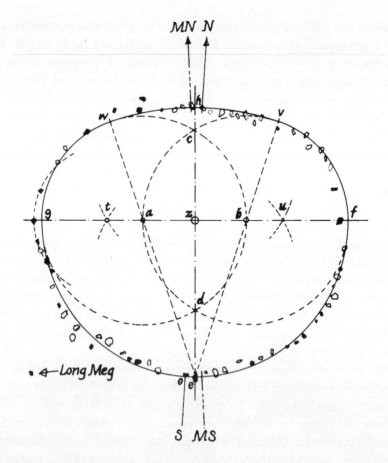

Figure 53. Long Meg

horseshoe may have been constructed at Stonehenge, and the
vesica which Bligh Bond identified in the Lady Chapel at Glastonbury? Is there any significance in the fact that the vesica, with its
√3 ratio, is only known to have been used for planning in two
architectural traditions in the world, the megalithic and the Gothic
and that these, though separated by over 3,000 years, arose on the
very same soil of North Western Europe?

From this excursion into the broad field of Professor Thom's
researches, we can conclude that not only is the geometry of the
stone circles Pythagorean, but that this is so much the case that
one might suspect that there was indeed some actual historic
connection between those who built them and those who 2,000
years later in Greece, gathered round Pythagoras himself. If we

follow the logic of geometric proof *per se*, then this possibility can be legitimately entertained. Yet to do so would be to imply that Pythagoras gave his name to a system of numero-geometric knowledge which he had inherited and not discovered. But this is precisely what Clement of Alexandria implied when he told us that philosophy 'flourished in antiquity among the barbarians, shedding its light over the nations and afterwards it came to Greece.' It was argued earlier that what Clement called philosophy could be called the philosophy-wisdom tradition of which Pythagoreanism formed a considerable part. If this was the case then all that we have discovered about the Pythagoreanism of megalithic Britain could give substance to the fact that both Clement and Diogenes Laertius list 'the Druids among the Gauls ... and the philosophers of the Kelts' amongst those who had this philosophy-wisdom before it came to Greece. It would also help to explain the claim which Clement made, based on Alexander Polyhistor's 'On the Pythagorean Symbols,' that 'Pythagoras was a hearer of the Galatae' which could be construed as 'student of the Gauls or Druids.'

It was of course no secret that Pythagoras had learnt his philosophy-wisdom from others, and not invented it himself. As noted earlier, his later biographers tell of him spending many years travelling to all the known wisdom centres of the ancient world particularly Egypt and Babylon. Indeed, since Alexander Polyhistor also says that 'Pythagoras was a pupil of Nazaratus the Assyrian' and that he was a 'hearer of the Brahmins' as well as the Galatae, we might reasonably assume that he had learnt from the wise men of *all* the countries listed by Clement and Diogenes Laertius as being illuminated by philosophy before the Greeks. As discussed in Chapter 7, Pythagoras was seen as the one through whom the wisdom of the barbarian countries was brought to Greece. Among those from whom it was believed he had inherited it were clearly the Druids and the Celtic philosophers. The implication from this would appear to be that the Druids were Pythagoreans and that they were themselves the heirs and inheritors of the proto-Pythagoreanism which we have identified in the megalithic stone circles. Neither of these two propositions are as tenuous as they appear. Both have in fact now become far more substantial than when they were first demonstrated in Chapter 6, 'The Pythagorean Option.'

Assuming therefore that we can take Druid-Pythagoreanism and Druid-megalithic continuity of culture, as having been reasonably proved, we can go on to ask if there is any actual evidence for an historic or legendary link between the Greek Pythagoreans and ancient Britain. Strangely enough there is and it is focused on the presumed identity of Pythagoras himself.

17
Apollo of the Hyperboreans

Although there is widespread ignorance today about the true identity of Pythagoras, in the ancient world it was generally accepted that he was, as Aelian said, 'of higher than mortal origin' and that he was, in fact, no less than the incarnation of a god. There also appears to have been a general agreement as to which god he embodied for Aelian also states 'Aristotle says that Pythagoras was hailed by the people of Croton as Hyperborean Apollo' and Diogenes Laertius asserts that 'it was the opinion of his disciples that he was Apollo, come from the Hyperboreans.' Iamblichus also claimed that 'One of the *acousmata* was "Who are you, Pythagoras?" For they say he is the Hyperborean Apollo.' Thus there seems to be no question that, whatever or whoever else they thought he was, the ancients took him to be the embodiment of Hyperborean Apollo. Commenting on these quotations, J.A. Philip in *Pythagoras and Early Pythagoreanism* explains that:

> Pythagoras is said to be Apollo because Apollo is the god of purification, and probably also because he is the law-giver. He is also called 'Hyperborean Apollo' because the Apollo of Delphi comes from a land in the distant north where he is perfectly worshipped.[1]

This classical consensus as to the divine origin of Pythagoras' identity raises the questions: who were the Hyperboreans and where did they come from? Scholars have varied greatly in their answers. Stuart Piggott, somewhat predictably, following Heroditus, believes they were purely mythical in the sense that they didn't really exist, and that their location was a Never-Never-Land comparable to the Elysian plains or Homer's realm of Rhadamanthus. He has good reason for this since numerous authors describe Hyperborea in idealistic, mystical terms such as Pindar who says that it was never deserted by the Muse, that everywhere girls were dancing, the sound of harps and flutes were to be heard, its people knew neither sickness or old age and instead of working or fighting, spent their time feasting. Pliny likewise claims:

> ... their country is open upon the sun, of a blissful and pleasant temperature, void of all noisome wind and hurtful airs. Their habitations be in woods and groves, where they worship the gods both by themselves, and in companies and congregations: no discord know they, no sickness are they acquainted with.

On the basis of such fanciful descriptions Piggott can call the Hyperboreans 'the most distinguished of all claimants for the title of Noble Savage in antiquity' and can dismiss those ancient and modern scholars who have been under the illusion of their historical actuality as having fallen victim to the dreaded 'soft primitivism' which, as we saw earlier, he considered to have been such a scourge among the Alexandrians in their exultation of the Druids.[2]

For the Greek traveller and priest of Apollo, Aristeas, however, in the seventh century BC, Hyperborea was a this-wordly place. He had heard of this legendary land whose people lived peaceful, happy, virtuous and vegetarian lives worshipping Apollo, and he set out to find it. His journey took him north-east to Sythia where he was told that he should go no further and that Hyperborea lay to the north beyond gold-bearing mountains. According to Ward Rutherford in *Celtic Mythology*, these must have been the Altai range which, since earliest times, have been associated with high magic and shamanism:

> It is from the peoples living there that we get the word 'shaman' — and surely if anyone can claim to have a special relationship with the divine, it is the shaman. It is the region of the Bon magicians who helped to shape Chinese Taoism and Hindu Tantrism as well as Tibetan Buddhism, and within it stands the sacred Mount Meru, dwelling place of the Seven Sages, mentioned in the *Rig Veda*. It is a great centre ... A place where our own world and the Other World meet. Indeed Mount Meru is actually called 'The Centre of the World'.[3]

Rutherford has been greatly influenced in his opinion as to the Altaic location of Hyperborea by Geoffrey Ashe, who, in *The Ancient Wisdom* and other more recent publications such as *Avalonian Quest*, has made out a persuasive case for it having originated in that area. Although there have been scholars who have equated it with many other lands such as Libya and China, it is Ashe's theory that would appear to carry most weight because it goes together with an assumption that the body of esoteric knowledge originally associated with that zone, later became diffused over a vast geographical area, an assumption which seems to fit the similarities between Taoism, Tantrism, Tibetan Buddhism and Shamanism as Rutherford has indicated. Summarizing the Western aspect of his theory in *Mythology of the British Isles*, Ashe says:

After Aristeas, more Greeks wrote of the Hyperboreans. Losing sight of the pioneer explorer, and the Altaic home he had identified, they shifted them westwards and confused them with other peoples. They had no serious grounds for doing so, yet this gradual extension over an immense area matched the apparent drift of Altaic influence. Hyperboreans were located in Scythia, and on the upper Danube, and in the Alps. They turned up in the Celtic west and showed signs of becoming Celtic.[4]

Thus according to Ashe, the Greeks located Hyperborea further and further west, which corresponded to 'the apparent drift of Altaic influence.' This explains why, by the third century BC, Diodorus Siculus, following the fifth century traveller Hecateus, could claim that Hyperborea was an 'island opposite Gaul' which, as Robert Graves in *The Greek Myths* asserts, along with others, is 'clearly identified' as Britain.[5] The conclusion which Ward Rutherford makes, following Ashe, is that if the Hyperboreans were 'an actual as opposed to an Other World people, that those in Britain, could have been a migrating group who preceded the Celts in the British Isles.'[6] This seems very reasonable for although Hyperborea may well have been originally located in the Altai mountains, by the fifth century BC it *could* well have been identified as Britain as evidenced by Hecateus quoted by Diodorus.

Geoffrey Ashe's theory may be right in substance but there may also be evidence arising out of the Hecateus-Diodorus description which would boost the case for a much earlier association of Hyperborea with Britain. If we bear in mind all that has already been said in this enquiry about the Druids and the Pythagoreans, it could be argued that although the Hecateus-Diodorus source is regarded as late, it may nevertheless be based on a tradition which is much older than is usually supposed, as a close examination of the text appears to reveal. This is what Diodorus says:

> Now for our part, since we have seen fit to make mention of the regions of Asia which lie to the north, we feel that it will not be foreign to our purpose to discuss the legendary accounts of the Hyperboreans. Of those who have written about the ancient myths, Hecateus and certain others say that in the regions beyond the land of the Celts (i.e. Gaul) there lies in the ocean an island no smaller than Sicily. This island, the account continues, is situated in the north and is inhabited by the Hyperboreans, who are called by that name because their home is beyond the point whence the north wind (Boreas) blows; and the island is both fertile and productive of every crop, and since it has an unusually temperate climate, it produces two harvests every year.[7]

Diodorus then goes on to mention the legends that Hecateus tells regarding Apollo's link with Hyperborea:

> Moreover, the following legend is told concerning it: Leto (the mother by Zeus, of Apollo and Artemis) was born on this island, and for that reason Apollo is honoured among them above all other gods; and the inhabitants are looked upon as priests of Apollo, after a manner, since daily they praise this god continuously in song and honour him exceedingly.[8]

This is obviously the source, or an example of the type of source from which the belief grew up quoted by Aristotle, Aelian, Diogenes Laertius, Iamblichus and other classical authorities cited above that Pythagoras was the incarnation of Hyperborean Apollo. The rest of the Diodorus-Hercateus section is of such importance that it must be examined sentence by sentence. The next paragraph speaks of an ancient friendship between the Hyperboreans and the

Figure 54. Precinct of the Hyperborean Maidens, Delos

Greeks, as seen in the visit of Abaris. This is the Abaris referred to by Martin Hengel in connection with Pythagorean sources, cited in Chapter 12:

> The Hyperboreans also have a language, we are informed, which is peculiar to them, and are most friendly disposed towards the Greeks, and especially towards the Athenians and the Delians, who have inherited this good-will from most ancient times. The myth also relates that certain Greeks visited the Hyperboreans and left behind them there costly votive offerings bearing inscriptions in Greek letters. And in the same way Abaris, a Hyperborean, came to Greece in ancient times and renewed the good-will and kinship of his people to the Delians.[9]

In connection with these ancient reciprocated visits between the Delians and the Hyperboreans, it is fascinating to note that to this day on Delos, near the ruins of the precinct of Apollo, can be seen a small, walled enclosure labelled the 'Graves of the Hyperborean Virgins.' Geoffrey Ashe in *The Ancient Wisdom* picks up on this:

> There was also a story told at Delos of two Hyperborean maidens, called Arge or Hekaerge, and Opis. They came at the time when the Apollo-Artemis cult was founded there and died on the island. Their supposed tomb was in or behind, Artemis' temple, and semi-divine honours were paid to them.[10]

The strength of this tradition is also attested to in a recent study *Karistos: City State and Country Town* by William Philip Chapman. Karistos, on a neighbouring island, was evidently a staging post on the pilgrimage from Hyperborea to Delos for he writes 'Meeting Hall in Karistos — there are archaeological remains where a priest presided over the Hyperborean offerings. Heroditus tells us that they were placed on a ship at Karistos annually and conveyed to Tinos and then to Delos.' He also says 'The identity of Karistos as a city may have been strengthened by a tradition of Northern immigration and Dryopian descent closely connected with the worship of Apollo.'[11]

The visit of Abaris is mentioned so often in the biographies of Pythagoras, that it is important to find out more about him before going on with the quotation from Diodorus. Iamblichus mentions this 'Scythian who came from the Hyperboreans' to Pythagoras as an example of the discretion the Master used in the correction and education of visitors from other lands 'according to their individual abilities.' He explains that because Abaris was an old man and was 'unskilled and uninitiated in the Greek learning,' Pythagoras 'did not compel him to wade through introductory theorems, the period of silence, and long lectures, not to mention other trials but considered him to be fit as an immediate listener to his doctrines, and instructed him in the shortest way, in his treatise *On Nature*, and one *On the Gods*.'[12] All of this confirms the opinion of the Alexandrian school of commentators on the Druids, that they learnt their philosophy from Pythagoras. Iamblichus continues: 'At that time he was returning from Greece to his country, in order to consecrate the gold which he had collected, to the God of his temple among the Hyperboreans. As therefore he was passing through Italy, he saw Pythagoras, and identified him as the God of whom he was the priest.' On account of this startling identification and in homage, Abaris gave Pythagoras a sacred dart or arrow, which he accepted 'without amazement ... as if he really was a God.'[13]

This dart or arrow which he gave Pythagoras seems to have been rather like a witch's broomstick because it had the power to carry Abaris over inaccesible places 'such as rivers, lakes, marshes, mountains and the like.' It also gave him power to expel winds and pestilence from cities. In another passage, Iamblichus tells us that Abaris was called an *air-walker* because of this apparent ability to fly on it. Many people came to think that Pythagoras could do the same because he was seen chatting to his disciples on the same day in two widely differing places. This passage makes the dart seem like a simple explanation for the actual known phenomena of bilocation reported by Yogis in the east and also among contemporary gurus such as Sai Baba and the Catholic mystic the late Padre Pio. It is also possibly linked to the traditional power among Celtic seers of activating their 'co-walker' or doppelgänger.

If we can legitimately interpret Abaris' dart as a simple, graphic explanation for his ability to levitate, travel out of his body, activate his co-walker, or whatever particular psychic gift one likes to call it, then perhaps there is an equally intelligible explanation of the story of Pythagoras' golden thigh which is mentioned in several places, but particularly in connection with Abaris: 'Then he took Abaris aside, and showed him his golden thigh, as an indication that he was not wholly mistaken in his estimate of his real nature.' Porphyry, telling the same story says: 'It is well known that he showed his golden thigh to Abaris the Hyperborean, to confirm him in the opinion that he was the Hyperborean Apollo, whose priest Abaris was.'[14] It has been suggested by various authors that the golden thigh might have been a birthmark, a tattoo or some sort of hip replacement, all of which are too mundane explanations. Thinking along more symbolic Pythagorean lines, it is noteworthy that in the tradition of ancient Chinese mathematics dating from *c.*1100 BC, Chou Kung, the author of one of the oldest scientific treatises, writes about the *Chow-pi*,[15] the 'Thigh-bone of Chow.' This odd nomenclature was derived from two characters (composite letters) Keu and Koo which were used to designate the base and height of a triangle and which meant originally the Leg and the Thigh. Although this may seem a distinctly outré reference, it is with surprise that we learn that the *Chow-pi* is in fact an essay on what we call in the West, the theorem of Pythagoras.

If we were to entertain such a parallel symbolism, then 'golden thigh' would be a code for 'most important theorem.' In addition, when we remember how 'the section' came to be called 'the divine proportion' or 'the golden section' or 'the golden rule,' the use of the word 'golden' might indicate that Pythagoras revealed the innermost secret of his sect, the φ (phi) ratio, and how it had 'magic properties' as in the triangle of base 1, height $\sqrt{\varphi}$ and hypotenuse φ which, as explained in Chapter 10, was the secret geometry behind the Great Pyramid's proportions. Fanciful as this might seem, we must get used to the idea that just as the Greek myths spoke a symbolic language which was separate from but also linked to the abstractions of the philosophers, so in the life of Pythagoras, the legends are separate from but also linked to mathematical and cosmological secrets.

These stories of Abaris are enough to confirm a link between Pythagoras and the Hyperboreans which, although stated as if it was that of only teacher and grateful disciple, was also a two-way exchange of wisdom for, as we have seen, Abaris had mantic arts to teach Pythagoras. As Ward Rutherford says in *Pythagoras* 'One can hazard the opinion that Abaris was himself a psychic medium and if he did not actually help Pythagoras develop his talents, he at least recognized him as one like himself.'[16] Thus already we have an indication that not only was Pythagoras a 'hearer of the Galatae,' as Clement of Alexandria claimed, but also that through Abaris, the ancient Greeks shared some distant kinship with the ancient Britons. We now return to finish the section on the Hyperboreans in Diodorus Siculus:

> The account is also given that the god visits the island
> every nineteen years, the period in which the return of the
> stars to the same place in the heavens is accomplished; and
> for this reason the nineteen-year period is called by the
> Greeks the 'year of Meton.' At the time of this appearance
> of the god he both plays on the cithera and dances continu-
> ously the night through from the vernal equinox until the

rising of the Pleiades, expressing in this manner his delight in his successes.[17]

This passage, if taken literally, yields as little comprehension as the notion that Pythagoras' golden thigh was a birthmark, tattoo or hip replacement. It is intriguing but not illuminating. If however we speculate symbolically as to its meaning, much may be revealed.

Giorgio de Santillana and Hertha von Dechend, in *Hamlet's Mill*, were led to startling conclusions in their world-wide search for the origin of mythology, which can perhaps help us understand why Apollo should travel to Hyperborea for a special moon festival every nineteen years. Summarizing their findings, Santillana and von Dechend declared:

> First, all the great myths of the world have a common origin. Next, the geography of myth is not that of the earth. The places referred to in myth are in the heavens and the actions are those of celestial bodies. Myth, in short, was a language for the perpetuation of a vast and complex body of astronomical knowledge.[18]

Now although these assertions are surprising, they are also in a sense self-evident because we all know that the Greek and Roman gods and goddesses were often either planets or constellations. For instance, the planets were Zeus or Jupiter, Chronos or Saturn, Hermes or Mercury etcetera. Also the constellations of the Zodiac, though ruled by planetary divinities, had divine characteristics of their own.

Santillana and von Dechend scarcely mention Apollo but their main proposition that 'the places referred to in myth are in the heavens and the actions are those of celestial bodies' is worth applying to Apollo. If we began to adopt this celestial, astronomical symbolism to what Diodorus and Hecateus tell us about him coming to Hyperborea for the festival of the Metonic Year, the first radical step we would have to take would be to propose that, in some sense, he *was* the Metonic Year; that is to say, his actions 'are those of celestial bodies,' in this case, the moon synchronizing with the sun. Ward Rutherford in *Celtic Mythology* believes this to be the case and points to a connection with Stonehenge and also the Druids. Commenting on this Diodorus-Hecateus passage he says:

The reference to nineteen years is significant as this is the period of the Metonic cycle, named after the Greek astronomer Meton, who used it as a means of bringing lunar and solar years into synchronicity. Nineteen years is roughly the period between one eclipse and another (it is actually 18 years 11⅓ days). Professor Fred Hoyle has shown that the so-called Aubrey Holes at Stonehenge, the circle of fifty-six pits outside the trilithons, may have been designed for eclipse prediction by using a system of markers and, though the movement of these is quite complex, they could have operated with considerable accuracy. Furthermore, this may well explain Apollo's nineteen-year incarnations, for if the period is that between eclipses, what could be more logical — the sun being absent from the sky — than that it was because its ruling deity was visiting his earthly worshippers? But the Coligny calendar — the key archaeological evidence of Druidic astronomy — is also based on the nineteen-year or Metonic cycle and, as Piggott points out, it may well have been that the training course, which Caesar said lasted twenty years, actually lasted nineteen, thus corresponding with the Druid's epoch.[19]

This passage from Rutherford is most relevant to our enquiry for in one paragraph he has linked the Apollo of the Metonic cycle with the Druids, and with Stonehenge.

Fred Hoyle's theory that the 56 Aubrey Holes were used for eclipse prediction, like other theories, has been contested. Nevertheless it is significant, as Robin Heath points out in *The Key to Stonehenge*, that 56 is a solar and a lunar number if the solar year is taken as 364 days, for $28(56 \div 2) \times 13 = 364$. Thus, if the sun marker is moved 2 holes every 13 days and the moon marker 2 holes each day, the Sun pole will complete exactly one circuit of the Aubrey Holes each year and the Moon pole exactly 13.[20]

In this connection, it is odd that the Essenes were also known to have used a 364 day Calender as detailed by Yigael Yadin in *The Temple Scroll*.[21] Scholars have usually called this a solar year as distinct from the lunisolar one, observed by mainstream Judaism. Actually, as described by Robin Heath above, the 364 day year is the only one which synchronizes the solar with the lunar year with

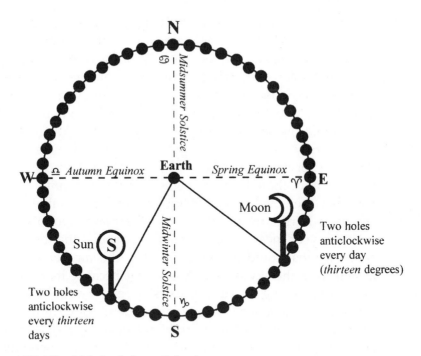

Figure 55. The 56-hole Aubrey Calendar

any degree of precision. The Essenes claimed that they observed an older, more sacred system which had been subverted by the Temple priests in Jerusalem. How old was it and where had it come from? Do the speculations which follow in this chapter and the next offer possible answers?

Even if this interpretation of the Aubrey Holes might seem a little strained, there is general agreement that the 40 Causeway Post Holes mark the most northerly point of the moon's cycle, while the Heel Stone, whose orientation is only sightly different, approximates closely to the midsummer sunrise. Thus, however contentious the purpose of the Aubrey Holes may be, it can be claimed that, since the Post Holes and the Heel Stone also date from Stonehenge I circa 3000, the earliest astronomical purpose of Stonehenge was to attempt to synchronize the moon with the sun. How precise this was is debatable, but in essence it would appear that modern archaeological research, particularly Archaeo-astronomy confirms the Diodorus-Hecateus description if Apollo, in this sense, is taken to be a mythological personification of the lunisolar cycle.

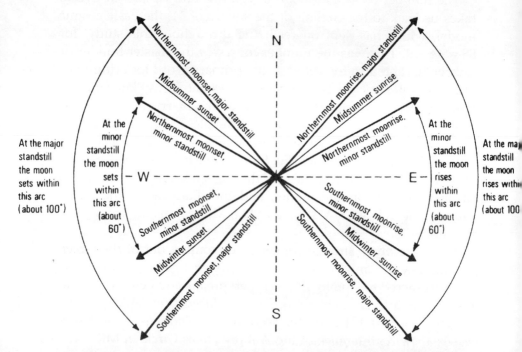

Figure 56. Directions of sunrise, sunset, moonrise and moonset at Stonehenge.

Strangely this lunisolar synchronization is echoed in the Hebrew gematria of the Lesser Canon because, as shown earlier, *chodesh* and *lebanah*, which mean new moon and full moon respectively, both have the number 33, while *shemesh* sun, is 55. These two together give 88 which equals *Apollon* in the Greek Lesser Canon. It may seem highly inappropriate to jump from Greek mythology to Hebrew gematria and then back again, but enough should have been said by now to indicate that the numerology of the two languages is much more closely linked than has been realized, particularly in relation to the Lesser, as distinct from the Greater Canon. Now that we have established, in the last chapter, that the Pythagorean or proto-Pythagorean system of numerical knowledge can be traced back as far as the stone circles of megalithic Britain to at least 3000 BC, it should be legitimate to conjecture that both languages later arose as distinct, but related, expressions of the same ancient wisdom. Precisely *how* this happened is not clear but *that* it was so, is attested by the many numero-geometric connections that have been noted.

The number 88 as sun-moon in Hebrew and *Apollon* in Greek, takes us back to the circling of the square of 11, the basic cosmic model, which has kept on recurring throughout this study, for 88 = 44 × 2. This was the number for *tektōn* the master builder or 'carpenter' and also for *arithmos*, the primary word for arithmetic, number and numeration which Simone Weil told us Plato equated with Logos. Now we can also see it as the marriage of sun and moon, the masculine and feminine principles.

It is also extraordinary how closely these simple numbers agree with the actual measurements of Stonehenge because we can recall that the inner circumference of the Sarsen circle is 45 MR, as distinct from 44 in the model, and the diameter of the Outer Bluestone Circle is 29 MY ÷ 2.5 = 11.6 MR, as distinct from 11 in the model.

There are other strange coincidences coming out of the Greek gematria which might indicate that Stonehenge was indeed the precinct sacred to Apollo of the Hyperboreans and hence to Pythagoras. For instance, Hyperboreans is *Huperboreoi* which, in the Lesser Canon, is 131 and this, according to Thom, is 'almost precisely' the circumference of the Aubrey Holes Circle in MR.

The temple of Apollo is given by Liddell and Scott as *Apollonion* which in the Lesser Canon is 128. This is 2^7 ($2 \times 2 \times 2 \times 2 \times 2 \times 2 \times 2$) and is the number associated with the seventh octave and hence the Pythagorean Comma, the musical discrepancy between tuning in octaves and tuning in fifths, an harmonic anomaly which fascinated the ancients. By analogy this was taken as the microcosmic expression of the macrocosmic discrepancy between the lunar and

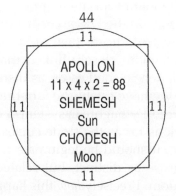

Figure 57. *Apollon as Sun:Moon ratio*

the solar year as David Tame points out in *The Secret Power of Music*.[22] So once again, it could be argued that this number might represent a correspondence between the synchronization of the sun with the moon in the gematria of *Apollonian* and between the Post Holes and Heel Stone alignments at Stonehenge.

Putting *Apollonion* together with *Huperboreoi*, we get 128 plus 131 which equals 259. This factorizes as 37×7 which brings together 37, the number for *chokmah* wisdom in the Hebrew Lesser Canon with 7, the number associated with the Moon's quarter, for $7 \times 4 = 28$ the lunar month. Not only this but 37 can also be associated with Apollo. Apollo as distinct from Apollon, the variant spelling, as noted earlier, is 74 in the Greek Lesser Canon. 74 as 2×37 can claim the same root prime as *chokmah* and thus, according to the logic of gematria, can be considered to be built or founded on it, as indeed can 37×64, the number for Jesus Christ. According to this interpretation wisdom, as the expression of the root prime 37 itself, would have come first. Apollo, as 74 or 37×2 would have been a development of this and Jesus Christ as 2368 or 37×64 would have been a still later embodiment. Since the mean diameter of the Sarsen Circle could be taken to be 'the great measure' of Stonehenge III, and this is 37 MY, it could be said that the dedication would have been to wisdom first and then to Apollo. John Michell gives the circumference of the outer bank as 370 MY, which would agree with this from the earlier period of Stonehenge I. So also would the fact that if we add the definite article to *Apollonion Huperboreoi*, making it *To Apollonion Huperboreoi*, we get 296 which is 37×8. This is a very powerful number whose symbolism could lead us in a number of directions, but which for our present purposes can be taken either as a square of 74 ($74 \times 4 = 296$) representing Apollo, or a circled square of 37. Of the two the latter is perhaps the more significant because it is yet another expression of the marriage of heaven and earth in relation to the root prime for wisdom, Apollo, Jesus Christ, and the Sarsen Circle. Either way it is the gematria of 'The Temple of Apollo-Hyperboreans' and it is surely remarkable that, as a whole and in its constituent parts it coincides with such significant measurements at Stonehenge.

Is it remarkable, or is it to be expected? We have already shown that Stonehenge, like other lesser-known rings of megalithic Britain, fits a proto-Pythagorean analysis, implying that proto-

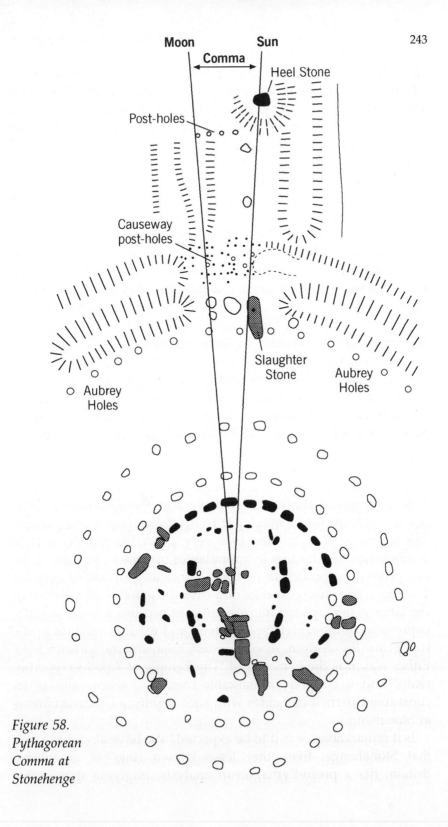

Figure 58.
Pythagorean
Comma at
Stonehenge

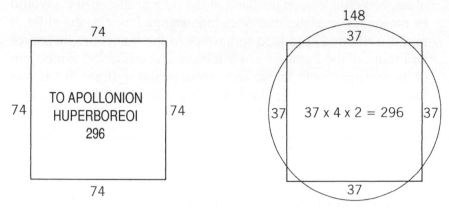

Figure 59. To Apollonion Huperboreoi: The Temple of Apollo of the Hyperboreans

Pythagoreans built it. We have also shown that according to the legends recorded by Diodorus and Hecateus, there were many links between ancient Britain and ancient Greece. Perhaps it is now time to propose that behind these legends there lay real historical events; that hidden within the mythology, there lay truths which were too complex and primeval to communicate in any other way. Perhaps it is time to propose that the link between the proto-Pythagoreans who built Stonehenge and Pythagoras himself can best be explained by the belief of his disciples, that he was indeed 'Apollo, come from the Hyperboreans' and that Abaris' recognition that he was the God of whom he, Abaris was priest, was correct. Perhaps Diodorus was accurate in his account of Hecateus, and perhaps Hecateus was recording some actual truth regarding the transmission of an ancient Apollonian wisdom from Hyperborea to Greece. The fact that Pythagoras, from other authorities, was regarded as a 'hearer of the Druids of the Gauls and the philosophers of the Celts' along with all the other sources from which he is reputed to have learned, would suggest this. So would the sheer age of Stonehenge. In fact the age factor alone would be enough not only to indicate that the Pythagorean wisdom was brought from Hyperborea to Greece, but also that it may have originated there because Stonehenge I is usually dated to around 3000 BC, which is considerably earlier than the Great Pyramid's usual dating of around 2600 BC. These dates are contested by some who claim that the Pyramids if not the stone circles are much, much older. Nevertheless, on the basis of the current consensus, it would be reasonable to claim that since Stonehenge I may be the older, it might well have been held to have been the home, origin, source and fount of the Pythagorean tradition. The numerical symbolism of its measurements, as we have seen, would indicate that it was indeed the Temple of Apollo of the Hyperboreans. This would also seem to be precisely what Diodorus and Hecateus is indicating when he goes on to speak of Apollo's temple in the final paragraph of his famous passage.

> And there is also on the island both a magnificent sacred precinct of Apollo and a notable temple which is adorned with many votive offerings and is spherical in shape. Furthermore, a city is there which is sacred to this God and the majority of its inhabitants are players on the citheria; and these continually play on this instrument in the temple and sing hymns of praise to the god glorifying his deeds.[23]

Wherever the 'sacred precinct' and the 'city' might have been, it is reasonable to suppose that the 'notable temple' which is 'spherical in shape' refers to Stonehenge. It has been objected that Stonehenge is not spherical but circular, but couldn't the Greek words *sphairoeide to schemati* which are used, mean that it pertained not to an architectural dome but to the sphere of the heavens? In the light of all that has been claimed for Stonehenge as an observatory, I believe that it could.

This being so, we may conclude that Stonehenge was indeed the Temple of Hyperborean Apollo and that as such, together with the other monuments of the megalithic civilization of which it was the chief, it was considered to be the home, origin, source and fount of the Pythagorean tradition.

It was argued in Chapter 12 'The Essene Connection,' that Jesus, whatever else he was, was most probably an Essene Pythagorean. What if he were not so much *a* Pythagorean but *the* Pythagorean? What if he was Pythagoras himself — the *new* Pythagoras? The striking similarities between his teachings and those of the Essenes, and between the Essenes and the Pythagoreans as outlined, would strongly suggest this possibility. If he came to embody, fulfil and renew the tradition of Gentile as well as biblical philosophy-wisdom, of which the Pythagorean system was an integral part, then it is just as permissible to suggest that he was the new Pythagoras as the new Joshua or the new Moses. And if there is any truth in this, then couldn't it also be suggested that he was the new Apollo of whom Pythagoras was said to have been an incarnation? This identification was in fact not unknown among the early Church fathers. And if he could in some sense be said to be the new Apollo, couldn't he also be said to be the new *Hyperborean* Apollo? If Pythagoras was generally thought to be not just Apollo but *Hyperborean* Apollo, then Jesus likewise as the new Pythagoras himself, could also be thought to be the new Hyperborean Apollo. If this were the case, then it would have been very important for him to come to Hyperborea-Britain, for to do so would have been to tap into the fount of Pythagorean-Apollonion wisdom. It would have been to return to the source of this mighty river which had flowed south over the millennia spreading its life-giving waters over all the known world. It would have been to acknowledge the origin of the truth he had come to embody. It would have been, humanly speaking, to return home.

According to this interpretation the question 'And did those feet?' would have to be answered very definitely in the affirmative. William Blake's psychic seership leapt intuitively to a rhetorical question which it has taken us another two hundred years to answer. Likewise Dobson's contention that Jesus came for the Druids, would have to be affirmed because, as we have seen, the Druids were the heirs and guardians of this ancient wisdom.

Perhaps Apollo's 'sacred precinct' which Diodorus speaks of was Avebury. Perhaps the'city' was Glastonbury. No one can tell, but what we can say is that a body of legends that Jesus did come with Joseph, have survived the depredations of the centuries and testify to the fact that he may have visited all these ancient sites. As we can now see, these legends, like those of Diodorus and Hecateus, also testify to a wisdom tradition which goes right back to at least 3000 BC. This tradition, this wisdom, could truly say through Jesus 'Before Abraham was, I am.'

18
The Pillars of Wisdom

What of the Hebrew connection with Stonehenge? Is it completely fanciful and far-fetched, or is there some evidence comparable to the legends of Hyperborean Apollo, which might persuade us that such a link is not totally fictitious? It was noted earlier that 116, the mean circumference of the Sarsen Circle in MY, was the number for 'Joshua Messiah' and 'Holy of Holies' in the Hebrew of the Lesser Canon. It was also noted that 37, the mean diameter of the Sarsen Circle in MY, was the number for 'wisdom' and 'Holy'; that 29, the diameter of the Outer Bluestone circle corresponded to 'Adonai,' Lord, and that, 116 could be seen as 29 × 4 and hence as the notional square, equal to the Sarsen circumference, which exactly enclosed the Outer Bluestone Circle. Are all these symbolic equivalences pure chance, or do they speak of some forgotten cross-cultural connection?

I don't believe it is possible to answer this question with anything like the plausibility with which the Greek connection could be assessed. There do not seem to be any texts equivalent to

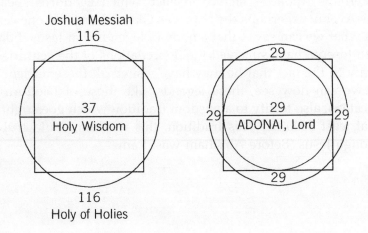

Figure 60. Hebrew Divinities at Stonehenge

Diodorus and Hecateus to go on. Nevertheless, there are certain indications which, while not amounting to anything more than possibility, are worth examining. The most arresting of these is the presence of a row of standing stones at Tel Gezer, near Tel Aviv in Israel. Some of these are over 10 feet in height, others are much smaller and all together they are a most imposing spectacle.

The generally accepted theory about these stones, as described by Carl F. Graesser in a major article in *The Biblical Archaeologist* 'Standing Stones in Ancient Palestine,'[1] is that they, like many other smaller stones excavated round the country, were memorials to important historical events such as victories, theophanies, covenants or burials. Called *masseba*, plural *massebot*, the Tel Gezer stones were thought to be a memorial to ten towns or local Canaanite tribes who had come into some form of confederation or legal covenant, each stone representing a town or tribe. However, this interpretation is evidently pure conjecture because there is not a

Figure 61. Tel Gezer

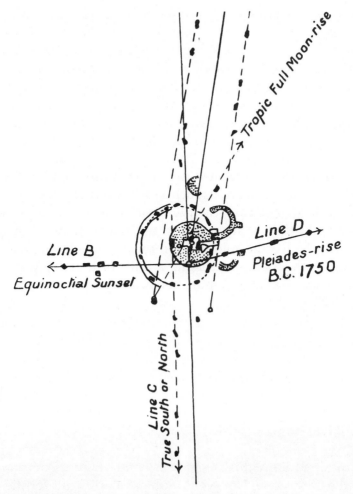

Figure 62. The north-south Stone Row, Callanish

scrap of evidence to support it. There are no inscriptions on the stones and there is no mention of any of the ten local Canaanite towns or tribes.

Looking at the stones with a fresh eye, they are morphologically so similar to the megalithic monuments of north-west Europe, that they look completely out of place. It is difficult *not* to think that they are of European origin. They are dated between 1800 and 1600 BC which would coincide with the third, or late phase of megalithic building. Furthermore they are lined up to point due north-south which is immediately reminiscent of stone rows in ancient Britain, particularly the one aligned north-south at Callanish,

Lewis, about which Professor Thom commented at the very start of his researches:

> This was an extraordinary thing, because I knew that four thousand years ago there was no Pole Star there to help them set out this line. How did they do it? ... I can only think that they may have used plumb-lines to sight with and observe the stars slowly revolving around the pole.

The date given for this alignment by Thom is round 1800 BC, exactly the same as that given for Tel Gezer.[2]

Although archaeologists have compared the *massebot* at Tel Gezer to much more diminutive stones such as those set up by Joshua at Gilgal, they also call them and the area round them 'the high place.' They do this because, as William Dever points out, it is widely conjectured that it was a 'prototype of the pagan "High Places" which the Israelite prophets abhorred, but with *stone* uprights rather than the cultic poles (*asheroth*) which represented the Goddess Asherah.'[3] Carl Graesser, following this opinion, grapples with the question: if the stones were an example of a Canaanite high place, then why weren't they destroyed along with all the other high places, by the invading, iconoclastic devotees of Yahweh? His answer is ingenious for he says that because the *massebot* had no inscriptions:

> ... different individuals could easily attach *diverse* meanings to the *same* stone. Nor would it be at all difficult for the understanding of a given *masseba* to change over the course of changing generations. The diverse opinions regarding *massebot* in the Old Testament offer a good example of this fluidity and shift of meaning.[4]

This would seem to be the only obvious answer except perhaps that the inhabitants of Tel Gezer might have continued to favour the old religion of Canaan as well as the new religion of Israel. This is at least implied in the references in Joshua and Judges which state that Yahweh was angry because his followers had not destroyed Gezer as instructed. (Joshua 16:10, Judges 1:29).

Or could it be that what was later called 'Canaanite' had, at an earlier period, been an integral part of the Israelite religion? This is the explanation which it is possible to infer from Margaret Barker in *The Great Angel* who holds that there was an 'Older Testament' in Israel which was superseded, and to a large extent suppressed, by a Reformation in the seventh century BC. This Reformation, associated with a group collectively known as the Deuteronomists, branded many genuine features of traditional religion as 'Canaanite,' and therefore heathen. Amongst these was the feminine aspect of the deity usually called *Asherah* and associated with pillars called *Asherim*. These Asherim were traditionally linked with sacred trees, stones and altars. They were all banned by the reformers:

> The patriarchs set up rural altars and had sacred trees
> and pillars; all these practices were forbidden by the
> Deuteronomic reformers at the end of the seventh
> century, yet this prohibition is in itself proof that such
> pillars, trees and altars were still a part of popular piety at
> the time.[5]

Barker goes on, by implication, to extend this interpretation to the standing stones at Tel Gezer when she says that the reformers demanded that all local cult sites be absorbed 'into the collective memory of the people' and that they become 'memorials to events in Israel's past.'[6] In other words, while the High Place at Tel Gezer *may* have survived the iconoclasm of the devotees of Yahweh because, being without inscriptions, it could easily have been reinterpreted as a memorial to an event in Israel's past, it is more likely that it survived because it remained a local cult site of the old religion for those who, down succeeding centuries, continued to believe that the Deuteronomists had been usurpers, not reformers, of the ancient faith.

Seen as the survival of a typical High Place *not* of Canaanite heathenism, but of the 'Older Testament' of Israel and Judah which, according to a minority, or even a majority, of the people at the time and subsequently, was held to be the true religion, the monoliths at Tel Gezer take on a completely new meaning and importance. They become freed from the interdict under which they have lain for 2500 years and become acceptable for what they are — the Asherim of a pre-Deuteronomic Israelite local cult site. In so doing, they cease to be marginal and become central, for they

represent the many hundreds of local cult sites which the reformers branded as Canaanite and ordered to be destroyed in the
name of their centralized, masculine monotheism. In liberating Tel
Gezer from this condemnation, Asherah herself is also allowed to
once again become the ancient consort of Yahweh as she is described in the inscriptions recently discovered at Kuntillet Cajrud,
upon which, together with other evidence, Margaret Barker bases
her theory. She is, or she represents, the Mother goddess called
variously Asherah, Anath and Ishtar. Barker says that so many
fragments of the old Israelite religion do survive that it is possible
to assert that 'the ancient goddess was indistinguishable from
Yahweh, being simply the female aspect.'[7] This female aspect of
Yahweh, although officially banished, survived in the form of
wisdom, *chokmah* and in the wisdom tradition which spawned the
wisdom literature of the Inter-Testamental period, with which we
have already become familiar in this study. The main elements of
this suppressed tradition gathered in strength until in the New
Testament they became central:

> The reform of Josiah/the Deuteronomists, then,
> reconstructed as best we can from both biblical and non-
> biblical sources, seems to have been a time when more than
> pagan accretions were removed from the Jerusalem cult.
> Wisdom was eliminated, even though her presence was
> never forgotten, the heavenly ascent and the vision of God
> were abandoned, the hosts of heaven, the angels, were
> declared to be unfit for the chosen people, the ark (and the
> presence of Yahweh which it represented) was removed,
> and the role of the high priest was altered in that he was
> no longer the anointed. All of these features of the older
> cult were to appear in Christianity.[8]

The implication of all that Margaret Barker says is that the New
Testament and the figure of Jesus himself, cannot be understood
without the acknowledgement that he embodied the chief elements
of this suppressed, older religion and that this was what brought
him into conflict with the religious authorities, who represented
the tradition of the Deuteronomic reformers. Although she says
nothing explicitly about this older faith being related to the
Pythagorean and proto-Pythagorean tradition as we have described

it, much of her thesis could be accounted for in these terms. This becomes clear if we apply what she says about wisdom to what has been said already about the ancient wisdom, particularly with regard to its universal dimensions. If she is right in claiming that the main purpose of the Deuteronomic reformers was to throw out all aspects of their traditional religion that resembled the religions of the Gentiles, then they would effectively have been replacing a broad international, ecumenical spirituality with a narrow, chauvinist sectarianism. In this case wisdom, whose very nature was universal, would have to have been robbed of her true character and nationalized. This was evidently done by making her synonymous with Law, Torah, and as far as possible denying that she was feminine.

But although made legalistic and neutered, her true nature lived on in the nation's consciousness and had re-emerged strongly in the second century BC, particularly in the *Wisdom of Solomon* where she became once more the consort of Yahweh, who loved her.

> She glorifies her noble birth by living with God,
>   and the Lord of all loves her.
> For she is an initiate in the knowledge of God,
>   and an associate in all his works. (*Wisdom*, 8:3f, JB)

In a passage such as this, it is possible to recognize the same wisdom figure from Prov.8, whom we encountered earlier as the one who was beside Yahweh in the work of creation as *'amon*, the master craftsman. This recognition is even more obvious in the *Wisdom of Solomon*, Chapter 7 where she is presented as the one who had formed everything: 'for Wisdom, the fashioner of all things taught me' (*Wisdom*, 7:22). In fact, it is this chapter more than any which brings together what Margaret Barker has proposed, with the concept of the ancient wisdom as described earlier, for she says:

> The power to create or control and order the creation was intimately bound up with knowledge of the creation. It was this issue of creative power which lay at the heart of the crisis in Israel's wisdom tradition. Knowledge of the natural order gave power over the creation and thus gave to the wise man a godlike status.[9]

Wisdom was bound up with knowledge of the natural order. 'These were the secrets known to Solomon, the secrets of the healing arts, astronomy ...' and most importantly cosmology:

> It was Yahweh who gave me true knowledge of all that is,
> who taught me the structure of the world and the
>   properties of the elements,
> the beginning, end and middle of the times,
> the alternation of the solstices and the succession of the
>   seasons,
> the revolution of the year and the position of the stars,
> the natures of animals and the instincts of wild beasts,
> the powers of spirits and the mental processes of men,
> the variety of plants and the medical properties of roots.
> All that is hidden, all that is plain, I have come to know
> instructed by Wisdom who designed them all.
>
> (*Wisdom*, 7:17–21, JB)

Although Margaret Barker does not examine the cosmological dimension in detail, it is clear from this passage that we are dealing with a tradition which could just as easily be called Pythagorean as Wisdom. In specifying the structures of the world, properties of the elements, alternating solstices, seasons of the year and positions of the stars, we can recognize the cosmological mindset of the Pythagoreans, just as we can in the itemizing of knowledge of animals, humans, spirits and healing plants. We can also recognize Martin Hengel's itemization of the subjects studied by the Essenes and indeed we can also hear a recognizable echo of the *disciplina* of the Druids, as described by the Roman and Alexandrian sources. We are in fact back within the conceptual framework of what we have called earlier, the philosophy-wisdom tradition, of which the Pythagorean system formed an important part.

We have claimed a universal provenance for this tradition, from Egypt to Scythia, from India to Hyperborea. We have also proposed that wisdom, *chokmah* 37, is not only the root prime for Apollo and Jesus Christ but, as 37 MY, is also the mean diameter of the Sarsen Circle and hence the Great Measure and tutelary spirit of Stonehenge III. After all that has been cited from Margaret Barker, it may not seem as unreasonable as it did, to hold to the initial idea, based on morphological similarity, that there might be a link between the monoliths at Tel Gezer and those in north-west Europe, especially the stone row at Callanish erected at approximately the same time. The question may therefore be asked, is there any other evidence that might help to turn this idea from morphological speculation to something a little more substantial? There is, and it is based on the fact that the Tel Gezer stones are orientated north-south. They have all been moved and replaced during excavations but there is no doubt about their original alignment. Whether they were lined up on true north or not, will probably never be definitely known, nevertheless an ordinary compass reading on site confirms the opinion of R.A.S. Macalister, early this century, that they were aligned on magnetic North.[10] Why should this be so important? Because amongst the Hebrews of the older pre-Deuteronomic religion, there was a mythology about the North as powerful and mysterious as that of Hyperborea amongst the Greeks.

The Hebrew word for 'north' is *tsaphon* and its use in the Old Testament is usually straightforward. However, there are a few texts which betray a more complex meaning. Among these the most striking is 'the mount of assembly in the far north' in Isaiah's vision of the mountain of the gods. The heathen king has become so arrogant that he aspires to ascend to the gods:

> You said in your heart,
> 'I will ascend to heaven;
> above the stars of God
> I will sit on my throne on high;
> I will sit on the mount of assembly in the far north;
> I will ascend above the heights of the clouds,
> I will make myself like the Most High.' (Isa.14:13)

There was evidently a mythological mountain in the far north where the gods held their assembly. This sounds like a Semitic Olympus and indeed scholars are agreed in accepting this comparison. Some go further and liken it to other holy mountains of the ancient world. According to A.F. Kirkpatrick, this sacred mountain in the far north corresponding to 'the Olympus of the Greeks, was the *Meru* of the Indians, the *Alborg* of the Persians, the *Aralu* of the Assyrians and the Babylonians.'[11] It was also associated with Mount Zion, for in Psalm 48 we read:

> Great is the Lord and greatly to be praised
> in the city of our God!
> His holy mountain, beautiful in elevation,
> is the joy of all the earth,
> Mount Zion, in the far north,
> the city of the great King. (Ps.48:1f)

Commentators have pointed out that 'in the far north' cannot be a geographical description of Mount Zion, but must refer to this Asiatic mythology. As H.C. Leupold says: 'The writer seems to use the expression as one that is generally known and by the use of it implies that what the fables of the Gentiles imagined was a reality in Zion; God really dwelt there.'[12]

Where was this other holy mountain in the north, this other mythological Zion, the abode of the gods? Was it located at Mount *Meru* or the *Alborg*, or the *Aralu*, or were all these, like Mount Zion itself, pointing towards a common prototype much further north? Ezekiel's famous vision of the chariot may give us a clue here because the vision itself came not just from the north but on a stormy wind *from* the north: 'And as I looked, behold, a stormy wind came out of the north, and a great cloud, with brightness round about it ...' (Ezekiel 1:4) This image of a strong wind from the north bears a striking resemblance to Boreas, the north wind of the Greeks. Put this together with the belief that there was a paradise garden on the mountain of God (Ezekiel 28:11–16), and that the north quarter of the heavens was believed to contain a garden of righteousness (Enoch 77:3), and something like a biblical version of Hyperborea, the land beyond the north wind, whose happy inhabitants knew no discord or sickness, begins to emerge.

Nor does this striking likeness end here, for in the same verse which speaks of the 'stormy wind from the north,' there is possibly another equally strong connection with Hyperborea. The whole verse reads:

> As I looked, behold, a stormy wind came out of the north, and a great cloud, with brightness round about it, and fire flashing forth continually, and in the midst of the fire, as it were gleaming bronze.

Robert Graves in *The White Goddess*, points out that the Hebrew word translated in the RSV as 'gleaming bronze' is *hashmal* which is usually taken to mean 'amber' as the AV states. Geoffrey Ashe in *The Dawn Behind the Dawn* comments 'Amber, a northern stone from the Baltic, had connections — according to some — with the Hyperboreans ...'[13] From this and other snippets of evidence, Graves goes on to put forward the notion that Apollo of the Hyperboreans and Yahweh of Israel were, at least to a degree, the same.[14] Extraordinary though this may seem, it is clear that there was something very strange about the *Maaseh Merkabah*, the 'Work of the Chariot' judging by the way the Rabbis guarded its secret so fiercely. Graves' notion therefore may have some substance. I would agree that the two Gods are closely linked through the ancient, universal, pre-Deuteronomic wisdom tradition and through Wisdom herself, the goddess, the original consort of Yahweh whose number 37 is also the root prime for Apollo 74 (37 × 2). I have already argued that the Greek and the Hebrew traditions, while distinct from each other are nevertheless much more closely linked than they are usually thought to be. I have based this on comparing their Pythagorean traditions and have concluded that they are both derived from a common proto-Pythagorean source. I have identified this source as far as the Greek expression of this is concerned, as possibly being in megalithic Britain before 3000 BC. It would now appear that the Hebrew mythology of the far north, with its concepts of 'Mount Zion in the far north' and 'the stormy wind from the north,' can possibly also lead us back to the same source.

This is quite remarkable and yet is also to be expected if, as I have contended, we are dealing with different expressions of the same original wisdom tradition. Supposing this to be the case, is there any other dimension of evidence that might point us to this conclusion? There is, and it comes from the dimension of the stars. Returning to the proposition of Santillana and Dechend that 'The places referred to in myth are the in heavens and the actions are those of celestial bodies' and applying it to Wisdom herself, we may ask: who was Wisdom? Where was her northern abode, to which the more southerly wisdom centres referred? The answer which I have already given is that it was the Sarsen Circle at Stonehenge whose diameter or Great Measure is 37 MY, wisdom's prime. I have also claimed that because the number for *Chesed*, Holy, is also 37, we may say that the Sarsen Circle is dedicated to

Holy Wisdom. However, Santillana and Dechend's proposition also prompts the further question: where was the heavenly abode of wisdom of which the Sarsen Circle was the earthly counterpart? Perhaps the stone row at Tel Gezer and indeed at Callanish give us the clue, for in pointing north, they point towards the pole of the heavens. It was part of the mythology of all holy mountains that their summit touched or led to the celestial North Pole around which the stars rotated. Geoffrey Ashe says, regarding Mount Meru:

> Meru contained a paradise, like the Canaanite Safon, and an abode of Gods. Above its peak was the celestial pole, and the heavens rotated round it as a pivot. Iranian and other legends portray the same mountain. Among Buddhists it is usually called Sumeru. Sometimes it is said to have a temple on its summit. In some accounts the temple has a golden spire which we see as the Pole Star.[15]

The pillars, the Asherim, of Tel Gezer and of Callanish, point to the Pole star, but as Professor Thom rightly observed, when the stones were erected, there was no Pole star. So how could the Pole itself be identified? From the pointer stars of the Great Bear, Ursa Major, the most conspicuous circumpolar constellation. Again, Geoffrey Ashe:

> As Philo says, Ursa Major has a plain practical value to mankind because of its use in direction finding and navigation. The word 'arctic' is from the Greek for 'north' and means, literally, the Bear's place. More important still, the portion of sky which it dominates is more than a mere vague area. It is centripetal. The constellation sweeps round it. Ursa Major's two pointer-stars guide the eye inward to the celestial centre; some northern folklore speaks of the constellation as tied to Polaris. It was even more consciously seen as central when no single star defined the pole. Homer speaks of it as 'always wheeling round the same place.' Its circlings marked the hub of heaven, the axle, the pivot above the world-mountain.[16]

Ashe backs up all that he says about the astronomical and mythological importance of the Great Bear with a mass of references to the centrality of the number seven in ancient symbolism throughout the known world. This he demonstrates convincingly to be derived from, and indissolubly linked to, the seven stars of Ursa Major. From his extensive researches on this he concludes 'Ursa Major, not numerology, is the ultimate source of all the sevens' and quoting Gerald Massey the theosophical writer he agrees that 'The first form of the mystical SEVEN was seen to be figured in heaven by the Seven large stars of the Great Bear.'[17]

Returning to the Pythagorean side of this, it is intriguing to discover that *Arktos*, Bear in the Greek Lesser Canon is 88, the same as Apollon, *tektōn* and *arithmos-Logos;* while *He Arktos, The Bear,* is 96 which is the same as *Kosmos* and *Iesous,* also in the Lesser Canon. Once again, we may wonder whether this is pure chance and whether to even revert to any argument based on gematria is to muddy the waters. Nevertheless, it is even more intriguing to discover that where Job says 'who made the Bear and Orion' (Job 9:9) and 'can you guide the Bear?' (Job 38:32), the Hebrew word, which the Authorised Version translates 'Arcturus,' is *Ash*; Ayin Shin, whose number in the Lesser Canon is 37. Why should the number for the constellation of the Bear in the Hebrew gematria be 37? Why should the number for *chokmah*, wisdom also be 37? Without directly answering this question, it is nevertheless possible, according to the conventions of gematria which we have been observing, to claim that, insofar as the Bear and wisdom have the same number and both are associated with the number seven, the heavenly abode of Wisdom was in Ursa Major.

If this is the case, is it then possible to claim that the seven pillars of wisdom, are the seven stars of the Great Bear?

Wisdom has built her house,
She has set up her seven pillars. (Prov.9:1)

It would seem that it is, if we hold to the axioms of Pythagorean cosmology: 'as above, so below,' 'as in the greatest, so in the least' and 'the gods — (and goddesses) — are numbers.' So can we, from the same axioms, reasonably deduce that the Sarsen Circle at Stonehenge was a mesocosmic representation of the circumpolar revolutions of the Great Bear? I think we can and I think that we

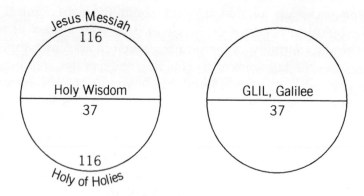

Figure 63. Holy Wisdom and Galilee-Glil Circles

can also infer that the circles and standing stones of the Megalithic Age, wherever they are to be found, while they may be dedicated to other numbers and other deities, could generally be called 'the Pillars of Wisdom.'

All this would support our earlier contention that the historical Jesus was the embodiment of the universal ancient wisdom which had been suppressed by the sectarian and chauvinistic Deuteronomic reformers. If the Sarsen Circle diameter represents Holy Wisdom, then the mean circumference of 116 MY represents the Holy of Holies, Kodesh ha Kodeshim 116, and Jesus Messiah, *Yehoshua Meshiach* 116. If there is any meaning at all in this numero-geometric symbolism then we can surely say that Jesus is related to wisdom as the circumference of a circle is related to its diameter. A haunting echo of this is found in the number for Galilee which, as GLIL, is 37 and means, quite simply, 'circle.'

From this perspective it is possible to see what William Blake might have meant when he asked 'Was Britain the Primitive Seat of the Patriarchal Religion?' We would have to give an affirmative answer to this on the understanding that the Druids were the heirs and guardians of the proto-Pythagorean tradition of megalithic Britain which might well have been the source, or one of the sources of the Hebrew wisdom, as well as the Greek. In this way we could assent to the possibility that the ancestors of the Jews might well have 'derived their origin from Abraham, Heber, Shem and Noah who were Druids ...' We might also find ourselves able to agree with the evidence he cites for this claim, for he goes on to say '... as the Druid Temples (which are the Patriarchal Pillars and

Oak Groves) over the whole Earth witness today.' We would have to remain agnostic about 'the whole Earth' and focus only on Israel. We would also have to substitute Matriarchal for Patriarchal for, as has been shown, the Pillars were sacred to the goddess, or at least to Yahweh *and* his consort. But with these caveats in mind, it is quite possible to interpret Blake along the lines which have been presented above.

But what about the 'Oak Groves'? Surely we have been talking about stone circles and stone rows, not trees. The Druids worshipped in groves, not stone circles, so how can there be a connection? The answer may lie in the assumption that, while the Druids did not build stone monuments, they may nevertheless have used them for their known cosmological and astronomical observations. Their worship and general studies however may have been conducted in groves and secluded woods. At any event the continuity of tradition between the Neolithic and Iron Age cultures, which was proposed earlier, would lead to the supposition that the stone monuments may have preceded wooden ones. In this regard it is intriguing that Margaret Barker's researches lead in this direction, for the Asherah, the symbol of the goddess she says, was often assumed to be made of wood and even to have been a grove:

> Asherah must have been something which represented the goddess. It is possible that it was something wooden, perhaps a tree or the representation of a tree since it could be planted (Deut.16:21), reformers could cut it down (Deut.7:5), or burn it (Deut.12:3). The Asherah was erected near or under a tree (1Kings 14:23, 2Kings 17:10). It was *made* (1Kings 14:15; 16:33; 2Kings 17:16). The LXX could translate the word either by 'tree' as at Isa.17:8 and 27:9 or, more frequently, by 'grove' as at 1Kings 16:33, where Ahab made a *grove*. Jewish tradition recorded in the Mishnah remembered that an Asherah could be either a sacred tree or a tree under which was an idol.[18]

All of which would appear to substantiate Blake's claim that the Asherah and Asherim were similar to, if not derived from, the Druid oak groves of ancient Britain. In fact so much is this the case that, thanks to Margaret Barker, it may be difficult to make sense of all these striking similarities in any other way.

19
The Sapphire Throne

William Blake entertained the prophets Isaiah and Ezekiel to dinner. During this singular and presumably clairvoyant occasion, the latter instructed him in the primacy of the poetic genius:

> Then Ezekiel said ... we of Israel taught that the Poetic Genius (as you now call it) was the first principle and all others merely derivative, which was the cause of our despising the Priests and Philosophers of other countries, and prophesying that all Gods would at last be proved to originate in ours and to be the tributaries of the Poetic Genius.[1]

Although Blake was the only Romantic privileged to have audio-visual access to the prophet, the actual Book of Ezekiel in the Old Testament, achieved cult status among the British literati of the later eighteenth century. It was widely read and found to be enormously inspiring. Brian Hepworth in *The Rise of Romanticism, Essential Texts*, lists it along with John Locke, George Berkeley, Joseph Addison and William Collins as a major influence on the change from a classical to a biblical understanding of sensibility, particularly with regard to the notion of 'the sublime,' which took place at this time. Ezekiel was considered to be the most sublime of all the Hebrew prophets because he was fierce, wild and terrible, and therefore produced the greatest sensation of 'pleasing horror' and awe. Hepworth goes so far as to claim: 'His appearance in eighteenth century literature describes an almost complete account of the path of creative imagination.' He explains:

> From the beginning Ezekiel's jewelled light symbolized the illumination of the infinite, a notion equally as influential in poetic imagery as any derived from Newton's *Optics*. For Burnet, Ezekiel's 'sapphire throne' indicated the 'Mundane

Egg,' a more sublime and elevated world than our present, finite one. For Joseph Spence his vision, parallel with Homeric prophecy, was *'an orientalism'* — the imaging of a revolution in a confusion of light in the heavens.[2]

It is clear from these and other references such as Young's *Night Thoughts*, Smart's *A Song to David* and Blake's *The Four Zoas*, that it was not the whole of Ezekiel's writings that was found to be so inspiring but only the first chapter which Hepworth cites in full. This is the famous vision of the chariot and of all its powerful imagery, it was the sapphire throne which was evidently the most enlivening. For instance, William Collins in *Ode on the Poetical Character* described the Creator placing the Muse of Poetry beside him 'on his sapphire throne,' Thomas Gray, in *The Progress of Poesy* spoke of the 'living throne, the sapphire blaze' and Wordsworth in *The Excursion* saw a great throne appearing out of the swirling mountain mist:

Right in the midst, where interspace appeared
Of open court, an object like a throne
Under a shining canopy of state
Stood fixed; and fixed resemblances were seen
To implements of ordinary use,
But vast in size, in substance glorified;
Such as by Hebrew Prophets were beheld
In vision — forms uncouth of mightiest power
For admiration and mysterious awe.

What was the reality behind Ezekiel's vision which was so important to these and other seminal Romantic works such as Keats' *Hyperion* and Macpherson's *Ossian*?

Cross-references in the Old Testament indicate that it was modelled on the experience which Moses had when he received the tablets of the Law on Mount Sinai:

Then Moses and Aaron, Nadab and Abihu, and seventy of the elders of Israel went up, and they saw the God of Israel; and there was under his feet as it were a pavement of sapphire stone, like the very heaven for clearness. (Exodus 24:9–10)

This Sinaitic derivation is confirmed by an equally clear reference to fire:

> Now the appearance of the glory of the Lord was like a devouring fire on the top of the mountain in the sight of all the peoples of Israel.

It would appear that Ezekiel had gone back six hundred years in his imagination and was reliving the great Mosaic theophany which had become paradigmatic for the people of Israel. Had he also gone even further back to a proto-typical experience of which Moses on Sinai had been a later expression? Such a question would be meaningless but for the evidence presented in the last chapter that the geographical Mount Sinai, like the geographical Mount Zion, might well have been seen as the southern, historical expression of a northern, mythological mountain of the Gods. Also that the whole of Ezekiel's vision came on 'a stormy wind out of the north' and that, in the midst of the vision, he saw a divine-human form who, from the waist upwards, was not 'gleaming bronze' but amber, the precious stone from north-west Europe which was sacred to Apollo not Yahweh.

Since there seemed to be some substance in these northern references insofar as they led to the possibility that the holy mountain in the far north might ultimately have been the celestial North Pole and that the heavenly residence of *chokmah*, wisdom, might have been the circumpolar constellation of the Great Bear, may we now ask whether Ezekiel's whole vision might well have been describing an essentially northern experience? This would also be an empty question but for the fact that, in a number of ways, the descriptions of the aurora borealis, the northern lights, given by Harald Falck-Ytter in *Aurora* bear striking resemblances to what the prophet saw. This might seem to be a far-fetched suggestion and yet the similarities are so marked that it is worth examining them in some detail.

Those who have experienced the full impact of the polar lights high up in the night sky, have always been overwhelmed by feelings of awe and wonder. Fridtjof Nansen, the Norwegian arctic explorer, is typical. Writing from his ice-packed ship, *Fram*, in 1904, he said:

I went on deck this evening in a rather gloomy frame of mind, but was nailed to the spot from the moment I got outside. There is the supernatural for you — the northern lights flashing in matchless power and beauty over the sky in all the colours of the rainbow! Seldom or never have I seen the colours so brilliant. The prevailing one at first was yellow, but that gradually flickered over to green, and then a sparkling ruby-red began to show at the bottom of the rays on the under side of the arch. And now from the far-away western horizon a fiery serpent writhed itself up over the sky, shining brighter and brighter as it came. It split into three, all brilliantly glittering. Then the colours changed. The serpent to the south turned almost ruby-red, with spots of yellow; the one in the middle yellow, and the one to the north, greenish white. Sheaves of rays swept along the sides of the serpents, driven through the ether-like waves before a storm wind. They sway backward and forward, now strong, now fainter again. The serpents reached and passed their zenith. Though I was thinly dressed and shivering with cold, I could not tear myself away till the spectacle was over ... When I came on deck later the masses of light had passed northward and spread themselves in incomplete arches over the northern sky. If one wants to read mystic meanings into the phenomena of nature, here surely, is the opportunity.[3]

Nansen saw the predominant colours as yellow, then green and then ruby-red, strangely reminiscent of traffic lights and thus suggesting amber rather than yellow! But more pertinently he speaks of the sheaves of rays being swept along 'driven through the ether-like waves before a storm wind.' Recent scientific theory explains the aurora as the electro-magnetic discharge which takes place when the earth's magnetosphere is disturbed by the mysterious emanation from the sun known as the solar wind. This may be the origin of Ezekiel's 'stormy wind from the north.' He also mentions the appearance of incomplete arches. Could these be the wheels, and the wheels within wheels of Ezekiel's 'chariot'?

Now as I looked at the living creatures, I saw a wheel upon the earth beside the living creatures, one for each of the four of them. As for the appearance of the wheels and their construction: their appearance was like the gleaming of a crystolite; and the four had the same likeness, their construction being as it were a wheel within a wheel. (Ezek.1:15f).

An eighteenth century Danish illustration tried to picture this.

Figure 64. Illustrations for an Essay on the Aurora 1745

Nansen starts by calling the aurora 'supernatural' and ends by suggesting it has 'mystic meanings.' He could thus be said to encourage the interpretation of Ezekiel's vision in these terms. This is strengthened when we realize that the key to its cosmic dimension is given in the description of the four living creatures, particularly their four faces. After the gleaming bronze-amber verse, Ezekiel continues:

> And from the midst of it came the likeness of four living
> creatures. And this was their appearance: they had the form
> of men, but each of them had four faces ... As for the like-
> ness of their faces, each had the face of a man in front; the
> four had the face of a lion on the right side, the four had
> the face of an ox on the left side, and the four had the
> face of an eagle at the back. Such were their faces.
> (Ezek.1:5f, 10f)

Although probably derived from the imagery of the Cherubim in Solomon's temple, these four living creatures symbolize unmistakably the four elements of air (man), fire (lion), earth (ox) and water (eagle) and also the four fixed signs of the zodiac, Aquarius (man), Leo (lion), Taurus (ox) and Scorpio (eagle, the exalted symbol). Since the fixed signs also represented the four directions and the four seasons, they were sometimes taken as shorthand for the whole zodiac in ancient cosmology. Thus, since they have such clear cosmic meanings, it is reasonable to suppose that the rest of the vision may be understood in cosmic terms.

If we accept that the four living creatures do indeed represent the four fixed signs of the zodiac, and by implication the whole zodiac, then we can assume that they define the totality of the vault of the heavens. This would be centred on the celestial North Pole. As such they would be like the ribs of an oval cage. They would be the fixed divisions of the dome of the skies. They would not move. But in the vision they move all the time, flying on wings 'And each went straight forward; wherever the spirit would go, they went, without turning as they went.' How can this contradiction be resolved? How could the signs of the zodiac move? Perhaps we are being told that they *appeared* to move, that the whole sky *seemed* to be alive with fire and coloured lights. This would agree with one of the important early scientific theories made by

Jean de Mairan (1678–1771) that the aurora originated in a 'lighting up of the zodiacal light in the earth's extended atmosphere.'[4] This zodiacal light is evidently seen in the ecliptic's outer space.

But it is the details of Ezekiel's description of *how* the four living creatures moved that resemble first-hand accounts of the northern lights. He says that in their midst 'there was something that looked like burning coals of fire, like torches moving to and fro among the living creatures.' (Ezek.1:13) These 'torches moving to and fro' between the signs of the zodiac look very much like the darting lights and living flame described in the Norwegian saga *The King's Mirror*:

> It [the aurora] also looks as if sharp points were shot from this flame up into the sky; these are of uneven height and in constant motion, now one, now another darting highest; and the light appears to blaze like a living flame.[5]

All those who have actually seen the northern lights describe this darting quality which could easily be likened to 'burning coals of fire, like torches moving to and fro.' In 'The Ancient Mariner,' Coleridge describes a display of the aurora, in this case the southern lights. The movement of his 'fire-flags' is very similar to Ezekiel's torches:

> The upper air burst into life,
>   And a hundred fire-flags sheen
> To and fro they were hurried about;
> And to and fro, and in and out,
>   The wan stars danced between. (307–311)

Ezekiel is at pains to emphasize this darting quality for, in the next verse he repeats: 'And the living creatures darted to and fro, like a flash of lighting.' (Ezek.1:14) He also repeats the reference to lightning which once again is characteristic of descriptions of the aurora. For instance, in one of the most ancient references from China, the term lightning is used as a metaphor for the northern lights as a whole. These descriptive similarities can also be extended to the appearance of a rainbow. In 1874, Karl Weyprecht, the arctic researcher, gave an extensive account from Franz Joseph Land in which he described bands of 'rainbow colours' and

Figure 65. Aurora's shooting Flames

'prismatic colours'[6] similar to Ezekiel's 'bow that is in the clouds on the day of rain, so was the appearance of the brightness round about.' (Ezek.1:28)

The only weak point in this comparison is the element of sound. Ezekiel says that the noise made by the wings of the four living creatures was like 'the sound of many waters, like the thunder of the Almighty, a sound of tumult like the sound of a host.' (Ezek.1:24) This contrasts sharply with the sound of silence which envelops the northern wastes as the cosmic fireworks display takes place above. Nevertheless, some sounds have been heard and there have also been testimonies to inner psychic sounds:

> Numerous traditions particularly those of the Indians, Eskimos and Lapps, but also later accounts, tell how the northern lights are often accompanied by different low but nevertheless distinct sounds. It is a hissing, crackling and piping ... A large part of the acoustic concomitant phenomena could be explained psychologically: the intensive and grandiose light and colour display also evokes sounds in the observer's psyche and sense of hearing. They are subjective and heard only inwardly. Nevertheless, a portion of the many descriptions points to an outer objective phenomenon.[7]

So much for Ezekiel's epiphenomena, all of which, apart from perhaps the sound, bear striking resemblance to accounts of the northern lights. Now we come to the focus, the heart of the vision which is described as having the 'likeness as it were of a human form.' (Ezek.1:26) Here we return to the gleaming bronze or amber and the sapphire throne:

> And above the firmament over their heads there was the likeness of a throne, in appearance like sapphire; and seated above the likeness of a throne was a likeness as it were of a human form. And upwards of what had the appearance of his loins I saw as it were amber, like the appearance of fire enclosed round about; and downward from what had the appearance of his loins I saw as it were the appearance of fire, and there was brightness round about him. (Ezek.1:26f)

Who was this celestial being? Who did Ezekiel see on the sapphire throne? Was it a chimera, a phantom similar to faces seen in clouds? Was it no more than a certain configuration of the shapes and colours of the aurora which, for a moment, seemed to appear like a man on a throne? In the excerpts from modern accounts quoted above we have had certain patterns and movements described as serpents, rainbows and arcs. Furthermore, Ezekiel is at pains to reiterate again and again that he didn't actually see a throne but only 'the likeness of a throne' which was not sapphire but was only 'in appearance *like* sapphire.' Neither did he see a human form but only a 'likeness as it were of a human form.' Note the double qualification of 'likeness' and 'as it were.' He could hardly qualify what he saw any more without actually admitting that none of it was more than pictures in the sky. Yet it seems as though he wants to come as close to saying precisely that as he can, for he goes on to say that he didn't see the being's loins but only their 'appearance.' Neither did he see amber but only 'as it were,' nor fire enclosed round about but only its 'appearance.' Thus, despite the robustness of his imagery, there is an insubstantial quality to everything he sees. It is never the thing in itself but only the appearance of it, as it were. If someone in modern speech were to keep using the phrase 'as it were' to qualify everything he said, we would think he had a communication problem and would offer some form of sympathetic help. Was Ezekiel in a stressed psychological state or was he genuinely attempting to describe the indescribable?

Assuming generously that it was the latter, an important observation can be made, that the constituent parts, namely amber and fire, of the being which had the likeness of a human form, were not in essence different from other constituent parts of the vision. The only difference was the form. Thus the being, whoever he was, was made of amber and fire in the same way as the other aspects of the vision were made of fire, crystals, rainbows and so on. In other words he was a being of light who was made of the same insubstantial material as all the epiphenomena round him. As such he could be described as the Spirit of the aurora, the Spectre of the northern lights.

Many northern tribes evidently had mythologies which featured such a being. For the Canadian Indians round Ottawa he was called the demigod Nanahboozho, for the Siberian Chuvasch he was the god Suratan-Tura and for the American Indians of the Pacific north-west he was the Chief of the Northern Lights. But most intriguingly from the point of view of this study, Harald Falck-Ytter states that for the Greeks, this being was Apollo and that he was associated with the land of Hyperborea:

> The Greeks also knew of a legendary people who lived
> in northern Europe. They spoke of the Hyperboreans. The
> name means beyond the north (the north wind). This far-
> northern people lived, like those inhabitants of the
> auroral world described by the Indians and Eskimos in a
> mild, sunny and fertile land, free from the weight of
> earthly destiny ... When the winter came in Greece, the sun-
> god Apollo moved to the land of the northern inhabitants
> in the land of Hyperborea.[8]

Falck-Ytter says there is a puzzle here. Why should the sun god, who represents light, move into the darkness and cold of the northern polar night? Although he makes no reference to Ezekiel, or to the celestial amber-coloured being on the sapphire throne, his answer perfectly fits an auroral interpretation of the prophet's vision:

In the traditions of ancient clairvoyance and the mystery
centres, the Greeks and their initiates did not, like modern
man, see only the external darkness, nor did they
experience only the physical cold of the terrestrial north.
They experienced how this part of the earth is permeated
by supersensory light-forces and occult heat activity.
Together with the outer sunlight, these forces are an
essential element of Apollo's being. In the Hyperborean
realm, supersensory light is transformed into visible
illumination, occult heat into the external colour flow of
the aurora.

Falck-Ytter concludes: 'It was, therefore, a spiritually perceived
sequence of events to see Apollo during the dark season in that
region of the earth where the supersensory sun-forces were just
then appearing outwardly in the aurora borealis.'[9]

This description of Apollo as the 'supersensible' Spirit of the
aurora is remarkable. So much so that it is hard to doubt that it
was some sort of Apollonian being which Ezekiel saw on the
sapphire throne. Striking though this identification seems to be,
there is one serious objection: this Apollonian spectre was experienced in the north, in Hyperborea, not in the south, in Israel. We
are not told that Ezekiel came north, so how could he have seen
the northern lights? The answer probably lies in the recorded fact
that they were seen very occasionally in Mediterranean lands and
were identified as coming from the north. For instance, Plutarch
saw them in 349 and 344 BC and, in his *Meterologia* wrote: 'On a
clear night a number of phenomena can be seen that take the
forms of chasms, trenches and blood-red colours.' Aristotle also
saw them and tried to explain them scientifically. Likewise Seneca
(*c.*4 BC–AD 65) in his *Naturales Questiones* (1,14,1):

Many kinds of them are seen. There are *bothyni* (abysses):
within a surrounding corona there is a great gap in the sky
like a hole dug in a circle. There are *pithiai* (casks): an
enormous round mass of fire, like a barrel, either darts by
or blazes in one place. There are *chasmata* (chasms): some
area of the sky settles and, gaping in hiding — so to speak
— sends out flame.[10]

If the northern lights were seen on rare occasions as far south as Rome and Greece, then it is quite possible they could have been seen a couple of hundred miles further south in the Levant. In fact the rarity of the sightings would have added enormously to their power to evoke the sense of theophany. It is therefore quite possible that this is what Ezekiel saw. Does this mean that the being whom he saw on the sapphire throne was more than an imaginary configuration of northern lights? The fact that this being was the colour of amber from the waist up would suggest that it symbolized Apollo and, as we have learnt from Falck-Ytter, Apollo was seen in, or as, the supersensory sun-forces of the aurora by the Greeks. Does this mean that he had effectively seen Apollo? Such a radical suggestion takes us back to Robert Graves who claimed that Apollo was cousin to Yahweh. This possibility would have to be conceded and would certainly explain why the gematria of the divine names fits equally well in the Greek as in the Hebrew in the symbolic measurements at Stonehenge and the numerology of the Great Bear. It would confirm the proposition made earlier that both the Greek and the Hebrew traditions were derived from a common proto-Pythagorean source which can be identified as megalithic Britain.

Does this mean that Apollo and Yahweh are the same? Probably not. Cousins yes, but the same, no. Their numbers are different and since 'the gods are numbers,' the implication is that their characters reflect that difference. Yahweh as 26 has 13 as his prime which links him with El 13 and Yah 15 ($15 \times \sqrt{3} = 26$). Apollo on the other hand as 74, has 37 as his prime and thus, as we have already seen, he is connected to *chokmah*, wisdom 37, and Jesus 888 (37×24). These three, Apollo, wisdom and Jesus, have already been linked to the north, so what is the new element that has entered our understanding of their interrelationship, through our discovery that Ezekiel's vision was of an Apollonian presence in the midst of a display of the northern lights? What does this add to what has already been claimed for Jesus as the embodiment of the ancient wisdom, as the new Pythagoras and the new Apollo of the Hyperboreans?

The answer to this lies in the fact that after Ezekiel's time, approximately the same vision came again to Daniel in the second century BC, but this time the indistinct Apollonian form on the sapphire throne had become distinct as 'one like a son of man'

(Daniel 7:13). It then came again to others during the two centuries before Jesus, particularly to the writer called Enoch. It came again to Jesus himself who identified himself specifically with this figure of the Son of Man. In other words the Apollonian auroral figure changed into the Son of Man figure which eventually became flesh in Jesus. But this also has already been implied in the numerical genealogy of Apollo as 37 × 2 developing from wisdom 37 and Jesus as 37 × 24 developing from Apollo, as noted earlier. So is there any genuinely new insight offered by the establishment of the link between this auroral vision and the concept of the Son of Man? There is, and it has to do with what is called 'the ascent.' This ascension or exultation was what we today would call an out-of-body experience in which the king or seer would ascend the mountain of the gods in his astral body, sit on the divine throne and acquire divine wisdom. This wisdom was associated with learning the secrets of the universe. Margaret Barker explains:

> 'Vision' and 'exaltation' are highly significant words, especially if the exaltation means 'rising up' in more than just the sense of conferring high status. There are many examples in the ancient Near East of royal figures being raised up into the presence of their Gods ... Emenduranki, for example, the legendary seventh king of Babylon, was summoned to the presence of the gods to learn the secrets of the creation and the divinatory techniques which were later the exclusive preserve of the kings ... Such ascending figures were fairly common ... there were flying king cults in India, in South-East Asia and in China.[11]

Margaret Barker then likens these flying kings to shaman figures who always seem to have been part of the universal experience of humanity. She goes on to describe their function and initiation:

> The heavenly journey reinforced the belief that the ordinary world of human existence and the upper world of their mythology were once in a harmony which had been destroyed by the action of evil forces. The shaman had to repel these forces and thus restore the cosmic harmony. As a result of his initiation he had enhanced powers of vision and hearing; he could see into the very nature of things

and understand the processes of life itself. Thus he became a healer. The commonest way to induce the experience of ascent was by fasting, lightening the body so that the soul could fly. Once the shaman figure had ascended to the heavenly places and knew the secrets of the creation, he enjoyed a life which had already passed through death, and he became a being from another world.[12]

Like Margaret Barker, Geoffrey Ashe has much to say about shamanism which he claims can be experienced today in certain parts of the world. In Siberia it is still evidently a central part of the communal religious life. He also makes an observation which is crucial, that the shaman climbs a pole or tree into the celestial realms:

The main feature of the shaman's universe is the cosmic centre, a bond or axis connecting earth, heaven and hell. It is often pictured as a tree or a pole holding up the sky. In a trance state, a shaman can travel disembodied from one region to another, climbing the tree into the heavens or following its downward extension. By doing so he can meet and consult the gods.[13]

This pole, axis or tree is in fact the axle of the cosmos which we encountered in our discussion about the holy mountains such as Meru, Olympus, Alborg and Aralu, of which Mount Zion and indeed Mount Sinai were also examples. These, we established, were linked to a prototype in the north which may well have been connected with Stonehenge or other megalithic sites, but which was ultimately identifiable as the celestial North Pole. This now appears to be the same pole, or *axis mundi* up which the shaman climbed or rather flew in his astral body, to the council of the gods. If we add this to what Margaret Barker says, then the implication is that Ezekiel, Daniel, Enoch and Moses on Sinai, not only had shamanic, out-of-body experiences of the ascent to the divine presence, but also that this was via the *axis mundi* up to the celestial pole, past the phantasmagoria of the northern lights and through the hole in the apex of the vault of heaven which St John in *Revelation* calls an 'open door.' (Rev.4:1)

The unmistakable implication is also that Jesus was himself the supreme initiate of this experience. Margaret Barker in *The Lost Prophet*, claims that this was why he called himself the Son of Man. He had not only made the ascent, he had already made the descent as that heavenly being who had first appeared as the shimmering Apollonian aurora and gradually been revealed as Joshua the Anointed, and as Jesus the Christ. Moses, Ezekiel, Daniel and Enoch had all made the ascent and then descended but it was only Jesus who first descended and then ascended for he was the heavenly being as well as the earthly incarnation. This is the meaning of: 'He who descended is also he who ascended far above all the heavens, that he might fill all things.' (Eph.4:10) Jesus had been there, he was there and he was going to be there. This was his identity as the Son of Man. Thus when the High Priest asked 'Are you the Christ, the Son of the Blessed?' he replied 'I am; and you will see the Son of Man seated at the right hand of Power' (Mark 14:61f) Again, Margaret Barker, quoting from John's Gospel:

> Jesus had been in the presence of God, and he speaks of what he has heard and seen there; 'Truly, Truly, I say to you, we speak of what we know, and bear witness to what we have seen' (John 3:11); 'He who comes from above is above all; he who is of the earth belongs to the earth, and of the earth he speaks; he who comes from heaven is above all' (John 3:31f); 'it is not I alone that judge, but I and he who sent me' (John 8:16); 'I declare to the world what I have heard from him' (John 8:26); 'the Father who sent me has himself given me commandment what to say and what to speak.' (John 12:49)[14]

And what about all the numbers with which this study has been littered? Do they matter or does the tradition of the shamanic, astral ascent stand apart from all our gematria? The answer would seem to be that the numbers matter very much and are integral to the shaman's consciousness. In fact they appear to determine which god or goddess the shaman will meet. They represent the stations on the heavenly journey. It is evidently important to know the number of your god's station otherwise you might meet the wrong god, for the gods are most definitely numbers. Geoffrey

Ashe's explanation of this goes a long way in confirming the theory, put forward earlier, that the various types of stone circle, as exemplified supremely at Stonehenge, were designed to embody the attributes of these numbers through particular geometrical patterns associated with each one:

> There is always a numerical factor. He (the shaman) climbs through a fixed number of celestial stages, or descends through a fixed number of infernal ones. His key number may be expressed in his costume — for example, in a set of bells which he attaches to it. The key number varies from shaman to shaman and from tribe to tribe ... In a typical Altaic descent to the nether world, the shaman goes down through seven levels to encounter Erlik Khan, lord of the dead, who has seven sons and seven daughters.[15]

This being so, it isn't surprising to find that Pythagoras, the father of numerology in the west, was associated with shamanism. This is shown in his feats of healing and bilocation, his founding of a mystical community which admitted women, a shamanic rather than Hellenic practice, and the legend of him taming a bear. The latter links him to the north and indeed to Apollo of the Hyperboreans of whom, as we have seen, he was believed to have been the incarnation. Mircea Eliade in *Shamanism* goes so far as to say that the few characters in Greek legend who are probably shamans, are related to Apollo. They all come from the north and include Abaris:

> And it is from the north, from the land of the Hyperboreans, from Apollo's country of origin, that they are said to have come to Greece. Such a one, for example, is Abaris. 'Carrying in his hand the golden arrow, the proof of his Apolline origin and mission, he passed through many lands dispelling sickness and pestilence by sacrifices of a magic kind, giving warnings of earthquakes and other disasters.' (Erwin Rohde, (*Psyche: the Cult of Souls and Belief in Immortality among the Greeks*, London, 1925, p.300) A later legend shows him flying through the air on his arrow, like Musaeus. The arrow, which plays a certain role in Scythian mythology and religion, is a symbol of magical flight.[16]

Once again we have been led back unexpectedly to the theme, considered in the chapter 'Apollo of the Hyperboreans,' of the ancient connection between the proto-Greeks and the proto-Pythagoreans in Hyperborea, which we established could have been Britain. This time the link is through shamanism. Was this why the early Romantics found Ezekiel's vision so inspiring? Was Ezekiel's experience of the ascent, really that of the shaman in other guise? Was Blake referring to this when he wrote 'Bring me my Chariot of fire'? Although his specific reference is to Elijah (2 Kings 2:11), not Ezekiel, Elijah was yet another prophet in the same tradition. His ascent to heaven in a chariot of fire with horses of fire caught up in a whirlwind, was so dramatic that his successor Elisha shouted 'My father, my father, the chariots of Israel and its horsemen.'

What were these 'chariots of Israel?' Were they the vehicles of the ascent for the shamanic initiates? Did they have 'the appearance as it were,' of fiery red flames because they were quite literally solar flares which had shot down to the earth from the aurora borealis? This interpretation is quite possible because there are traditions noted by Falck-Ytter, which believe that the northern lights can be called down to earth. For instance an Indian from the far north-west of Canada recalled:

> When I was a boy, people respected the northern lights as
> messengers of our spirits. People also said that some men
> and women can bring the northern lights down and make
> them obey their commands. You only have to walk outside,
> rub your hands together and whistle, then the northern
> lights will come down and sing and dance for you. When I
> was a young man I tried it once and it worked.[17]

There are also more reliable accounts of the aurora not only descending to earth but enveloping the tops of mountains. Was this the origin of the council of the gods in the far north coming down to meet with kings, prophets, seers and shamans as they sat atop their holy mountains? Dorothy Ray recorded such an experience in Alaska in August 1958:

> The Brooks range in Alaska one night in late August was
> as bright with the aurora as if it were dawn. After two

Figure 66. Aurora on the Mountain

years in the North, I had learned to view these dazzling displays with equanimity, but this one differed from others as much as a hamburger from a T-bone steak. The aurora had just accomplished the impossible. It had come down to meet the earth just a few miles from me. The top of the highest mountain in the vicinity, almost 9,000 feet (2,700 m) of vertical rock, was completely submerged in auroral gauze.[18]

She said that she thought she was seeing a mirage but it stayed there on the mountain for more than 20 minutes 'settling now and then with uncanny precision on its pinnacle. What I had witnessed was impossible according to science.'

In order to complete this Pythagorean-shamanic-auroral interpretation of the visionary experience of Ezekiel, Daniel, Enoch and Jesus, it is necessary to move back down to earth, from the macrocosm to the microcosm. What would be the microcosmic equivalent of all this in the life of the individual? Quite apart from all the symbolic numbers we have examined in relation to the numero-geometric alphabets, there is a dimension of subjective experience which seems to confirm all that has so far only appeared to be objective. This comes from the interpretation of dreams through which Carl Jung became convinced that numbers were intelligences which could work as powerfully in the inner psyche as in the outer world. Numbers featured so regularly in his patients' dreams that he came to the conclusion that they had an existence independent of our knowledge of them:

> It appears that whole numbers are individuals, and that they possess properties which cannot be explained on the assumption that they are multiple units. The idea that numbers were invented for counting is obviously untenable, since they are not pre-existent to judgement but possess properties which were discovered only in the course of centuries, and presumably possess a number of others which will be brought to light by the future development of mathematics.[19]

Jung also provides us with a most illuminating microcosmic interpretation of the Great Bear, for this too has appeared in dreams. In the light of all that has been said above, it is highly intriguing that he refers to this constellation as both 'the chariot' and 'the self.'

> The 'chariot' in the sky, Charles' Wain (Ursa Major or Big Dipper) ... marks the celestial Pole, which is of great significance in the history of symbols. It is a model of the structure of the self.[20]

It would thus appear that there really is a microcosmic equivalent to the macrocosmic vision which has been described, and that it is experienced in the inner life of the individual psyche. That this is indeed the case, is confirmed in relation to the shamanic ascent itself because many today who have had near-death experiences have recounted how they left their physical bodies and journeyed 'out-of-body' to far away places. Sometimes, they met a Being of

Light who has occasionally been identified as Jesus. Sometimes, they ascended to the heavens in outer space and saw the Celestial city, the New Jerusalem, which itself was seen in a similar experience by St John, as recorded in *Revelation*. Such a person was George Ritchie who, in *Return from Tomorrow* speaks in detail of how Jesus led him on such a journey:

> And then I saw, infinitely far off, far too distant to be
> visible with any kind of sight I knew of ... a city. A
> glowing, seemingly endless city, bright enough to be seen
> over all the unimaginable distance between. The brightness
> seemed to shine from the very walls and streets of this
> place, and from beings which I could now discern moving
> about within it. In fact, the city and everything in it seemed
> to be made of light, even as the Figure at my side was
> made of light. At this time I had not yet read the Book of
> Revelation.[21]

Like Jung's numbers and 'chariot' of the Great Bear, the Celestial City was experienced by George Ritchie in his out-of-body condition, as having an existence independent of his knowledge of it. It was experienced as an actuality; an objective reality within the profoundly subjective consciousness of his disembodied mind. Likewise, Jesus was experienced as being there, as 'the Figure by his side,' simultaneously objective and subjective at the same time; a being of Light who he described as a 'Man made out of light, though this seemed no more possible to my mind than the incredible intensity of the brightness that made up his Form.'

George Ritchie's experience has been one of the most important in recent years because it was his testimony which encouraged Raymond Moody to begin the research which led to the publication of *Life after Life* in 1975.[22] This was instrumental in effecting a revolution in the reappraisal and acceptance of the concept of life after death in the sceptical western world. His experience is also important for his conclusion because it confirms from the astral and etheric planes, the description of Jesus which we have arrived at through more pedestrian researches. For this being whom he encountered as 'a Man made out of Light,' whose form was made up of an 'incredible intensity of brightness,'[23] bears a remarkable resemblance to Ezekiel's being on the sapphire throne who had a human form surrounded 'as it were' with fire and 'brightness round about.'

This, I would conclude, is most probably the true identity of the being who inspired the Romantics, the biblical visions of the Son of Man and all the figures examined earlier — Joshua the Anointed One, Wisdom the master craftsman, and Jesus the Master Builder. It is also, most probably, the true identity of the young son of Mary who came to Britain with his 'uncle' Joseph to return to the source of that divine stream of consciousness which had originally come from the north; of the being who had to return in his physical body to the land on whose green mountains he had walked in his etheric body aeons before; of the individual who had to return to the north to where his Apollonian countenance had already shone forth for ages in auroral splendour; of the one who had to make the physical journey to the geographical north and on through the shamanic journey to the celestial north and the throne of God, for 'He who descended, is he who also ascended far above all heavens, that he might fill all things.'

References

Chapter 1
1. Thomas. p.35
2. Chadwick, Henry p.63
3. Gougaud p.20
4. Thomas p.44
5. Hardinge pp.1f
6. Barley and Hanson p.38
7. Tertullian p.87
8. Thomas p.43
9. Origen p.162
10. Thomas p.43
11. Moorman pp.3f
12. Collingwood and Myres p.270
13. Clement p.8
14. Irenaeus I,10
15. Foster p.16
16. Eusebius p.130
17. Gildas p.20
18. Deansley p.4
19. McNeill p.16
20. Ashe, *Arthur's Avalon*, p.37
21. Ussher p.54
22. Dorotheus of Tyre, p.479
23. Isidore of Seville, col. 152
24. Ashe, *Arthur's Avalon*, p.40
25. McNeill p.16
26. McNeill p.18
27. Deansley p.13

Chapter 2
1. Moorman p.3
2. Collingwood and Myres, p.270
3. Thomas p.42
4. Scott, John p.43
5. Giles p.21
6. Treharne p.36
7. Treharne p.116
8. Treharne p.119
9. Treharne p.119
10. Treharne pp.128f
11. Deansley pp.12f
12. Deansley p.14
13. Martin 1517
14. Ussher 1639
15. Ashe, *Arthur's Avalon*, p.47
16. Ashe, *Arthur's Avalon*, p.45
17. Ashe, *Arthur's Avalon*, p.45
18. Spelman p.5

Chapter 3
1. Treharne p.116
2. Ashe, *Avalonian Quest*, p.145
3. Ashe, *Avalonian Quest*, p.149
4. Ashe, *Avalonian Quest*, p.149
5. Ashe, *Avalonian Quest*, p.149
6. Ashe, Mythology p.252
7. Gransden p.143
8. Carley pp.1-15
9. Pagels p.22
10. Eisenman and Wise pp.1–16

Chapter 4
1. Ashe, *Arthur's Avalon*, p.301
2. Penhallurick p.142
3. Penhallurick pp.123–30
4. Dobson, Illustration
5. Caesar *De Bello Gallico* VI, 13
6. Crawford p.53
7. Baring-Gould p.57
8. Spelman p.5
9. Dobson pp.24f
10. Dobson p.26
11. Dobson p.27
12. Ashe, *Avalonian Quest*, p.147
13. Ashe, *Avalonian Quest*, p.147
14. Ashe, *Avalonian Quest*, p.147
15. Dobson p.27
16. Lewis, H.A. p.17

17. Dobson p.28
18. Lewis, H.A. p.10
19. Dobson, Illustration
20. Dobson p.34
21. Dobson p.34
22. Dobson pp.35–38
23. Dobson p.37
24. Dobson p.37
25. Ashe, *Arthur's Avalon*, p.302
26. Piggott p.162

Chapter 5
 1. Piggott p.163
 2. Piggott p.164
 3. Morgan p.67
 4. Piggott p.164
 5. Morgan p.73
 6. Piggott p.165
 7. Piggott pp.165-168
 8. Kendrick p.27
 9. Piggott p.159
10. Piggott p.10
11. Piggott p.20
10. Piggott p.10
11. Piggott p.20
12. Piggott p.9
13. Piggott p.23
14. Piggott p.114
15. Piggott p.95
16. Piggott ,p.96
17. Piggott p.96
18. Piggott p.117

Chapter 6
 1. Chadwick, Nora p.vii
 2. Chadwick, Nora p.11
 3. Piggott p.98
 4. Chadwick, Nora p.65
 5. Chadwick, Nora p.93
 6. Hippolytus I, xxv
 7. Kendrick p.107
 8. Chadwick, Nora pp.101f
 9. Piggott p.117
10. Ellis p.233
11. Ellis p.233
12. Caesar *De Bello Gallico*, VI, 14
13. Chadwick, Nora p.101

14. Clement, *Stromata* I,XV,70,1
15. Clement, *Stromata* I,XV,71,3
16. Chadwick, Nora p.64
17. Mackie p.228
18. Wood p.30
19. Wood p.32
20. Thom, *Megalithic Sites*, p.3
21. Atkinson p.51
22. Atkinson p.51
23. Burl, *Stone Circles*, p.40
24. Burl, *Stone Circles*, p.42
25. Burl, *Stone Circles*, p.38
26. Burl, *Stone Circles*, p.39
27. Burl, *Avebury*, p.152
28. Chippindale p.230
29. Heggie p.221
30. Heggie p.224
31. Heggie p.224
32. Heggie p.230
33. Heggie p.230
34. Hutton pp.113f
35. Mackie p.228
36. Mackie p.229

Chapter 7
 1. Philip pp.185-99
 2. Aristotle 985, b 23-6
 3. Fideler, *Pythagorean*, p.19
 4. Fideler, *Pythagorean*, p.93
 5. Aristotle 985, b 31-986, a 3
 6. Fideler, *Pythagorean* , p.60
 7. Fideler, *Pythagorean*, p.124
 8. Fideler, *Pythagorean*, p.140
 9. Philip p.3
10. Philip p.191
11. James, Jamie, *Music*, p.21
12. McLeish, *Number*, p.79
13. Neugebauer, p.93 and p.36
14. Tompkins, pp.186-87
15. Clement, *Stromata* I, xv, 71,3
16. Philip, p.188.
17. Caesar, *Conquest of Gaul* VI, 13
18. McClain, *Myth of Invariance*
    and *Pythagorean Plato*
19. Copleston Vol I, p.37
20. Butler, p.37
21. Ehrhardt p.44

22. Colson and Whitaker, p.13
23. Butler, p.24
24. Butler, p.24
25. Hopper, p.73
26. Proclus, L 14,8
27. Butler, p.49
28. Butler, p.49
29. Butler, p.49
30. Butler, p.49
31. Butler, p.51

Chapter 8
1. Weil, p.151
2. Weil, p.155
3. Weil, p.152
4. Weil, p.152
5. Weil, p.58
6. Weil, pp.157f
7. Weil, pp.159f
8. Weil, p.157
9. Weil, p.171
10. Weil, p.160
11. Weil, p.161
12. Weil, p.195 (See also: Plummer, p.314; Geldenhuys, p.344; Marshall, p.507; Goulder, p.525)
13. Bligh Bond and Simcox Lea, Gematria, p.16
14. Welburn, p.3
15. Welburn, p.98 and Smith, The Secret Gospel, p.15
16. Welburn, p.99
17. Welburn, p.25

Chapter 9
1. Bligh Bond and Simcox Lea, Apostolic Gnosis I, p.27
2. Bligh Bond and Simcox Lea, Apostolic Gnosis I, p.37
3. Pagels, p.27
4. Eliade, Encyclopaedia, Vol. 14, p.407 'Tertullian'
5. Encyclopaedia Judaica, Vol 7, p.370
6. Encyclopaedia Judaica, Vol 7, p.370-372

7. Bligh Bond and Simcox Lea, Gematria, p.3
8. Bligh Bond and Simcox Lea, Gematria, p.3
9. Crowley, Equinox, Vol. I, No.5. p.2
10. Michell, City of Revelation, p.7
11. James, John, p.108
12. Sendrey, p.69
13. Bligh Bond and Simcox Lea, Gematria, p.95
14. Bligh Bond and Simcox Lea, Gematria, p.95
15. Crossan
16. Vermes, Jesus the Jew
17. Mack
18. Lawlor, p.48 (See also, Huntley, Divine Proportion)
19. Bouleau, pp.74-76
20. Bligh Bond and Simcox Lea, Apostolic Gnosis I, p.24
21. Bligh Bond and Simcox Lea, Apostolic Gnosis I, p.24
22. Bligh Bond and Simcox Lea, Apostolic Gnosis I, p.27

Chapter 10
1. Strachan, Chapter 2
2. Michell, City of Revelation, p.60
3. Michell, City of Revelation, p.68
4. Tompkins, pp.195f
5. Smith, Jesus the Magician, p.48

Chapter 11
1. Liddell and Scott, p.797
2. Justin Martyr, Dialogue 88
3. Origen, Against Celsus, 6:36
4. Guelich Vol 34A, p.310; Branscomb p.100; Anderson p.159; Arindt and Gringrich p.816
5. Buchanan, p.178
6. Vermes, Jesus the Jew, p.21
7. Bligh Bond and Simcox Lea, Gematria, p.2
8. Case, pp.16-19
9. Case, p.19
10. Case, p.21

11. Case, p.18
12. Patey, 'Carpenter,' p.254
13. Patey,'Carpenter,' p.255
14. Patey, 'Jesus,' p.565
15. Patey, 'Jesus,' p.571
16. Patey, 'Jesus,' p.568
17. Vitrivius, Book III, Chap I, p.74
18. Vitrivius, Book III, Chapter I, p.75
19. Doczi, pp.106-8
20. Brandon, and Eisenman and Wise
21. Fideler, *Jesus Christ*, Chap 3
22. Meyers and Netzer, p.11

Chapter 12
 1. Hengel, p.250
 2. Hengel, p.210
 3. Hengel, pp.228f
 4. Hengel, p.229
 5. Hengel, p.230
 6. Hengel, p.232
 7. Hengel, p.236
 8. Hengel, p.238
 9. Hengel, p.241
10. Hengel, p.243
11. Hengel, p.211
12. Hengel, p.243
13. Hengel, p.244
14. Hengel, p.245
15. Hengel, p.246
16. Hengel, p.247
17. Dupont-Sommer, p.39
18. Cook, p.133
19. Vermes, *Dead Sea*, p.xxv
20. Vermes, *Dead Sea*, p.xxv
21. VanderKam, p.92
22. VanderKam, p.160
23. VanderKam, p.161
24. VanderKam, p.162
25. Baigent and Leigh
26. Freedman and Greenfield, p.77
27. Betz and Riesner, p.137
28. Betz and Riesner, p.146
29. Pixner, p.79

30. Pixner, pp.73f
31. Betz and Riesner, p.151
32. Pixner, pp.76f
33. Betz and Riesner, p.152
34. Yadin, pp.86-96
35. Betz and Reisner, p.153
36. Thiede and D'Ancona
37. Betz and Riesner, p.155

Chapter 13
 1. Rad, p.152
 2. Kidner, p. 81
 3. Oesterley, p.64
 4. Cohen, p.50
 5. Jones, p.102
 6. Scott, R.B.Y. pp.68-72
 7. Farmer, p.55
 8. Hengel, p.162
 9. Hengel, pp.162f
10. Hengel, pp.162f
11. Wilken, p.108
12. Baumgartner, p.19 (See also R.B.Y. Scott, p.23)
13. Diogenes Laertius, *Vitae*, introduction, I
14. Clement, *Stromata*, I, xv, 70, 1

Chapter 14
 1. Jenkins
 2. Boyer and Merchbach, p.62
 3. Morgan, Donn F. p.112
 4. Bligh Bond and Simcox Lea, *Apostolic Gnosis I*, p.26
 5. Bligh Bond and Simcox Lea, *Apostolic Gnosis II*, p.109
 6. Bligh Bond and Simcox Lea, *Apostolic Gnosis II*, p.115
 7. Fideler, *Jesus Christ*, Chapter 4
 8. Lawlor, p.35
 9. Lawlor, pp.33f
10. Bragdon p.71.
11. Bligh Bond and Simcox Lea, *Gematria*, p.99
12. Bligh Bond and Simcox Lea, *Gematria*, p.101

Chapter 15
1. Michell, *View*, pp.128f
2. Roberts, Chapters 6-8
3. Michell, *View*, Chapter 5
   (See also Michell, *New Light*,
   Part II)
4. Michell, *View*, p.123
5. Michell, *City*, Chapter 8
6. Michell, *City*, p.54

Chapter 16
1. Thom, *Megalithic Remains*,
   p.144
2. Thom, *Megalithic Remains*,
   p.146
3. Heath, p.36
4. Thom, *Lunar Observatories*, p.5
5. Chippindale, p.230
6. Thom, A.S., p.281
7. Thom, *Megalithic Sites*,
   pp.68–71
8. Cooper, p.179
9. Thom, A.S., pp.281-82
10. Thom, *Megalithic Remains*, p.18
11. Thom, *Megalithic Rings*,
    pp.300-302
12. Critchlow, *Time*, p.40
13. Thom, *Megalithic Remains*, p.18
14. Critchlow, *Time*, p.42

Chapter 17
1. Philip, p.156
2. Piggott, p.93
3. Rutherford, *Celtic*, p.126
4. Ashe, *Mythology*, p.129
5. Graves, *Greek Myths*, Vol I,
   p.80
6. Rutherford, *Celtic*, p.127
7. Diodorus Siculus, Book II,
   46.4-47.1. p.37
8. Diodorus Siculus, Book II,
   46.4-47.1. p.39
9. Diodorus Siculus, Book II,
   46.4-47.1. p.39
10. Ashe, *Ancient Wisdom*, p.132
11. Chapman
12. Fideler, *Pythagorean*, p.80

13. Fideler, *Pythagorean*, p.80
14. Fideler, *Pythagorean*, p.128
15. Midonick pp.71-73
16. Rutherford, *Pythagoras*, p.52
17. Diodorus Siculus, Book II,
    46.4-47.1. p.41
18. Santillana and Dechend, Front
    cover flap
19. Rutherford, *Pythagoras*, p.124
20. Heath, p.18
21. Yadin, pp.84-86
22. Tame, pp.249-250
23. Diodorus Siculus, Book II,
    46.4-47.1. p.39

Chapter 18
1. Graesser, pp.34-63
2. Thom, *Stone Rows* II, pp.411-12
3. Dever, p.70
4. Graesser, p.35
5. Barker, *Angel*, p.21
6. Barker, *Angel*, p.21
7. Barker, *Angel*, p.57
8. Barker, *Angel*, p.15
9. Barker, *Angel*, p.63
10. Macalister, Vol II, p.385
11. Kirkpatrick, p.264
12. Leupold, p.375
13. Ashe, *Dawn*, p.156
14. Graves, *White Goddess*, p.414
15. Ashe, *Ancient Wisdom*, p.95
16. Ashe, *Ancient Wisdom*, p.121
17. Ashe, *Ancient Wisdom*, p.124
18. Barker, *Angel*, p.55

Chapter 19
1. Kazan, p.256
2. Hepworth, 'Ezekiel'
3. Falck-Ytter, p.12
4. Falck-Ytter, p.53
5. Falck-Ytter, p.49
6. Falck-Ytter, p.26
7. Falck-Ytter, p.31
8. Falck-Ytter, p.40
9. Falck-Ytter, p.40
10. Falck-Ytter, p.46
11. Barker, *Angel*, p.39

12. Barker, *Angel*, p.39
13. Ashe, *Ancient Wisdom*, p.144
14. Barker, *Prophet*, p.57 (See also, Collins and Fishbane)
15. Ashe, *Ancient Wisdom*, p.144
16. Eliade, *Shamanism*, p.388
17. Falck Ytter, p.35

18. Falck-Ytter, p.30
19. Jung, p.328
20. Ashe, *Ancient Wisdom*, p.125
21. Ritchie, p.72
22. Moody, Dedication (See also Lorimer)
23. Ritchie, p.48

Bibliography

Anderson, Hugh, *The Gospel of Mark*, Oliphants, 1976.

Arindt, F.W. and F.W. Gingrich, *A Greek Lexicon of the New Testament*, University of Chicago.

Aristotle, *Metaphysics*.

Ashe, Geoffrey, *Avalonian Quest*, Collins/Fontana, 1982.

—, *King Arthur's Avalon*, Fontana, 1990.

—, *Mythology of the British Isles*, Methuen, London 1990.

—, *The Dawn Behind the Dawn*, Henry Holt, NY, 1992.

—, *The Ancient Wisdom*, Abacus Sphere Books, London 1979.

Atkinson, R.J.C. *Journal for the History of Astronomy*, 6, 1975.

—, *Stonehenge*, Hamish Hamilton, 1956.

Augustine, *De Civitas Dei*.

Ausonius, *Commem. Professorum*.

Baigent, Michael and Richard Leigh, *The Dead Sea Scrolls Deception*, Corgi, London 1991.

Baring-Gould, Sabine *A Book of Cornwall*, Methuen, 1912.

Barker, Margaret, *The Great Angel*, SPCK, 1992.

—, *The Lost Prophet*, SPCK, 1988.

Barley and Hanson (Ed.), *Christianity in Britain 300–700*, Leicester U. Press, 1968.

Baumgartner, W. *Israelitische und altorientalische Weisheit*, 1933. Cited in R.B.Y. Scott, *The Way of Wisdom*, Macmillan, London.

Bede *Ecclesiastical History of the English People*, trans. Leo Sherley-Price, Penguin, 1990.

Betz, O. and R. Riesner, *Jesus, Qumran and the Vatican*, SCM, 1994.

Blake, *see* Kazan.

Bligh Bond, F. and T. Simcox Lea, *Gematria*, RILKO, 1980.

—, *The Apostolic Gnosis I*, RILKO, 1979.

—, *The Apostolic Gnosis, Part II*, RILKO, 1985.

Bongo, *Numerorum Mysteria*.

Bouleau, Charles, *The Painter's Secret Geometry*. Hacker, NY 1980.

Boyer and Merchbach, *A History of Mathematics*, John Wiley, 1989.

Bragdon, Claude, *The Beautiful Necessity*, Quest, Wheaton, 1978.

Brandon, S.G.F. *Jesus and the Zealots*, Manchester UP, 1967.

Branscomb, B. Harvey, *The Gospel of Mark*, Hodder, 1964.

Buchanan, G. W. *Jesus, the King and His Kingdom*, Mercer UP, 1984.

Burl, Aubrey *Prehistoric Avebury*, Yale UP, 1979.

—, *Prehistoric Stone Circles*, Shire, 1979.

—, *see also* Thom, A. and Thom, A.S.

Butler, Christopher, *Number Symbolism*, RKP, 1970.

Caesar, *The Conquest of Gaul*.

—, *De Bello Gallico*.

Carley, James *Glastonbury Abbey*, Boydell, Woodbridge, Suffolk 1988.

Case, Shirley Jackson 'Jesus and Sepphoris,' *Journal of Biblical Literature*, Vol.45, 1926.

Chadwick, Henry *The Early Church*, Penguin, 1967.

Chadwick, N.K. *The Druids*, Cardiff and Connecticut, 1966.

Chapman, W.P. *Karistos: City State and Country Town*, Library of Congress Catalogue Card No.93-071318, 1993.

Chippindale, Christopher *Stonehenge Complete*, Thames and Hudson, 1994.

Cicero, *De Divinatione*.

Clement of Alexandria, *Stromata*.

Clement of Rome, *see* Harmer.

Cohen, A. *Proverbs*, Socina, Hindhead, 1945.

Collingwood R.G. and J.N.L. Myres, *Roman Britain and the English Settlements*, Oxford Clarenden, 1936.

Collins, John and Michael, Fishbane, eds, *Death, Ecstasy and Other Worldly Journeys*, State University, NY, 1995.

Colson, F.H. and G.H. Whitaker (trans), Philo *De Opificio Mundi*, Vol I.

Cook, Edward, *Solving the Mysteries of the Dead Sea Scrolls*, Paternoster, 1994.

Cooper, J.C. *An Illustrated Encyclopaedia of Traditional Symbols*, Thames and Hudson, London, 1978.

Copleston, Frederick, *A History of Philosophy*, Burnes Oates, 1956.

Crampton, Patrick *Stonehenge of the Kings*, John Baker, London, 1967.

Crawford, Deborah 'St Joseph in Britain: Reconsidering the Legends. Part 2,' *Folklore*, 1993.

Critchlow, Keith, *Glastonbury, A Study in Patterns*, RILKO, 1970.

—, *Time Stands Still*, Gordon Fraser, London, 1979.

Crossan, J.D. *The Historical Jesus: The Life of a Mediterranean Jewish Peasant*, T and T Clark, Edinburgh, 1991.

Crowley, Aleister, *777 and Other Qabalistic Writings*, Weiser, 1991.

Cyril of Alexandria, *Contra Julianum*.

Deansley, Margaret *The Pre-Conquest Church in England*, A & C Black, 1961.

Dever, W.G. 'The Gezer Fortifications and the "High Place",' *Palestine Exploration Quarterly*, London, 1973.

Dio Chrysostom, *Orations*, XLIX. Strabo, *Geographica*, IV, 4, c. 197, 4.

Diodorus Siculus, *In Twelve Volumes*, Loeb Classical Library, W. Heinemann, London 1967.

Diogenes Laertius, *Life of Pythagoras*.

—, *Vitae*.

Dobson, C.C. *Did Our Lord Visit Britain as they say in Cornwall or Somerset?* Covenant, London 1989.

Doczi, Gyorgy, *The Power of Limits*, Shambhala, Boulder 1981.

Dorotheus of Tyre *De Ss. Prophetis, Apostolis and LXX Christi Discipulis,* XXIX Aristobulus. In G. Gaulmin *De Vita et Morte Mosis,* 1714.

Dupont-Sommer, André, *The Dead Sea Scrolls: A Preliminary Survey,* Blackwell, Oxford 1952.

Ehrhardt, Arnold, *The Beginning,* Manchester UP, 1968.

Eisenman, Robert and Michael Wise, *The Dead Sea Scrolls Uncovered,* Penguin, 1992.

Eliade, Mircea, *Shamanism,* Princeton UP., 1974.

—, ed. *Encyclopaedia of Religion,* MacMillan, London 1987.

Ellis, Peter Beresford, *The Druids,* Constable, 1994.

Encyclopaedia Judaica, Jerusalem, 1971.

Eusebius *The Proof of the Gospel,* translated by W.J. Ferrar, SPCK, 1920 Book 3.

Falck-Ytter, Harald, *Aurora,* Floris, Edinburgh 1985.

Farmer, Kathleen, *Who Knows What is Good,* Eerdman's, Grand Rapids and Handsel, Edinburgh, 1991.

Fideler, David, *Jesus Christ, Sun of God,* Quest, Wheaton, USA, 1993.

—, ed. *The Pythagorean Sourcebook and Library,* (Trans. K.S. Guthrie), Phanes, Michigan, 1987.

Foster, John *They Converted Our Ancestors,* SCM, 1965.

Freedman, D.N. and J.C. Greenfield, *New Directions in Biblcal Archaeology,* Garden City, 1971.

Fuller, B.A.G. *A History of Philosophy,* Holt, N.Y., 1938.

Geldenhuys, Norval, *Commentary on the Gospel of Luke,* Marshall, Morgan and Scott, London, 1971.

Gildas *The Ruin of Britain,* London, David Nutt, 1899. Ed. by Hugh Williams.

Giles, J.A. (Trans.), William of Malmesbury *Chronicle of the Kings of England,* Henry Bohn, London 1847. .

Gougaud, Dom Louis *Christianity in Celtic Lands,* Sheed & Ward, 1932.

Goulder, Michael, *Luke, a New Paradigm* II Journal of Society of Old Testament Studies, Sheffield 1989.

Graesser, C.F. 'Standing Stones in Ancient Palestine,' *The Biblical Archaeologist.*

Gransden, Antonia *Historical Writings in England, c.550 to c.1307,* Ithaca: Cornell University Press, 1974.

Graves, Robert, *The Greek Myths,* Penguin, London 1955.

—, *The White Goddess,* Faber, London 1961.

Guelich, R. A. *World Biblical Commentary,* Vol 34A, Word Books, Dallas.

Guthrie, K.S. *The Pythagorean Sourcebook and Library, see* Fideler.

Hardinge, Leslie *The Celtic Church in Britain,* SPCK, 1972.

Harmer, J.R. (ed.) *The Apostolic Fathers,* MacMillan 1891.

Hawkins, Gerald *Stonehenge Decoded,* Souvenir, London 1966.

Heath, Robin, *A Key to Stonehenge,* Bluestone, St Dogmaels 1993.

Heggie, Douglas C. *Megalithic Science,* Thames and Hudson, 1981.

Hengel, Martin, *Judaism and Hellenism,* SCM, 1974.

Hepworth, Brian, *The Rise of Romanticism, Essential Texts*, 'Ezekiel,' Carcanet, Manchester 1978.

Hippolytus, *Philosophumena*.

Hopper, V.F. *Medieval Number Symbolism*, New York 1938.

Huntley, H.E. *The Divine Proportion*, Dover, NY 1970.

Hutton, Ronald *The Pagan Religions of the Ancient British Isles*, Blackwell, 1991.

Iamblichus, *The Life of Pythagoras*.

Irenaeus *Against Heresies*.

Isidore of Seville *De Obitu Patrum*.

James, Jamie, *The Music of the Spheres*, Abacus, 1995.

James, John, *Chartres, the Masons who built a Legend*, Thames and Hudson, 1982.

Jenkins, Vernon, *The Cracking of a Unique Code*, Cardiff, 1984 (Unpublished paper in the author's possession.).

Jones, Edgar, *Proverbs*, SCM, London 1961.

Jung, Carl J. *Letters* 1951-1961.

Justin Martyr, *Dialogue 88*.

Kaye, John, *Tertullian*, London 1845.

Kazan, Alfred (ed.), *The Essential Blake*, Chatto and Windus, London, 1968.

Kendrick, T.D. *The Druids*, Methuen, 1927, Studio Edn. London 1994.

Kidner, Derek, *Proverbs*, Tyndale, London 1964.

Kirkpatrick, A.F. *The Psalms*, Cambridge UP, 1933.

Klibansky, *Continuity of the Platonic Tradition in the Middle Ages*.

Lawlor, Robert, *Sacred Geometry*, Thames and Hudson, London 1982.

Leupold, H.C. *The Psalms*, Evangelical Press, London 1961.

Lewis, H.A. *Christ in Cornwall*, Lake, Falmouth 1939.

Lewis, L.S. *St Joseph of Arimathea at Glastonbury*, James Clarke, Cambridge 1922, 1955.

Liddell and Scott, *An Intermediate Greek-English Lexicon*, Clarendon, Oxford 1992.

Lorimer, David, *Whole in One*, Arkana, London 1990.

Lucan, *Pharsalia*.

Macalister, R.A.S. *The Excavation of Gezer 1902–5 and 1907–9*, John Murray, London 1912.

McClain, Ernest, *The Myth of Invariance*, Shambhala, 1978.

—, *The Pythagorean Plato*, N.Hays, Maine, 1984.

MacCulloch, J.A. *The Religion of the Ancient Celts*, Constable, London 1911 and 1991.

Mack, B.H. *A Myth of Innocence: Mark and Christian Origins*, Fortress, Philadelphia 1988.

Mackie, Euan *Science and Society in Prehistoric Britain*, Paul Elek, London 1977.

McLeish, John, *Number*, Flamingo, 1992.

McNeill, John T. *The Celtic Churches AD 200–1200*, U. Chicago, 1974.

Marshall, Howard, *The Gospel of Luke*, Paternoster, 1978.

Martin, Theodore *Disputatio super Dignitatem Angliae et Calliae in Concilio Constantiou*, Lovan, 1517.

Meyers, E. and C., Ehud Netzer, 'Sepphoris, Ornament of all Galilee,' *The Biblical Archaeologist*, March, 1986.

Michell, John, *City of Revelation*, Abacus, London 1973.

—, *New Light on the Ancient Mystery of Glastonbury*, Gothic Image, Glastonbury 1990.

—, *The View over Atlantis*, Abacus, London 1975.

Midonick, Henrietta, *The Treasury of Mathematics:1*, Pelican Books, London 1968.

Moody, Raymond, *Life after Life*, Bantam, London 1976.

Moorman, J.R.H. *A History of the Church in England*, A & C Black, 1953.

More,T. *Conjectura Cabbalistica.*

Morgan, Donn F. *Wisdom in the Old Testament*, Blackwell, Oxford 1981.

Morgan, Rev R.W. *St Paul in Britain*, Covenant, London 1925.

Nennius *British History and the Welsh Annals*, Ed. John Morris, London: Phillmore, 1980.

Neugebauer, Otto, *The Exact Sciences in Antiquity*, Dover, NY 1969.

Oesterley, W.O.E. *The Book of Proverbs*, Methuen, London 1929.

Origen *Homilies on Ezekiel*, in Marcel Borret S.J., *Homélies sur Ezékiel*, Paris 1989.

—, *Against Celsus.*

Pagels, Elaine *The Gnostic Gospels*, Penguin, 1990.

Patey, Richard, 'Is not this the Carpenter?' *New Testament Studies*, Vol. 30, 1984.

—, 'Jesus and the Theatre,' *New Testament Studies*, Vol. 30, 1984.

Penhallurick, R.D. *Tin in Antiquity*, Institute of Metals, London 1986.

Philip, J.A. *Pythagoras and Early Pythagoreanism*, Toronto, UP, 1968.

Philo, *De Opificio Mundi, see* Colson.

Piggott, Stuart *The Druids*, Thames and Hudson, 1968.

Pixner, Bargil, *With Jesus in Jerusalem*, Corazin, Rosh Pina, 1996.

Pliny, *Naturalis Historia.*

Plummer, Alfred, *Gospel According to St Luke*, T and T Clark, Edinburgh 1905.

Polyhistor, Alexander Cornelius, *Philosophon diadochai* and *De Symbolis Pythagoricis*, lost source for Greek authors.

Pomponius Mela, *De Situ Orbis.*

Porphyry, *The Life of Pythagoras.*

Posidonius, *Histories*, lost source for Latin authors.

Proclus, *Elements of Theology.*

Rad, Gerhard von, *Wisdom in Israel*, SCM, London 1972.

Ritchie, George, *Return from Tomorrow*, Kingsway, Eastbourne 1992.

Roberts, Anthony, ed. *Glastonbury, Ancient Avalon, New Jerusalem*, Rider, London 1978.

Rutherford, W. *Celtic Mythology*, Aquarian, Wellingborough, 1987.

—, *Pythagoras*, Aquarian, Wellingborough, 1984.

Rylaarsdam, J. Coert, *Revelation in Jewish Wisdom Literature*, Chicago UP.

Santillana, Giorgio de and Hertha von Dechend, *Hamlet's Mill*, Gambit, Ipswich 1969.

Scott, John *The Early History of Glastonbury: An Edition, Translation and Study of William of Malmesbury's De Antiquitate Glastonie Ecclesiae*, Boydele Press, Woodbridge 1981.

Scott, R.B.Y. *Proverbs — Ecclesiastes*.

Sendrey, Alfred, *Music in Ancient Israel*, Vision, London 1982.

Smith, Morton, *Jesus the Magician*, Harper Row, 1977.

—, *The Secret Gospel*, Gollancz, London 1974.

Spelman, Henrici; *Concilia, Decreta, Leges, Constitutiones, in re Ecclesiarum orbis Britannici*, London 1639.

Stephanus of Byzantium, *Ethnica*, fragment.

Strabo *Geographica*.

Strachan, Gordon, *Christ and the Cosmos*, Labarum, 1986.

Tacitus, *Annals*.

Tame, David, *The Secret Power of Music*, Turnstone, Wellingborough 1984.

Tertullian, *see* Kaye.

Theodoret, *see* Ussher.

Thiede, Carsten Peter and Matthew D'Ancona, *The Jesus Papyrus*, Weidenfeld and Nicolson, 1996.

Thom, A. *Megalithic Lunar Observatories*, Clarendon, Oxford 1971.

—, *Megalithic Sites in Britain*, Clarendon, Oxford 1967.

Thom, A. and Thom, A.S. *Megalithic Remains in Britain and Brittany*, Clarendon, Oxford 1978.

Thom, A. and A.S. Thom, Collated A. Burl, *Megalithic Rings*, BAR, British Series 81, Oxford 1980.

—, *Stone Rows and Standing Stones*, Part II, BAR International Series 560(ii), Oxford 1990.

Thom, A.S. *Walking in all of the Squares*, Argyll Pub., Glasgow 1995.

Thomas, Charles *Christianity in Roman Britain*, Batsford, 1981.

Tompkins, Peter, *Secrets of the Great Pyramid*, Harper Row, 1971.

Treharne, R.F. *The Glastonbury Legends*, Cresset, 1966.

Ussher, *Stillingfleet*.

—, *British Ecclesiastical Antiquities*.

VanderKam, James, *The Dead Scrolls Today*, Eerdmans-SPCK, 1994.

Vermes, Geza, *Jesus the Jew*, SCM, 1983.

—, *The Dead Sea Scrolls in English*, 4th ed. Penguin, 1995.

Vitruvius, *The Ten Books of Architecture*.

Weil, Simone, *Intimations of Christianity among the Ancient Greeks*, Ark, 1987.

Welburn, Andrew, *The Beginnings of Christianity*, Floris, 1991.

Wood, John Edwin *Sun, Moon and Standing Stones*, OUP, 1978.

Yadin, Yigael, *The Temple Scroll*, Weidenfeldt and Nicolson, 1985.

Index